HISTORY OF INDIA

HISTORY OF INDIA

Edited by

A. V. WILLIAMS JACKSON, Ph. D., LL.D.

VOLUME I

From the Earliest Times to the Sixth Century B.C.

BY

Romesh Chunder Dutt, C.I.E.

GYAN

Published by

Gyan Publishing House
5, Ansari Road
Daryaganj, New Delhi 110002
Phone: 011-47034999, 9811692060
E-mail: books@gyanbooks.com

Distribution Network
gyanbooks.com
India, USA, Canada, UK, Australia, France

ISBN : 978-81-212-6772-4 (Set)
978-81-212-6771-7 (PB)
First Published, 1906

2nd Impression 2022

Printed at: Gyan Press, Delhi.

HISTORY OF INDIA (VOL. I)
Author: ROMESH CHUNDER DUTT

The State Elephant of the Gaikwar of Baroda

The Gaikwar of Baroda, one of the few independent native princes of India, rules over a district of nearly five thousand square miles in the Bombay Presidency and traces the origin of his power to the early part of the eighteenth century. Like all Hindu rulers and high officials in India, this potentate has a special state elephant, which is adorned with magnificent trappings and surmounted by a howdah in which ride the prince and those whom he chiefly honours.

History of India

Edited by

A. V. WILLIAMS JACKSON, Ph. D., LL. D.
Professor of Indo - Iranian Languages in Columbia University

VOLUME I

From the Earliest Times to the Sixth Century, B. C.

By

ROMESH CHUNDER DUTT, C. I. E.

Of the Indian Civil Service; and of the Middle Temple, Barrister-at-law, Member of the Royal Asiatic Society of Great Britain and Ireland, and of the Asiatic Society of Bengal, Finance Minister to His Highness, the Maharaja of Baroda, India

INTRODUCTION BY THE EDITOR

Not the least historic of the ancient nations of the East is India, even when compared with Egypt and its monuments, China and its annals, or Assyria and Babylonia with their cuneiform tablets and their cylinders. India's earliest records, written in its literature, have been inscribed in the hearts of the people for more than three thousand years; and from that remote age its history is recorded in an almost unbroken line to this very century, so that he who will may follow its development through the early centuries that preceded the Christian era, onward through the mediæval period of Mohammedan rule, down to the days when the Europeans entered India and the country came under British dominion.

The aim of this series of volumes is to present a continuous narrative of the history of India from the dim ages of the past down to the present time, combining into an organic whole a succession of standard works by recognized authorities, each a master of the special period with which he deals, thus providing a complete picture of the development of the country whose teeming millions are now under the sceptre of Great Britain. In carrying out this design, the publishers and the editor have had the generous assistance of the scholars whose work is represented by these volumes. Special care has been taken to make such changes as were needed to meet the requirements of the series in a sympathetic manner and in such a way as to preserve all the essentials, thus giving the reader the results of the ripest scholarship in each field.

Ancient India and its civilization is discussed by the Honourable Romesh Chunder Dutt, of Baroda State, in a manner that will awaken interest in the life and history of our earliest kinsmen of Aryan blood. The second volume, written by Mr. Vincent Smith, recounts the history of the land of the Ganges from the time of Buddha to the first centuries after the Mohammedan conquest of Hindustan, when the history of Mediæval India begins. A comprehensive picture of the fortunes of the country under the rule of Islam is given in the volumes by Mr. Stanley Lane-Poole, and this is supplemented by a collection of the most characteristic descriptions of the period by Mohammedan writers themselves, as translated from their Arabic and Persian originals by Sir Henry M. Elliot, thus covering the history of India down to the time when the land was brought into direct contact with Europe. The settlements by the Portuguese, Dutch, French, and English, and the struggle for supremacy which resulted in England's triumph, are thoroughly treated in the volumes originally prepared by Sir William Hunter, and Sir Alfred Lyall relates the modern history of British dominion in India. A volume designed to give an objective view of the land and its people, as seen through the eyes of foreigners, presents a collection of the most striking descriptions of India by foreign travellers from ancient times to the eighteenth century, selected by the editor from Greek, Chinese, Persian, and Arabic sources, and from the accounts of the earliest European travellers and discoverers from the Western World.

Throughout the entire series the endeavour has been to eliminate the more technical matters and to omit detailed discussions of mooted points, while foot-notes have been almost universally avoided and diacritical marks omitted in the spelling of proper names. The illustrations of the various volumes have been chosen with great care, and many of them have been taken from photographs in my own collection, made during my travels in India. I am happy to have the opportunity to acknowledge my obligations to those scholars who have so kindly aided me by giving permission to make use of their works and to thank those who have allowed me to reproduce pictures which were their special property.

My thanks in particular are due to my friend and former pupil, Dr. Louis H. Gray, sometime Fellow in Indo-Iranian at Columbia University, for aid in the preparation of the text and for the indexing of the volumes. Mr. George C. O. Haas, formerly Scholar, now Fellow, in Indo-Iranian at Columbia, has also lent generous assistance in reading the proof-sheets and in various matters of detail.

A. V. Williams Jackson.

PREFATORY NOTE BY THE AUTHOR

The method by which this work has been written is very simple. My principal object has been to furnish the general reader with a practical and handy work on the Ancient History of India—not to compose an elaborate work of discussions on Indian antiquities. To study clearness and conciseness on a subject like this was not, however, an easy task. Every chapter deals with matters about which long researches have been made and various opinions recorded. It would have afforded some satisfaction to me to have given the reader the history of every controversy, the account of every antiquarian discovery, and the *pros* and *cons* of every opinion advanced. But I could not yield to this temptation without increasing the work greatly in bulk and thus sacrificing the very object with which it is written. To carry out my purpose, I have avoided every needless controversy and discussion, and I have tried to explain as clearly, concisely, and distinctly as I was able, each succeeding phase of Hindu civilization and Hindu life in ancient times.

But, while conciseness has been the main object, I

have also endeavoured to tell my story so that it may leave some distinct memories in the minds of my readers after they have closed the work. For this reason I have avoided details as far as possible and have tried to develop, fully and clearly, the leading facts and features of each succeeding age. Repetition has not been avoided, where such repetition seemed necessary to impress the cardinal facts—the salient features of the story of Hindu civilization.

The copious extracts which I have given (in translation) from the Sanskrit works may, at first sight, seem to be inconsistent with my desire for conciseness. Such extracts, however, have been advisedly given. In the first place, on a subject where there is so much room for difference of opinion, it is of the highest importance to furnish the reader with the text on which my conclusions are based, to enable him to form his own judgment, and to rectify my mistakes if my conclusions are erroneous. In the second place, it is a gain to the cause of historical knowledge to familiarize the reader with the texts of these ancient authors. It is scarcely to be hoped that the busy student will spend much of his time in reading the ancient and abstruse works in the original, or even in learned translations, and the historian who seeks to familiarize his readers with some portions at least of these ancient works, adds in so far to the accurate knowledge of his readers on this subject. And lastly, it has been well said, that thought is language, and language is thought; and if it be the intention of the historian to convey an idea of ancient thought—of what the ancient Hindus felt and believed—he cannot do this better than by quoting the words in which that ancient people expressed themselves. Such brief extracts very often give the modern reader a far more realistic and intimate knowledge of ancient Hindu society and manners and ways of thinking than any account that I could give at twice the length. And it is because I have desired the modern reader to enter into the spirit and the inner life of the ancient Hindus, that I have tried to bring the old composers of hymns and sutras face to face with the reader, and allowed them to speak for themselves. Such an intimate grasp of the inner life and feelings of the ancients is the very kernel of true historical knowledge, and I have felt it a hopeless task to impart this knowledge more accurately or more concisely than in the words of the ancients. It is for this reason mainly, and consistently with my anxiety to be concise, that I have quoted extensively from ancient works.

R. C. Dutt.

CONTENTS

CHAPTER		PAGE
I.	Ancient India and the Rig-Veda	1
II.	The Indo-Aryans and Their Literature	6
III.	Agriculture, Pasture, and Commerce	13
IV.	Food and Art in the Vedic Age	21
V.	Wars and Dissensions	30
VI.	Social Life	44
VII.	Vedic Religion	62
VIII.	The Brahmanic Period and Literature	82
IX.	The Epic Age — The Mahabharata	97
X.	The Epic Age — The Ramayana	112
XI.	Aryans and Non-Aryans	126
XII.	Caste in the Brahmanic and Epic Age	134
XIII.	Social Life in Brahmanic and Epic Times	143
XIV.	Law, Astronomy, and Learning	155
XV.	The Sacrificial Rites of the Brahmanas	159
XVI.	The Religious Doctrines of the Upanishads	172
XVII.	The Age of Laws and Philosophy	184
XVIII.	Expansion of the Hindus	197
XIX.	Administration, Agriculture, and Arts	208
XX.	Laws	220
XXI.	Caste in the Age of Laws and Philosophy	230
XXII.	Social Life in the Age of Philosophy	238
XXIII.	Sankhya and Yoga	253
XXIV.	Nyaya and Vaisesika	262
XXV.	Purva Mimamsa and Vedanta	268
XXVI.	Buddhist Sacred Literature	274
XXVII.	Life of Gautama Buddha	284
XXVIII.	Doctrines of Gautama Buddha	304
XXIX.	Moral Precepts of Gautama Buddha	312
XXX.	History of Buddhism	318
XXXI.	History of Jainism	323

LIST OF ILLUSTRATIONS

	PAGE
The State Elephant of the Gaikwar of Baroda	*Frontispiece*
Primitive Manner of Grinding Corn	8
Khaiber Pass, a Gateway from Afghanistan into India	9
Bridge of Boats on the Indus	10
Original Text of a Vedic Hymn	12
Ploughing in Ancient India	14
Primitive Indian Well	16
Old Indian Jewelry	19
Sacrifice of a Goat	22
The Horse-sacrifice (Asvamedha)	23
The Soma-plant	24
Fort Jamrud — Peshawar	27
Indian Elephant of State	28
Colonnade of Hindu Pillars	29
An Indian Scene	35
Women Drawing Water	36
Ancient Indian Head-dress	40
Scene on an Indian River	45
Primitive Indian Boats	46
Women of Salsette	47
Hindu Women	53
Nautch Girl	55
Burning Ghats	59
A Scene in the Himalayas	66
Indra	68
Surya	70
A Late Conception of Vishnu	71
Agni	72
Sculptures in the Cave Temple at Karli	76
Kali as worshipped to-day	77
Type of the Sudra Caste	84
Sacrificial Implements used in the Funeral Rites	87
Utensils for Religious Ceremonies	88
A Lake Scene in India	92
Overlooking Indrapat, the Ancient Pandu Capital	94

	PAGE
The Opening Page of the Bombay edition of the Mahabharata, reduced	97
The five Pandus and Draupadi	101
Winning the hand of the Princess	104
The Ill-fated Gambling-match	106
The reputed birthplace of Krishna at Mathura	107
Draupadi dragged into the Assembly	108
The Pandus and Kurus in Battle	109
After the Battle of Eighteen Days	110
The Closing Page of the Bombay edition of the Mahabharata, reduced	111
A Place Hallowed by Rama	113
Scene in Ceylon	115
Temple dedicated to Rama at Pushkar near Ajmere	118
Sacred Tank of Rama at Nasik	119
Ravana	121
Abduction of Sita	122
Hanuman	123
Hanuman and the Vanars rejoicing at the restoration of Sita	124
Rama with Sita, Lakshmana, and Hanuman	125
Hindus of Western Deccan	129
A Rajput Descendant of the Kshatriya Caste	131
The Monkey Temple at Benares	134
Shop of a Merchant of the Vaisya Caste	137
Brahman Types	140
A Hindu Youth	145
Hindu Women Bathing in a Pool	147
A Country Bullock-cart	148
A Type of Brahman Woman	153
The Astronomical Observatory, Yantra Samantra, at Delhi	156
Rail in the Gautamiputra Cave, Nasik	159
Sacred Tank of the Temple at Madura	160
Ceremonial bathing in the Ganges	161
Cremation on the Banks of the Ganges at Benares	164
The Fish Avatar of Vishnu	167
Siva Slaying Kamadeva, or Cupid	170
Vishnu	171
An Indian Scene	177
Gold Wire-drawers	180
Brahma	183
Sculpture from the Buddhist Tope near Benares	185
Law Code of Manu — A page of the text	187
Travelling in the Nilgiri Hills	199
Capital of Half Column from a temple in Orissa	203
An Indian Scene	209
Bhil Women of Kathiawar	212
Fresco in the Sheesh Mahal, at Rajgarh	217
Ganesa	219
Water Scene in India	224
Woman carrying water	231

PAGE

Sylvan Scene 235
The Vedi, or Marriage Altar 240
Ascetic at Benares 242
Propitiation of the Serpents 249
Swastika 253
Ascetic at Nasik 255
A Hindu Devotee 258
Undergoing Yogi Penance 260
Indian Scenery 265
Indian Carving 268
The Golden Temple at Benares 274
Western Gateway of the Buddhist Tope at Sanchi 277
Brass image of Gautama Buddha from Ceylon 287
Buddhist Rock-temple at Karli 294
Ruins of the Sakiya Tope 302
Footprints of Buddha 310
Buddhist Tope at Sanchi 318
Buddhist carving at Anuradhapura 320
Jain Temple of Vimala Sah, Mount Abu 325
Jain Temple at Ahmadabad 327

CHAPTER I

ANCIENT INDIA AND THE RIG-VEDA

THE history of Ancient India is a history of thirty centuries of human culture and progress. It divides itself into several distinct periods, each of which, for length of years, will compare with the entire history of many a modern people.

The earliest date claimed by modern scholars for its oldest literary monument, the Rig-Veda, is about 2000 B.C. Even at that remote age, Hindu civilization must have been hundreds or thousands of years old, and from that time the literary works of successive periods form a continuous picture of the culture and the history of India for three thousand years, so full, so clear, that he who runs may read. The oldest records were not written on parchment or inscribed on stone; they were written in the faithful memory of the people, who handed down the precious heritage from century to century with a scrupulous exactitude that would be considered, in modern days, a miracle.

Scholars who have studied the Vedic hymns historically are aware that the materials they afford for constructing a history of civilization are fuller and truer than any accounts which could have been recorded on stone or papyrus. And those who have pursued Hindu literature through the different periods of ancient Hindu history are equally aware that they form a complete and comprehensive story of the progress and gradual modifications of Hindu civilization, thought, and religion through three thousand years. The philosophical historiān of human civilization need not be a Hindu to think that the Hindus have preserved the fullest, the clearest, and the truest materials for his work.

We wish not to be misunderstood. We have made the foregoing remarks simply with a view to remove the very common and very erroneous impression that Ancient India has no history worth studying, no connected and reliable chronicle of the past which would be interesting or instructive to the modern reader.

Ancient India has a connected story to tell, and so far from being uninteresting, its special feature is its intense attractiveness. We read in that ancient story how a gifted Aryan people, separated by circumstances from the outside world, worked out their civilization under natural and climatic conditions which were peculiarly favourable. We note their intellectual discoveries age after age; we watch their religious progress and development through successive centuries; we mark their political career, as they gradually expand over India and found new kingdoms and dynasties;

we observe their struggles against priestly domination, their successes and their failures; we study with interest their great social and religious revolutions and their far-reaching consequences. And this great story of a nation's intellectual life is nowhere broken and nowhere disconnected. The great causes which led to great social and religious changes are manifest to the reader, and he follows the gradual development of ancient Hindu civilization through thirty centuries, from 2000 B. C. to one thousand years after Christ.

The story of India's success is not more instructive than the story of her failure. The hymns of Visvamitra, the philosophy of Kapila, and the poetry of Kalidasa have no higher lessons for the modern reader than the decadence of her political life and the ascendency of priests. The story of the religious rising of the people under the leadership of Gautama Buddha and Asoka is not more instructive than the absence of any efforts after popular freedom. And the great heights to which the genius of Brahmans and Kshatriyas soared are not more suggestive and not more instructive than the absence of genius in the people at large in their ordinary pursuits and trades—in mechanical inventions and maritime discoveries, in sculpture, architecture, and arts, in manifestations of popular life and the assertion of popular power.

The history of the intellectual and religious life of the ancient Hindus is matchless in its continuity, its fulness, and its philosophical truth. But the historian who paints only the current of that intellectual life performs but half his duty. There is another and a sadder portion of Hindu history, and it is necessary that this portion of the story, too, should be faithfully told.

We have said before that the history of Ancient India divides itself into several distinct and long periods or eras, marked by great historical events. We shall begin with the earliest period of India's history, that of Aryan settlements in the Panjab. The hymns of the Rig-Veda furnish us with the materials for a history of this period, which we may call the *Vedic*, and which we may approximately date from 2000 to 1400 B. C., or later according to some authorities.

In this priceless volume, the Rig-Veda, we find the Hindu Aryans as conquerors and settlers on the banks of the Indus and its five branches; and India beyond the Sutlaj was almost unknown to them. They were a conquering race, full of the self-assertion and vigour of a young national life, with a strong love of action and a capacity for active enjoyments. They were, in this respect, far removed from the contemplative and passive Hindus of later days; they rejoiced in wealth and cattle and pasture-fields; and, with their strong right arm, they won by force new possessions and realms from the aborigines of the soil, who vainly struggled to maintain their own against the invincible conquerors. Thus the period was one of wars and conflicts with the aborigines; and the Aryan victors triumphantly boast of their victories in their hymns, and implore their gods to bestow on them wealth and new possessions and to destroy the barbarians.

It is needless to say that the entire body of Aryans was then a united community, and the only distinction of caste was between the Aryans and the aborigines. Even the distinction between professions was not very marked; and the sturdy lord of many acres, who ploughed his fields and owned large herds in times of peace, went out to defend his village or to plunder the aborigines in times of war, and often composed spirited hymns to the martial gods in his hours of devotion. There were no temples and no idols; each patriarch of a family lighted the sacrificial fire on his own hearth, and offered milk and rice offerings, or animals, or libations of the Soma juice to the fire, and invoked the "bright" gods for blessings and health and wealth for himself and his children. Chiefs of tribes were kings and had professional priests to perform sacrifices and utter hymns for them; but there was no priestly caste and no royal caste. The people were free, enjoying the freedom which belongs to vigorous pastoral and agricultural tribes.

CHAPTER II

THE INDO-ARYANS AND THEIR LITERATURE

THE site of the early home of the Aryans has been a subject of endless controversies among scholars. Into this mooted problem we cannot enter here. Suffice it to say that enthusiastic and patriotic Hindu scholars will not admit that the first home of the Aryans was anywhere outside of India; while equally patriotic European scholars would place the abode of the primitive Aryans on the shores of the Baltic Sea. We need hardly say that it is not our object to enter into this discussion, and we merely repeat here that it is universally granted that the civilization, religion, language, and literature of the Hindus, from the earliest ages to the present day, are centred in India, and in India alone. There are, however, a number of facts about the life of the primitive Aryans regarding which there is no dispute.

The domestic economy among the early Aryans was much the same as it is to-day. The historian of man does not find in Aryan history any traces of hetairism (or of promiscuous relationship between the sexes), of families being reckoned on the mother's side, or of inheritance by the female line. On the contrary, the father was the protector and the nourisher of the family, the mother looked after and fed the children, the daughter milked the cattle, and relationship by marriage was recognized. Probably the primitive Aryans had already reached a higher state of civilization than promiscuous living would imply. The family, and not the tribe, was the unit of society, and the father was the head of the family.

Many of the useful animals had been domesticated, as, for example, the cow, the bull, the ox, the sheep, the goat, the swine, the dog, and the horse. The wild bear, the wolf, the hare, and the dreaded serpent were known. Similarly among birds, the goose, the duck, the cuckoo, the raven, the quail, the crane, and the owl were well known to the early Aryans.

The various industries were still in their infancy; but a commencement in manufactures and arts had been made. The Aryans built houses, villages, and towns, made roads, and constructed boats for communication by water or for a humble kind of trade. Weaving, spinning, and plaiting were known, and furs, skins, and woollen fabrics were made into garments. Carpentry must have made considerable progress, and dyeing was known.

It need scarcely be stated that agriculture was practised by the primitive Aryans, and it was this occupation which probably gave them their name (*ārya* = cultivator). Corn was ground, prepared, and cooked in various ways, while the flocks of sheep and cows by which every family was surrounded afforded milk and meat. There can be little doubt that, although

PRIMITIVE MANNER OF GRINDING CORN.
Copyright by Underwood and Underwood, N. Y.

agriculture was largely resorted to, many patriarchs of families used also to rove about from place to place with their attendants and flocks in search of new pastures, and a fairly large portion of the early Aryans led a nomad life.

War was not infrequent in those primitive times, and weapons of bone and of wood, of stone and of metal, were known. The bow and the arrow, the sword and the spear seem to have been the weapons of war.

Khaiber Pass, a Gateway from Afghanistan into India.
From a Photograph.

It argues some advance in civilization that the use of gold and of silver was undoubtedly known to the early Aryans, and, with the simplicity of early races, they called gold by the name "yellow" and silver by the name "white." A third metal (*ayas*) was also known, but it is doubtful whether it was iron.

It is perhaps impossible to conjecture the sort of government which obtained in those olden days. Patriarchs of tribes and leaders of men undoubtedly obtained ascendency, and the simple subjects looked up to them and called them the protectors or nourishers of men, or the chiefs (*pati*, *vispati*, *rāja*) in war as well as in peace. The natural feelings of civilized man distinguished between right and wrong, and custom and a vague perception of what was good for the nation had the force of law. And lastly, the primitive religion of the Aryans was largely suggested by that which was beautiful and striking in the phenomena of nature.

Adventurous bands of Aryans left their primitive home from time to time in quest of food or pasture, of kingdoms or plunder. The exact order in which the different nations left has not been ascertained and may never be ascertained. All that is even approximately certain from the historian's standpoint is that a branch of the Aryans, designated as Indo-Iranians, appeared at an unknown epoch in the land of Asia, but it is not yet known whether they were immigrants or indigenous to the soil. They travelled southward together, but became separated by religious, social, or tribal conditions, before they reached India. Only the Hindus, the worshippers of the Devas as gods, made their way to the River Indus and the land of the Five Rivers, the Panjab.

It was these worshippers of the Devas who composed those hymns which are known as the Rig-Veda, and we shall say a few words here about this ancient work. Probably there is not another work in the litera-

BRIDGE OF BOATS ON THE INDUS.

ture of mankind which is so deeply interesting, so unique in the lessons it imparts. The hoary antiquity of this ancient monument, the picture it affords of the earliest form of civilization that the Aryans developed in any part of the world, and the flood of light it throws on the origin of the myths and religions of all Aryan nations, make the Rig-Veda deeply interesting. It is, moreover, the oldest work in the Aryan world. It gives us a picture of the oldest civilization that the

Aryans developed, and it enlightens and clears up much that is dark and obscure in the religions and myths of Aryan nations all over the world.

To the Hindus the Rig-Veda is a work of still higher importance. It explains the whole fabric of the later Hindu religion; it solves all the complications of later mythology; it throws light on the history of the Indian mind from its earliest stage of infancy. The Hindu learns from this ancient and priceless volume that Vishnu, the supreme preserver, and his three steps, which cover the universe, mean the sun at its rise, its zenith, and its setting; that the terrible god Rudra, the supreme destroyer, originally meant the thunder or thunder-cloud; and that Brahma, the supreme creator, was originally prayer or the god of prayer.

The Rig-Veda consists of 1028 hymns, comprising over ten thousand verses. The hymns are divided into ten Mandalas or Books, and with the exception of the first and last books, every one of the remaining eight books contains hymns said to have been composed or rather proclaimed by one Rishi, by which we may understand one family or line of teachers. Thus the second book is by Gritsamada; the third is by Visvamitra; the fourth is by Vamadeva; the fifth is by Atri; the sixth is by Bharadvàja; the seventh is by Vasishtha; the eighth is by Kanva; and the ninth is by Angiras. The first book contains 191 hymns, which, with scattered exceptions, are composed by fifteen Rishis; and the tenth book also contains 191 hymns, which are mostly ascribed to fictitious authors.

The whole or the greater portion of the tenth book seems to have been the production of a later period, but was thrown in and preserved with the body of the older hymns. The hymns of the Rig-Veda were handed down from father to son or from teacher to pupil for centuries together, and it was in a later age, in the Epic Period, that they were arranged and compiled. By the close of this period, every verse, every word, and every syllable of the Rig-Veda had been counted. The number of verses, as computed, varies from 10,402 to 10,622; the number of words is 153,826; and there are altogether 432,000 syllables.

प्र पर्वतानामुशती उपस्थादश्वे इव विषिते हासमाने ।
गावेव शुभ्रे मातरा रिहाणे विपाट्छुतुद्री पयसा जवेते ॥ १ ॥
इन्द्रेषिते प्रसवं भिक्षमाणे अच्छा समुद्रं रथ्येव याथः ।
समाराणे ऊर्मिभिः पिन्वमाने अन्या वामन्यामप्येति शुभ्रे ॥ २ ॥
अच्छा सिन्धुं मातृतमामयासं विपाशमुर्वीं सुभगामगन्म ।
वत्समिव मातरा संरिहाणे समानं योनिमनु संचरन्ती ॥ ३ ॥

ORIGINAL TEXT OF A VEDIC HYMN.

Rig-Veda 3.33.

CHAPTER III

AGRICULTURE, PASTURE, AND COMMERCE

THE main industry of the ancient Hindus was agriculture; and the very word *ārya*, "cultivator," is the one term in the Rig-Veda which distinguishes the conquerors as a class from the aborigines of the country. There are, however, two other words in the Rig-Veda, which are synonymous, not with the Aryan tribe, but rather with man generally; and both of them come from roots which indicate cultivation. These are *charshana* and *krishti*, and both come from modifications of the root *krish*, to cultivate.

There are numerous direct allusions in the Rig-Veda to agriculture, but the most remarkable among them is found in the fourth book in the fifty-seventh hymn, which is dedicated to a supposed god of agriculture, the Lord of the Field, as he is called, and which we translate in full:—

"We will win (cultivate) this field with the Lord of the Field; may he nourish our cattle and our horses; may he bless us thereby.

"O Lord of the Field! bestow on us sweet and pure and butter-like and delicious and copious rain, even as cows give us milk. May the Lords of the water bless us.

"May the plants be sweet unto us; may the skies and the rains and the firmament be full of sweetness; may the Lord of the Field be gracious to us. We will follow him, uninjured by enemies.

PLOUGHING IN ANCIENT INDIA.
From a Buddhist sculpture.

"Let the oxen work merrily; let the men work merrily; let the plough move on merrily. Fasten the traces merrily; ply the goad merrily.

"O Suna and Sira! accept this hymn. Moisten this earth with the rain you have created in the sky.

"O fortunate Furrow! proceed onwards, we pray unto thee; do thou bestow on us wealth and an abundant crop.

"May Indra accept this Furrow; may Pushan lead her onwards. May she be filled with water, and yield us corn year after year.

"Let the ploughshares turn up the sod merrily; let the men follow the oxen merrily; may Parjanya moisten the earth with sweet rains. O Suna and Sira! bestow on us happiness."

We shall seek in vain in the entire range of later Sanskrit literature for a passage in which the humble hopes and wishes of simple agriculturists are so naturally described; and equally naïve is another hymn, also relating to agriculture, part of which may be translated thus:—

"Fasten the ploughs, spread out the yokes, and sow the seed on this field which has been prepared. Let the corn grow with our hymns; let the scythes fall on the neighbouring fields where the corn is ripe.

"The ploughs have been fastened; the labourers have spread the yokes; the wise men are uttering prayers to gods.

"Prepare troughs for the drinking of the animals. Fasten the leather string, and let us take out water from this deep and goodly well which never dries up.

"The troughs have been prepared for the animals; the leather string shines in the deep and goodly well which never dries up, and the water is easily got. Take out water from the well.

"Refresh the horses; take up the corn stacked in the field; and make a cart which will convey it easily. This well, full of water for the drinking of animals, is one *drona* in extent, and there is a stone wheel to it. And the reservoir for the drinking of men is one *skanda.* Fill it with water."

Irrigation and cultivation in the Panjab are only possible by means of wells, and wells are reserved also for the drinking of men and of beasts; and it is not surprising therefore that we should find references to wells in the Rig-Veda. Another remarkable fact is that horses were used for cultivation in those days, a custom still common in Europe, but not in India in modern times. In yet another hymn we are told how

PRIMITIVE INDIAN WELL.

water was raised from wells for irrigation. The contrivance was the same as is still in vogue in Northern India; a number of pots are tied to a string, and as the pots go up and down by the movement of a wheel, they are filled in the well and pulled up and emptied and sent down again. One hymn of the tenth book alludes to irrigation of fields by means of canals which were replenished with water by means of a *drona;* and in another we are told that cultivators who irrigated their fields kept away birds by uttering loud cries.

Allusions to pasturage, however, are by no means so frequent as allusions to agriculture. Pushan is the god of shepherds—he is the sun as viewed by shepherds—and is supposed to protect them and travellers generally in their wanderings over the country. And here and there in a hymn to Pushan, we find that the Aryans of India had brought with them recollections and songs about those migrations which they occasionally undertook in their primitive home, if not after their settlement in India. We translate one such hymn below:—

"O Pushan! help us to finish our journey, and remove all dangers. O Son of the Cloud, do thou march before us!

"O Pushan! do thou remove from our path him who would lead us astray, who strikes and plunders and does wrong.

"Do thou drive away that wily robber who intercepts journeys.

"Do thou trample under thy foot the vile carcass of him who plunders us in both ways (by stealth and by force) and who commits outrages.

"O wise Pushan, destroyer of enemies! we implore of thee the protection with which thou didst shield and encourage our forefathers.

"O Pushan, possessed of all wealth, possessed of golden weapons, and chief among beings! bestow on us thy riches.

"Lead us so that enemies who intercept may not harm us; lead us by an easy and pleasant path. O Pushan! devise means (for our safety) on this journey.

"Lead us to pleasant tracts covered with green grass; let there be no extreme heat by the way. O Pushan! devise means (for our safety) on this journey.

"Be powerful in thy protection; fill us with riches; bestow on us wealth; make us strong and give us food! O Pushan! devise means (for our safety) on this journey.

"We do not blame Pushan; but we extol him in our hymns. We solicit wealth from the handsome Pushan."

There is also another interesting hymn on the practice of taking out cattle to pasture-fields and bringing them back. A few verses are worth translating:—

"We call the cowherd, let him take out these cows; let him pasture them in the fields; let him know and pick out the animals; let him bring them back to the house; let him pasture them on all sides.

"The cowherd seeks for the cows and brings them back to the house; he pastures them on all sides. May he come home safe.

"O cowherd! pasture the cows in all directions and bring them back. Pasture them in various parts of the earth and then bring them back."

References to trade and commerce must necessarily

be rare in a collection of hymns to gods; but, nevertheless, we are here and there surprised by passages which throw a curious light on the manners of the times. Loans and usury were well understood in those days, and in one remarkable verse we are reminded of the finality of a sale-transaction, when once the sale is completed:—

" One sells a large quantity for a small price, and then goes to the purchaser and denies the sale and asks for a higher price. But he cannot exceed the price once

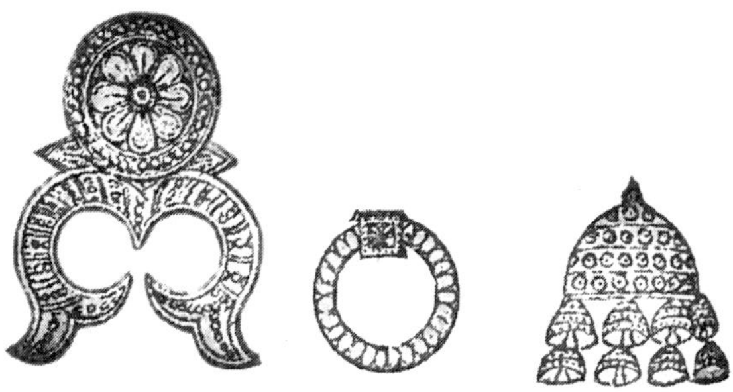

OLD INDIAN JEWELRY.

fixed, on the plea that he has given a large quantity. Whether the price was adequate or inadequate, the price fixed at the time of sale must hold good."

A passage like this would indicate the existence of current money for the purposes of buying and selling. We have instances of Rishis, or Vedic bards, acknowledging the gift of a hundred pieces of gold, and there can be no doubt that pieces of gold of a certain fixed value were used as money as indicated in these passages. At the same time it must be admitted that there is no distinct allusion to coined money in the Rig-Veda.

The word *nishka* is often used in the Rig-Veda with a connotation that is by no means clear. In some passages it means money, in others it implies a golden ornament for the neck. The two interpretations are not necessarily contradictory, for in India pieces of gold which serve as money have been used as ornaments for the neck from times immemorial.

On the other hand, there are distinct references to voyages by sea, though of course the words used may mean rivers only, and not the sea. The shipwreck of Bhujyu and his deliverance by the gods Asvins, is constantly alluded to, and the god Varuna is said to know the paths of the birds through the sky and the paths of the ships over the sea. Allusion is also made to the "people who, desiring to acquire wealth, pray to the sea before undertaking a voyage"; and another passage runs:—

"When Varuna and I went on a boat and took her out to sea, I lived in the boat floating on the water and was happy in it, rocking gracefully (on the waves)."

While there are these and other distinct allusions to voyage, there is absolutely no prohibition against it in the Rig-Veda, such as prevailed in later times and still holds among the orthodox of India.

CHAPTER IV

FOOD AND ART IN THE VEDIC AGE

BARLEY and wheat seem to have been the chief produce of the field, and the principal articles of food. The names of grain found in the Rig-Veda are somewhat misleading, as they have come to bear a different signification in modern days from what they had in the ancient times. Thus the word *yava*, which in modern Sanskrit implies barley only, was used in the Veda to imply food-grains generally, including wheat and barley. And the word *dhāna*, which, in Bengal at least, now means paddy or rice, implies in the Rig-Veda fried barley, which was used as food and offered to the gods. There is no allusion to rice (*vrīhi*) in the Rig-Veda.

We also find mention of various kinds of cakes prepared from these grains and used as food and offered to the gods. The term *pakti* (from *pach*, to cook, or to prepare) means prepared cakes, and various other terms, such as *purodāsa* (sacrificial cake), *apūpa* (cake), and *karambha* (barley groats), are also used.

It may easily be imagined that animal food was largely used by the early Hindus of the Panjab, and we have frequent allusions to the sacrifice and to the cooking of cows, buffaloes, and bulls. Mention is also made of a slaughter-house where cows were killed, as well as of the sacrifice of horses, bulls, and rams. The allusions to the sacrifice of the horse are extremely rare, showing that, although the custom was introduced

SACRIFICE OF A GOAT.

into India by the early Aryans from their primitive home, the flesh of horse as an article of food soon fell into disuse. In later times the asvamedha, or sacrifice of the horse, was performed on rare occasions with great pomp and circumstance by powerful kings, after they had subdued their neighbours and assumed a title answering to the imperial title in Europe. There can be no doubt that this great imperial rite rose out of the simple sacrifice of the horse practised in primitive times when the horse was still an article of food, but the pomp and ceremony, as well as certain revolting rites connected with the horse-sacrifice of later days, were unknown in Vedic times.

A fairly complete account of the sacrifice of the

THE HORSE-SACRIFICE (ASVAMEDHA).

horse, as it prevailed in Vedic times, is to be found in the one hundred and sixty-second hymn of the first Mandala of the Rig-Veda. The body of the horse was marked with a cane and was then dissected along the lines marked, and the ribs and the different limbs were separated. The meat was roasted and boiled, while the soul of the horse was supposed to go to the gods. In later times an endless amount of pomp, ceremony, and detail was woven about this rite of the horse-sacrifice, in contrast to the simplicity of Vedic days.

The fermented juice of the plant called *Soma* appears to have been the only intoxicating drink used in Vedic times. So much were the ancient Aryans addicted to this drink, that Soma was soon worshipped as a deity both in India and in Iran (under the name *Haoma* in the latter country), and we find one entire Mandala, or Book, of the Rig-Veda, dedicated to this deity. The Aryans appear to have been more habituated to fermented and intoxicating Soma than their peaceful brethren of Iran, and some allusions in the Avesta are thought to refer to the hated customs of their Indian brethren. Some antiquarians think that this was one great reason of those dissensions which broke out among the southern Aryans and led to the final separation of the Iranians from the Hindus.

THE SOMA-PLANT.

The process by which the Soma juice was prepared is fully described in the sixty-sixth hymn of the ninth book of the Rig-Veda, from which the following verses are selected:—

"O Soma! you have been crushed; you flow as a stream to Indra, scattering joy on all sides; you bestow immortal food.

"Seven women stir you with their fingers, blending their voices in a song to thee; you remind the sacrificer of his duties at the sacrifice.

"You mix with water with a pleasing sound; and the fingers stir you over a woollen strainer, and filter you. Your particles are thrown up then, and a sound arises from the woollen strainer.

"The woollen strainer is placed on a vessel, and the fingers repeatedly stir the Soma, which sends down a sweet stream into the vessel.

"O Soma! you are then mixed with milk. Water runs toward you with a pleasing sound."

From this description it would appear that the juice of Soma used to be taken mixed with milk. The poets of the Rig-Veda go into ecstasy over the virtues and the exhilarating powers of the Soma, and some of their descriptions have developed into the strange Puranic legends of the churning of the ocean and the discovery of the *Amrita*, or immortal drink. The sky in the Veda is considered watery and is often confused with the sea, and the milking of Soma from the sky is transformed in the Purānas into the churning of the ocean for the *Amrita*.

It would appear from many passages in the Rig-Veda that many arts were carried to a high state of excellence. Weaving was well known, of course, and deft female fingers wove the warp and woof. In one curious passage the seer laments his ignorance of the mysteries of religious rites by saying: "I know not the warp and I know not the woof" of religious rites; and elsewhere the weaving and bleaching of sheep's wool are attributed to the god Pushan, who, as we have already seen, is the god of shepherds.

Every Aryan village had probably its barber then as now, and the clearance of forests by fire is in one passage described as the shaving of the earth. Carpentry was also well known, and we have frequent allusions to the construction of carts and chariots. The use of iron, of gold, and of other metals was well known, and the Rig-Veda contains references to the work of the blacksmith and the goldsmith.

But we get a better idea of working in metals in Vedic times from the descriptions of various gold ornaments and iron utensils and implements of war which are to be found throughout the Rig-Veda. The allusions are numerous, and we select only a few as illustrations. We are told of armour used in war and of golden helmets, while mention is also made of armour for the shoulders or arms, probably a shield. The lightning is compared not only to a javelin, but also to a sword or battle-axe, and to bows and arrows and quivers. Three thousand mailed warriors are mentioned; feathered, sharp-pointed, shining shafts are described; and sharp-edged swords are noted, as well as war-chariots and kettle-drums. And lastly, we have a spirited account of the arms and accoutrements of war, which we shall translate for our readers further on.

The steeds of war had golden caparisons, and the warriors had golden ornaments about their necks. The lightning ornaments of the Maruts are compared to jewelry, necklaces, golden breastplates, and bracelets and anklets. We also learn of anklets for the feet, and of

FORT JAMRUD — PESHAWAR.

golden breastplates for the breast, as well as of golden crowns for the head.

Thus it will be seen that a very considerable advance had been made in the manufacture of arms, weapons, and various kinds of ornaments. We have references also to vessels of skin and iron vessels, as well as to iron towns, which must be taken in a figurative sense as signifying strong forts, and there are likewise allusions to a hundred stone-built towns.

There can be no doubt that in the various rocky

and mountainous tracts where the early Hindus established their colonies, they soon learnt to utilize stone as a durable and cheap material for architecture, and there can be little difficulty in believing that in some of the Vedic towns there were structures and surrounding walls of stone. That the art of building was carried to some degree of excellence appears from many

INDIAN ELEPHANT OF STATE.
From a Buddhist sculpture.

allusions to mansions with a thousand pillars, but at the same time it must be admitted that there is no distinct allusion in the Rig-Veda to the art of sculpture properly so called, and the researches of antiquarians have failed to discover in any part of India traces of sculptured stone much anterior to the Buddhist era.

Most of the animals domesticated at the present day were domesticated in India in the remote period

Colonnade of Hindu Pillars.
From a Photograph.

of the Rig-Veda, including cows, goats, sheep, buffaloes, and dogs (the latter used in carrying burdens), while one passage alludes to a king riding with his ministers on an elephant.

The war-horse, too, received his meed of praise, and so highly was he esteemed by the early Aryans in their battles against the aborigines, that under the name of Dadhikra he soon became an object of worship. It is evident, moreover, that the war-horses of the early Aryans inspired the aborigines with dire terror, as is shown by the following passage from the Rig-Veda:—

"As people shout and raise a cry after a thief who has purloined a garment, even so the enemies yell and shout at the sight of Dadhikra! As birds make a noise at the sight of the hungry hawk on its descent, even so the enemies yell and shout at the sight of Dadhikra careering in quest of plunder and cattle!

"Enemies fear Dadhikrā, who is radiant and destroying as a thunderbolt. When he beats back a thousand men around him, he becomes excitable and uncontrollable in his strength."

CHAPTER V

WARS AND DISSENSIONS

WHEN the early Hindus wrested the fertile tracts on the banks of the Indus and its tributaries from the primitive races of the Panjab, the aborigines did not give up their birthright without a struggle. Retreating before the more civilized organization and valour of the Hindus in the open field, they still lurked in fastnesses and forests near every Aryan settlement and village, harassed their conquerors in their communications, waylaid and robbed them at every opportunity, stole their cattle, and often attacked them in considerable force.

Unfortunately for themselves, however, they had no poet to hand down their story to later ages, and our only account of this long war of centuries is from the conquering Hindus. The conquest by the Aryans meant a widening of the area of civilization; waste and jungle lands were reclaimed and dotted with villages and towns, and the barbarians either submitted to the conquerors or retreated to those hills and mountains where their descendants still live. History repeats itself, and the banks of the Indus were cleared of these non-Aryan aborigines less than eighteen hundred years before Christ in much the same manner as the banks of the Mississippi have been cleared of their non-Aryan tribes in modern times eighteen hundred years after Christ.

To these wars with the aborigines we have frequent allusions in the Rig-Veda, and a translation of some of these passages will give a better idea of these interminable hostilities than any account that we can give of them. The allusions are so numerous that our only difficulty is in making a selection. Thus we read:—

"Indra, who is invoked by many, and is accompanied by his fleet companions, has destroyed by his thunderbolt the Dasyus and Simyus who dwelt on earth, and then he distributed the fields to his white-complexioned friends (Aryans)." Or again: "Indra with his weapon, the thunderbolt, and in his vigour, destroyed the towns of the Dasyus, and wandered at his will. O holder of the thunderbolt be thou cognizant of our hymns, and cast thy weapon against the Dasyu, and increase the vigour and the fame of the Arya."

One of the hymns of the Rig-Veda contains a curious allusion to aboriginal robbers who dwelt on the banks of four small streams called the Sipha, the Anjasi, the Kulisi, and the Virapatni. These robbers, led by Kuyava and Ayu, issued from their fastnesses and harassed the civilized Aryan villages, much in the same way as a true descendant of those aborigines, the

Bhil Tantia in our own times, harassed the peaceful villages of Central India.

Other passages alluding to these early struggles read as follows:—

"Indra protects his Arya worshipper in wars. He who protects him on countless occasions, protects him in all wars. He subdues the people who do not perform sacrifices for the benefit of men. He flays the enemy of his black skin and kills him and reduces him to ashes. He burns down all who do injury and all who are cruel."

"O destroyer of foes! collect together the heads of these marauding troops, and crush them with thy wide foot! Thy foot is wide!

"O Indra! destroy the power of these marauding troops! Throw them into the vile pit—the vast and vile pit!

"O Indra! thou hast destroyed three times fifty such troops! People extol this thy deed, but it is nothing compared to thy prowess!

"O Indra! destroy the Pishachis, who are reddish in appearance and utter fearful yells. Destroy all these Rakshasas.

"O Indra! the poet prays to thee for pleasant food. Thou hast made the earth the bed (burial-ground) of the Dasas. Indra has beautified the three regions with his gifts; he has slain Kuyavacha for King Daryori.

"O Indra! Seers still extol that ancient deed of prowess! Thou hast destroyed many marauders to put an end to war; thou hast stormed the towns of enemies who worship no gods; and thou hast bent the weapons of foes who worship no gods.

"O Asvins! destroy those who are yelling hideously like dogs and are coming to destroy us! Slay those who wish to fight with us! You know the way to destroy them.

"The far-famed god Indra has raised up the (Aryan) man. Strong, mighty, and triumphant, he has brought low the head of the malignant Dasa!

"Indra, who slew Vritra and stormed towns, has destroyed the troops of the black Dasas, and has made the earth and the water for the (Aryan) man, and fulfilled the wishes of the sacrificer."

It would seem from numerous passages in the Rig-Veda that Kutsa was a powerful warrior and a mighty destroyer of the black aborigines. Thus we are told that the god Indra, in order to bestow wealth on Kutsa, slew the "Dasyu, who is wily and impious"; that he helped Kutsa and came to his house with the object of slaying the Dasyu; and that he slew fifty thousand "black-complexioned enemies" in battle. We also learn that Indra made the Dasyus devoid of all virtues, and the object of hatred of all men; and that Indra destroyed five hundred and a thousand Dasas.

We have similar allusions to the subjugation and destruction of Dasyus or Dasas in other passages, while there is a curious reference to an unknown region inhabited by the Dasyus which deserves translation:—

"O ye gods! We have travelled and lost our way

and come to a region where cattle do not pasture. The extensive region gives shelter to Dasyus only. O Brihaspati! lead us in our search for cattle. O Indra! show the way to your worshippers who have lost their way."

We have already mentioned Kuyava and Ayu, two aboriginal robbers who dwelt in fastnesses surrounded by rivers, and harassed the Aryan villages. We likewise have frequent allusions to another powerful aboriginal leader called Krishna, or Black, probably because of his black complexion. One of the passages relating to him is here rendered:—

"The fleet Black warrior lived on the banks of the Ansumati River with ten thousand troops. Indra of his own wisdom became cognizant of this loud-yelling chief; he destroyed the marauding host for the benefit of (Aryan) men.

"Indra said: 'I have seen the fleet Krishna. He is lurking in the hidden regions near the Ansumati, like the sun in a cloud. O Maruts! I desire you to engage in fight and to destroy him.'

"The fleet Black warrior then appeared shining on the banks of the Ansumati. Indra took Brihaspati as his ally and destroyed the fleet and godless army."

Not only have the aborigines been described as howling, yelling, and devoid of a language, but they are considered scarcely human. We are told in one place:—

"We are surrounded on all sides by Dasyu tribes. They do not perform sacrifices; they do not believe in anything; their rites are different; they are not men! O destroyer of foes, kill them! Destroy the Dasa race!"

Elsewhere Indra proclaims that he deprived the Dasyu race of the name of Arya; that he destroyed Navavastva and Brihadratha of the Dasa race; and that

AN INDIAN SCENE.

he cut the Dasas in twain—"it is for this fate that they have been born!"

Such were the aborigines with whom the early Hindus carried on interminable war, and such was the fate to which they consigned their less civilized neighbours, the primeval owners of the Indian soil! It is abundantly evident that no love was lost between the conquerors and the conquered. It was by ceaseless fighting that the conquerors protected themselves in their newly conquered country, gradually extended the limits of cultivation, built new villages, threw out new colonies in primeval jungles, and spread the fame of their prowess around, and thus Aryan history moves forward.

On the other hand, the stubborn barbarians had their revenge. Retreating before the more civilized valour of the Hindus, they hung about in every fastness and

WOMEN DRAWING WATER.

every bend of a river, they waylaid and robbed travellers, harassed villages, killed or stole cattle, and sometimes fell on the Aryans in great hordes. With that dogged tenacity which is peculiar to barbarians they disputed every inch of ground as they retreated, they interrupted the religious rites of the conquerors, despised their gods, and plundered their wealth. But in spite of every resistance, the colonies of the more civilized races extended in every direction, the area of civilization widened, jungles and wastes were brought under cultivation and dotted with villages and royal towns, and the kingdoms of the early Hindus extended over the whole of the Panjab. The barbarians either were exterminated or retreated before the ever-advancing line of Aryan civilization into those hills and fastnesses which their children still inhabit.

It may be imagined, however, that some of the weaker barbarians preferred subjection to extermination or exile; and the Rig-Veda contains allusions to Dasyus who at last owned the domination of the more powerful race and who adopted their civilization and their language. These, then, were the first Hinduized aborigines of India.

On the other hand, the Aryan conquerors were not always at peace among themselves. Sudas was an Aryan king, lord of the Tritsu tribe, and a mighty conqueror. We are frequently told that various Aryan tribes and kings combined against him, but he was victorious over them all. The allusions to these internecine wars among Aryan races, and to the particular tribes who fought against Sudȧs, especially in the famous battle known as the Battle of the Ten Kings, are historically among the most important passages in the Rig-Veda. The united armies of ten allied kings, aroused to combat by the priest Visvamitra, who had himself once been a warrior, met Sudas at the river Ravi (then called Parushni). Sudas is aided by divine help, invoked by his priest Vasishta, and by the river whose flood sweeps the foe to destruction. The following are verses from the pæan that celebrates the victory:—

"The wily foes planned destruction and broke down the embankment of the Adina (to cause an inundation). But Sudas filled the earth with his prowess, and Kavi, the son of Chayamana, fell like a victim.

"For the waters of the river flowed through their old channel and did not take a new course; and Sudas's horse marched over the country. Indra placed the hostile and talkative men and their children under Sudas.

"Sudas earned glory by killing twenty-one men of both regions. As the young priest cuts the kusa grass in the house of sacrifice, even so Sudas cut his enemies. The hero Indra sent the Maruts for his succour.

"The sixty-six thousand six hundred and sixty-six warriors of Anu and Druhya, who had desired cattle and were hostile to Sudas, were laid low. These deeds proclaim the glory of Indra!"

Another hymn relating to Sudas runs thus:—

"O Indra and Varuna! Your worshippers, relying on your help and seeking to win cattle, have marched eastwards with their weapons. Crush, Indra and Varuna, your enemies, whether Dasas or Aryas, and defend Sudas with your protection.

"Where men raise their banners and meet in battle, where nothing seems to favour us, where the men look up to the sky and tremble, there, O Indra and Varuna! help us and speak to us words of comfort.

"O Indra and Varuna! the ends of the earth seem to be lost, and the noise ascends to the skies! The troops of the enemy are approaching. O Indra and

Varuna! who ever listen to prayers, come near us with your protection.

"O Indra and Varuna! you pierced the yet unassailed Bheda, and saved Sudas. You listened to the prayers of the Tritsus. Their priestly vocation bore fruit in the hour of battle.

"O Indra and Varuna! the weapons of the enemy assail me in all directions, the foes assail me among marauding men. You are the owners of both kinds of wealth! Save us in the day of battle.

"Both parties invoked Indra and Varuna for wealth at the time of war. But in this battle you protected Sudas with the Tritsus who were attacked by ten kings.

"O Indra and Varuna! the ten kings who did not perform sacrifices were unable, though combined, to beat Sudas.

"You bestowed vigour, Indra and Varuna, on Sudas, when surrounded by ten chiefs; when the white-robed Tritsus, wearing braided hair, worshipped you with oblations and hymns."

Another remarkable hymn gives an account of the weapons used in war in those days. We make some extracts:—

"When the battle is nigh and the warrior marches in his armour, he appears like the cloud! Warrior, let not thy person be pierced; be. victorious; let thy armour protect thee!

"We will win cattle with the bow, we will win with the bow; we will conquer the fierce and proud enemy with the bow! May the bow foil the desires of the enemy! We will spread our conquests on all sides with the bow!

"The string of the bow when pulled approaches the ear of the archer, making way in battle. It whispers words of consolation to him and with sound it

ANCIENT INDIAN HEAD-DRESS.
(From a Gandhara sculpture.)

clasps the arrow, even as a loving wife clasps her husband.

"The quiver is like the parent of many arrows; the many arrows are like its children. It makes a sound and hangs on the back of the warrior and furnishes arrows in battle and conquers the enemy.

"The expert charioteer stands on his chariot and

drives his horses wheresoever he will. The reins restrain the horses from behind. Sing of their glory.

"The horses raise the dust with their hoofs and career over the field with the chariots, with loud neighings. They do not retreat, but trample the marauding enemies under their feet.

"The arrow is feathered; the deer (horn) is its teeth. Well pulled and sent by the cow-leather string, it falls on the enemy. Wherever men stand together or are separate, there the shafts reap advantage.

"The leather guard protects the arm from the abrasion of the bow-string, and coils round the arm like a snake in its convolutions. It knows its work, and is efficient, and protects the warrior in every way.

"We extol the arrow which is poisoned, whose face is of iron and whose stem is of Parjanya."

Before concluding our extracts, we will make one more from a hymn about the coronation of victorious kings. It is commonly regarded as a later hymn, but it has an interest for the student of history and of customs.

"O king! I place you in the station of a king. Be the lord of this country! Be immovable and fixed! Let all your subjects cherish you! Let not your kingdom be destroyed!

"Remain here fixed as the mountain; do not be dethroned! Remain fixed like Indra and support the kingdom!

"Indra has received the sacrificial offerings and supports the newly crowned king! Soma blesses him.

" The sky is fixed, the earth is fixed, the mountains are fixed, this universe is fixed. He also is fixed as king among his subjects!

" May King Varuna make you immovable! May the good Brihaspati make you immovable! May Indra and Agni support you and make you immovable!

" See, I mix these immortal offerings with the immortal Soma-juice. Indra has brought your subjects under your rule, and made them willing to pay you revenue."

These extracts are enough. We have elsewhere shown that the warriors used not only armour and helmets, but also protecting armour for the shoulder, probably shields. They used javelins and battle-axes, and sharp-edged swords, besides bows and arrows. All the weapons of war known elsewhere in ancient times were known in India four thousand years ago. Drums assembled men in battle, banners led them on in compact masses, and the use of war-horses and chariots was well known; but it does not appear that elephants were regularly used in war in the Vedic Period, as they were in the third and fourth centuries before Christ when the Greeks came to India.

For the rest, it was a turbulent time when the Vedic warriors lived and fought. They had not only to wage unceasing war against the aborigines, but the Hindu states were divided among themselves, and a powerful leader was often bent on annexing his neighbour's state. Rishis engaged in sacrifices asked for prowess to conquer their foes or prayed to the gods for sons who would win victory in battles. Every able-bodied man was a warrior and was ever prepared to defend his home and his fields and his cattle with his strong right arm. Every Hindu colony or tribe, while attentive to the worship of the gods and to the cultivation of the various arts of peace, was at the same time alive to the fact that its national existence depended on constant readiness for war. And the great conglomeration of Hindu tribes, which spread from the banks of the Indus to the banks of the Sarasvati, consisted of hardy, brave, and warlike peoples who maintained their footing in the land and their independence and national existence by constant struggles and a determination to win or die.

CHAPTER VI

SOCIAL LIFE

IT was by such continuous wars against the aborigines of the soil that the Aryans at last conquered the whole of the Panjab from the Indus to the Sarasvati, and from the mountains probably to the sea. As might be expected, we have in the Rig-Veda frequent allusions to the Indus and its five tributaries, especially in the seventy-fifth hymn of the tenth book, which we translate in full:—

"O ye streams! The bard celebrates your excellent prowess in the house of the worshipper. They flow in three systems, seven streams in each system. The prowess of the Indus is superior to that of all others.

"O Indus! when you ran towards land rich in food, Varuna opened out the way for you. You flow over a spacious path on the land. You shine above all flowing rivers.

"The mighty sound of the Indus ascends above the earth to the sky! She flows with mighty force and in radiant form. Her mighty sound is heard as if rains were descending from the clouds with great noise. The Indus comes roaring like a bull.

"As cows bring milk to their calves, even thus, O

Indus, the other streams come sounding to you with their waters! As a king marches with his forces to battle, even thus you march in front with two systems of rivers flowing by your side!

"O Ganga! O Yamuna and Sarasvati and Sutudri (Sutlaj) and Parushni (Ravi)! share this my praise among you! O river combined with Asikni (Chinab)!

SCENE ON AN INDIAN RIVER.

O Vitasta (Jihlam)! O Arjikiya (Beas), combined with Sushoma (Indus)! hear my words.

"O Indus! first thou flowest united with Trishtáma, then with Susartu and Rasa and the Sveti. You unite Krumu (Kurum River) and Gomati (Gomal River) with Kubha (Cabul River) and Mehatnu. You proceed together with these rivers.

"The irresistible Indus proceeds straight, white and dazzling in splendour! She is great, and her waters fill all sides with mighty force. Of all the flowing rivers, none is flowing like her! She is wild like a mare, beautiful like a well-developed woman!

"The Indus is ever young and beautiful. She is rich in horses, in chariots, and in garments; she is rich in gold and is beauteously clad! She is rich in corn and in wool and in straw, and has covered herself with sweet flowers.

"The Indus has fastened horses to her easy chariot

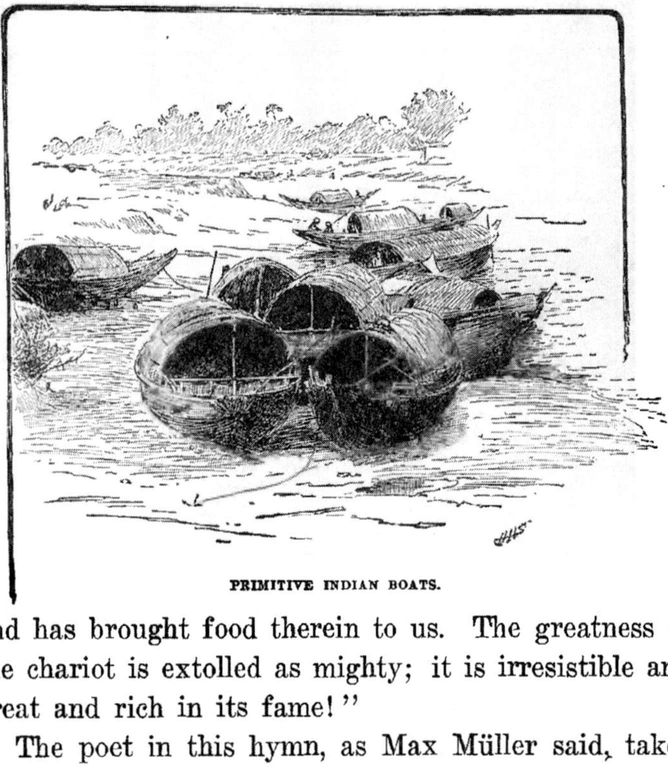

PRIMITIVE INDIAN BOATS.

and has brought food therein to us. The greatness of the chariot is extolled as mighty; it is irresistible and great and rich in its fame!"

The poet in this hymn, as Max Müller said, takes in at one swoop three great river-systems, those flowing from the northwest into the Indus, those joining it from the northeast, and in the distance the Ganges and the Jumna with their tributaries. "It shows the widest

WOMEN OF SALSETTE

geographical horizon of the Vedic poets, confined by the snowy mountains in the north, the Indus and the range of the Suleiman Mountains in the west, the Indus or the sea in the south, and the valley of the Jumna and Ganges in the east." The hymn has historical significance, therefore, with regard to the expansion of the Aryans.

The rivers of the Panjab are sometimes spoken of together as the "seven rivers," and in one passage the seven rivers are said to have the Indus for their mother and the Sarasvati as the seventh. The Indus and its five branches still water the primeval home of the early Hindus, but the Sarasvati, which was the most sacred of ancient rivers and was worshipped even in that remote time as a goddess, has since ceased to flow. Its bed remains visible near Kurukshetra and Thanesvar, however, and these places are still considered sacred by the Hindus.

There is one somewhat curious passage in which the sage Visvamitra, accompanied by chariots and horses and the booty-seeking host of the Bharatas, finds difficulty in crossing the confluence of the Bias and the Sutlaj and pours out an entire hymn to appease the anger of the roaring flood. The rivers yield to the honeyed words of the priest and lower their courses so that the raiding host crosses in safety.

While references to the rivers of the Panjab are thus frequent, allusions to the Ganges and the Jumna are rare, the former being mentioned only twice and the latter three times, but with sufficient clearness to show that the Aryans had at least begun to push as far to the south and east as this territory.

Thus the land of the five rivers was the earliest home of the Aryan settlers in India, and it would seem that the settlers in the Panjab gradually formed themselves into five tribes or nations, especially as the "five lands," "five cultivating tribes," and "five peoples" are frequently mentioned in the Rig-Veda.

We now turn to the interesting and pleasing subject of the social and domestic manners and the home life of these five tribes of the Panjab. The first thing that strikes us here is the absence of those unhealthy rules and restrictions, those marked distinctions between man and man and between class and class, which form the most unpleasant feature of later Hindu society. We have already seen that the sturdy Hindus of the Vedic Period recognized no restrictions against the use of beef, and that they referred with pride to their merchants' going to sea. We have seen, too, that the Rishis did not form a separate and exclusive class and did not pass their lives apart from the world in penance and contemplation. On the contrary, the Rishis were practical men of the world who owned large herds of cattle, cultivated fields, fought against the aboriginal enemies in time of war, and prayed to their gods for wealth and cattle, for victory in war, and for blessings on their wives and children. Every father of a family was, in fact, a Rishi on a small scale, and worshipped his gods in his own house in his own fashion, while the women of the family joined in the worship and helped in the performance of the ceremonies. Some among the community were of course prominent in the composition of hymns and the performance of great sacrifices, and kings and rich men sent for them on great occasions, and rewarded them handsomely. But even these great composers—these great Rishis of the Rig-Veda—did not form an exclusive caste of their own. They were worldly men, who mixed and married with the people, shared property with the people, fought the wars of the people, and were of the people; nor is there a shadow of evidence to prove that they formed a caste of their own, different from the fighters and cultivators. Except for the ninetieth hymn of the tenth book, written long after the Vedic period, there is not a single allusion to caste in the entire collection of the Rig-Veda, composed during six hundred years and more, and replete with references to the habits and manners and customs of the people, to agriculture and pasture and manufacture, to wars against aborigines, to marriage and domestic rules, to the duties and position of women, to religious observances and to the science of the time. But if this be negative proof, there is positive evidence as well, and various passages in the Rig-Veda show that the caste system did not exist at the time when the hymns were written and compiled. The very word *varna*, which in later Sanskrit denotes caste, is used in the Rig-Veda to distinguish the Aryans and the non-Aryans, and nowhere indicates separate sections in the Aryan community. The word *Kshatriya*, which in later Sanskrit means the military caste, is used in the Rig-Veda simply as an adjective which means strong, and is applied to gods. The word *Vipra*, which in later Sanskrit denotes the priestly caste, is used in the Rig-Veda merely as an adjective which means wise and which is applied to gods. And the word *Brāhmana*, which in later Sanskrit connotes also the priestly caste, is used in a hundred places in the Rig-Veda to imply the composers of hymns, and nothing else.

As we have seen, every father of a family was his own priest, and his home was his temple. There is no mention of idols in the Rig-Veda, none of temples or places of worship where the people were to congregate. The sacred fire was lighted in the house of every householder, and he chanted the hymns which we now find collected in the Rig-Veda. We have a pleasing picture of women who assisted at these sacrifices, who ordered the necessary things, prepared them with pestle and mortar, extracted the Soma-juice, stirred it with their fingers, and strained it through a woollen strainer. In numerous places we find mention of wives that joined their husbands and performed the sacrifice together with them, as is shown in the following hymn:—

"O ye gods! The married couple who prepare oblations together, who purify the Soma-juice and mix it with milk,

"May they obtain food for their eating and come united to the sacrifice. May they never have to go in quest of food.

"They do not make vain promises of offerings to the

gods, nor withhold your praise. They worship you with the best offerings.

"Blest with youthful and adolescent offspring, they acquire gold, and they both attain to a mature age.

"The gods themselves covet the worship of such a couple who are fond of sacrifices, and offer grateful food to the gods."

HINDU WOMEN.

From a painting by Edwin Lord Weeks. Copyright, 1895, by Harper & Brothers.

Still more charming is the picture of women who themselves acted as Rishis, and composed hymns and performed sacrifices like men. For there were no harmful restrictions placed on women in those days, no attempt to keep them secluded or uneducated or debarred from their legitimate place in society. There is mention of veiled wives and brides, but no reference to the enforced seclusion of women. On the contrary, we meet them everywhere in their legitimate spheres of action, taking a share in sacrifices and exercising their influence on society. We cherish the picture of the cultured lady Visvavara, which has been handed down to us through thousands of years—a pious woman who composed hymns, performed sacrifices, and with true fervency invoked the god Agni to regulate and keep within virtuous bounds the mutual relations of married couples. We meet with the names of other women also who were Rishis of the Rig-Veda.

In Vedic times, the relations of life were determined by the needs and requirements of individuals rather than by cast-iron rules, as in later days, and there was no religious obligation, therefore, that every girl must be married. On the contrary, we find allusions to unmarried women who remained in the homes of their fathers and naturally claimed and obtained a share of the paternal property. On the other hand, we have frequent references to careful and industrious wives who superintended the arrangements of the house and who possessed those domestic virtues for which Hindu wives have always been noted from the earliest to the present times. Occasionally we have allusions to women who went astray, to maidens who had no brothers to watch over their morals, and to wives who were faithless to their husbands, while elsewhere we are told of the wife of a ruined gambler who becomes the object of other men's lust.

It would seem that girls had some voice in the selection of their husbands. Their selection was not always happy, for " many a woman is attracted by the wealth of him who seeks her. But the woman who is of gentle nature and of graceful form selects, among many, her own loved one as her husband." There can be no doubt, however, that fathers always exercised a wise control in the selection of husbands for their daughters, and, as at the present day, fathers gave the maidens away adorned and decked with golden ornaments.

NAUTCH GIRL.

The ceremony of marriage was an appropriate one, and the promises which the bridegroom and the bride made to each other were suitable to the occasion. It is happily described in a hymn in the later portion of the Rig-Veda, which proves that the custom of child-marriage was then unknown, and that girls were married after they had attained their youth. The following verses from it show the Vedic marriage ritual:—

"O Visvavasu (god of marriage)! arise from this place, for the marriage of this girl is over. We extol Visvávasu with hymns and prostrations.

"O Visvavasu! arise from this place. We worship thee, bending in adoration. Go to an unmarried maiden whose person is well developed; make her a wife and unite her to a husband.

"Let the paths by which our friends go in quest of a maiden for marriage be easy and free of thorns. May Aryaman and Bhaga lead us well. O gods! may the husband and wife be well united.

"O maiden! the graceful sun had fastened thee with ties (of maidenhood), we release thee now of those ties. We place thee with thy husband in a place which is the home of truth and the abode of righteous actions.

"We release this maiden from this place (her father's house), but not from that place (her husband's house). We unite her well with that place. O Indra! may she be fortunate and the mother of worthy sons.

"May Pushan lead thee by the hand from this place. May the two Asvins lead thee in a chariot. Go to thy (husband's) house and be the mistress of the house. Be the mistress of all and exercise thine authority over all in that house.

"Let children be born unto thee, and blessings attend thee here. Perform the duties of thy household with care. Unite thy person with the person of this thy husband; exercise thy authority in this thy house until old age.

"First Soma accepts thee; then Gandharva accepts thee; Agni is thy third lord; the child of man is the fourth to accept thee.

"Soma bestowed this maiden on Gandharva, Gandharva gave her to Agni, Agni has given her to me with wealth and progeny.

"O bridegroom and bride! do ye remain here together; do not be separated. Enjoy food of various kinds; remain in your own home and enjoy happiness in the company of your children and grandchildren.

" (The bride and bridegroom say) May Prajapati bestow on us children; may Aryaman keep us united till old age. (Address to the bride) O bride! Enter with auspicious signs the home of thy husband. Do good to our male servants and our female servants, and to our cattle.

" Be thine eyes free from anger; minister to the happiness of thy husband; do good to our cattle. May thy mind be cheerful, and may thy beauty be bright. Be the mother of heroic sons and be devoted to the gods. Do good to our male servants and our female servants, and to our cattle.

" O Indra! make this woman fortunate and the mother of worthy sons. Let ten sons be born of her, so that there may be eleven men in the family with the husband.

" (Address to the bride) Mayest thou have influence over thy father-in-law and over thy mother-in-law, and be as a queen over thy sister-in-law and brother-in-law."

Polygamy was allowed among kings and the rich in Vedic times, as it was allowed in olden times in all countries and among all nations. Domestic dissensions were the natural result, and we have hymns in the latter part of the Rig-Veda in which wives curse their fellow wives. The evil seems, however, to have grown in the latter part of the Vedic Age, for there are scarcely any allusions to it in the earlier hymns.

There are two curious verses which seem to lay down the law of inheritance and are therefore of peculiar interest. We give a translation of them here:—

"The father who has no son honours his son-in-law, capable of begetting sons, and goes (*i. e.* leaves his property) to the son of his daughter. The sonless father trusts in his daughter's offspring and lives content.

"A son does not give any of his father's property to a sister. He gives her away to be the wife of a husband. If a father and mother beget both son and daughter, then one (*i. e.* the son) engages himself in the acts and duties of his father, while the other (the daughter) receives honour."

This is the first germ of the Hindu law of inheritance, which makes the son, and not the daughter, the inheritor of his father's property and religious duties, and which allows the property to go to the daughter's son only in the absence of male issue. We think we discover the first germs of the Hindu law of adoption, too, in such passages as the following:—

"A son begotten of another may yield us happiness, but can never be regarded or accepted as one's own. And verily he ultimately goes back to his own place. Therefore may a son be newly born unto us who will bring us food and destroy our foes."

We will now supplement our account of domestic customs by making some extracts with regard to funeral rites. Yama in the Rig-Veda is the god of the heaven of the righteous, the god who rewards the virtuous man in a happy land after his death. His two dogs, however, are objects to be avoided or propitiated.

"O thou deceased! proceed to the same place where our forefathers have gone, by the same path which they

BURNING GHATS.

followed. The two kings, Yama and Varuna, are pleased with the offerings; go and see them.

"Go to that happy heaven and join the early forefathers. Join Yama and the fruits of thy virtuous deeds. Leave sin behind, enter thy home.

"O ye ghosts! leave this place, go away, move away! for the forefathers have prepared a place for the deceased. That place is beautiful with day, with sparkling waters, and with light; Yama assigns this place to the dead.

"O thou deceased! these two dogs have four eyes each, and a strange colour. Go past them quickly. Then proceed by the beautiful path to those wise forefathers who spend their time in joy and happiness with Yama."

These verses give us some idea of the belief in future happiness as it prevailed among the Hindus of the Vedic Age. The rites of cremation and burial are alluded to in the following passages:—

"O fire! do not reduce this deceased to ashes; do not give him pain. Do not mangle his skin or his person. O fire! send him to the home of our fathers as soon as his body is burnt in thy heat."

"O thou deceased! go to the extended earth who is as a mother; she is extensive and beautiful. May her touch be soft as that of wool or of a female. You have performed sacrifices; may she save thee from unrighteousness.

"O earth! rise up above him, do not give him pain. Give him good things, give him consolation. As a mother covers her child with the hem of her garment, so cover the deceased.

"Let the earth, raised on him as a mound, lie light. Let a thousand particles of dust rest on him. Let them be to him as a house filled with butter, let them form a shelter to him."

It remains only to allude to one more remarkable verse of this hymn, the eighteenth in the tenth book, which distinctly sanctions the marriage of widows:—

"Rise up, woman, thou art lying by one whose life

is gone; come to the world of the living, away from thy husband, and become the wife of him who holds thy hand and is willing to marry thee."

It is with pain and regret that we refer to another passage belonging to the same hymn in the tenth book from which this last verse is cited. The passage in question may be thus translated:—

"May these women not suffer the pangs of widowhood. May they who have good and desirable husbands enter their houses with collyrium and butter. Let these women, without shedding tears and without any sorrow, first proceed to the house, wearing valuable ornaments." In itself this verse is perfectly harmless, yet by the change in it of *agre* ("first") to *agneh* ("of the fire") sanction was found in later times for the institution of suttee, or the burning of the widow on the pyre of her husband, though in the original form of the stanza—and this cannot be too strongly emphasized—the cruelest of all Hindu institutions finds no support whatever.

CHAPTER VII

VEDIC RELIGION

THE religion of the Rig-Veda is well known. It was pre-eminently the worship of nature in its most imposing and sublime aspects. The sky which bends over all, the beautiful and blushing dawn which like a busy housewife wakes men from slumber and sends them to their work, the gorgeous tropical sun which vivifies the earth, the air which pervades the world, the fire which cheers and enlightens man, and the violent storms which in India usher in those copious rains which fill the land with plenty—these were the gods whom the early Hindus loved to extol and to worship. And often when an ancient Rishi sang the praises of any of the gods, he forgot that there was any other god besides, and his hymn had the character and the sublimity of a prayer to the one God of the universe. Indeed the seers themselves often rose higher than the level of nature-worship and boldly declared that the different gods were but different manifestations or different names of the one Primal Cause.

The sky was naturally the most prominent object of worship, and as the sky assumes various aspects, various names were given to it, and the conception of various deities was formed. The oldest is probably Dyu, but in India he soon lost his place, and the sky in one of its peculiar functions soon usurped his place. For in India the annual rise of rivers, the fertility of land, and the luxuriance of crops depend, not on the sky which shines above us, but on the sky that rains, and Indra soon became the first among the Vedic gods.

Another ancient name of the sky was Varuna, the sky which covered the earth, probably the sky without light, the nightly sky. Both the idea and the name of Varuna as a god of sky were known to the ancestors of the Aryan nations before the Indo-Aryans and the Iranians separated. In that remote period Varuna was the highest and holiest of the gods, and represented the spiritual aspect of religion. After the separation had taken place, this deity of righteousness was translated in Iran into Ahura Mazda, the supreme deity, while to the Hindu Varuna the Vedic bard sang:—

"O Varuna! the birds that fly have not attained thy power or thy vigour; the water which flows ceaselessly and the moving wind do not surpass thy speed.

"King Varuna of unsullied power remains in the firmament and holds on high the rays of light.

"King Varuna has spread out the path for the course of the sun. He has made the path for the sun to traverse in pathless space.

"O King Varuna! a hundred and a thousand medicinal drugs are thine; may thy beneficence be vast and deep. Keep unrighteousness away from us, deliver us from the sins we have committed.

"Yonder stars which are placed on high and are seen by night—where do they go by day? The acts of Varuna are irresistible; the moon shines brightly by his mandate."

Elsewhere, in more ethical strain, the poet prays forgiveness for his sins:—

"O Varuna! with an anxious heart I ask thee about my sins. I have gone to learned men to make inquiry; the sages have all said to me, 'Varuna is displeased with thee.'

"O Varuna! what have I done that thou wishest to destroy thy friend, thy worshipper? O thou of irresistible power, declare it to me, so that I may quickly bend in adoration and come unto thee.

"O Varuna! deliver us from the sins of our fathers. Deliver us from the sins committed in our persons. O royal Varuna! deliver Vasishtha, like a calf from its tether, like a thief who has feasted on a stolen animal.

"O Varuna! all this sin is not wilfully committed by us. Error or wine, anger or dice, or even thoughtlessness, has begotten sin. Even an elder brother leads his younger astray; sin is begotten even in our dreams.

"Freed from sin, I will faithfully serve, as a slave, the Varuna who fulfils our wishes and supports us. We are ignorant, may the Arya god bestow on us knowledge. May the wise deity accept our prayer and bestow on us wealth."

Still more poignant is the entreaty:—

"O King Varuna! may I never go to the earthen home! O thou of great power! have mercy, have mercy!

"O Varuna with thy weapons! I come trembling even like a cloud driven by the wind. O thou of great power! have mercy, have mercy!

"O rich and pure Varuna! I have been driven against righteous acts through weakness. O thou of great power! have mercy, have mercy!

"Thy worshipper hath thirsted even when living in water. O thou of great power! have mercy, have mercy!

"O Varuna! we are mortals. In whatever way we have sinned against gods, in whatever manner we have through ignorance neglected thy work—O do not destroy us for these sins."

Despite the sanctity invariably ascribed to Varuna, however, he was less popular than Indra, who is peculiarly Indian and is unknown to other Aryan nations. One of the most famous legends about Indra, probably the most famous legend in the Aryan world, is the myth of his destruction of the demon Vritra, who confined the waters and would not let them descend until Indra struck the monster with his thunderbolt. The captive waters then descended in copious showers, rivers rose almost instantaneously, and gods and men rejoiced over the changed face of nature. The Maruts, or storm-gods, helped Indra in the battle; sky and earth trembled at the noise. Vritra long waged an unequal combat, only to fall and die at last—the drought was over, and the rains began. Many are the hymns in the Rig-Veda which recount this conflict, but here we have space to cite only one:—

"We sing the heroic deeds which were performed by Indra the thunderer. He destroyed Ahi (the cloud-serpent) and caused rains to descend and opened out the paths for the mountain streams to roll.

"Indra slew Ahi, who rested on the mountains; Tvashtri had made the far-reaching thunderbolt for him. Water in torrents flowed towards the sea, as cows run eagerly towards their calves.

"Impetuous as a bull, Indra quaffed the Soma-juice; he drank the Soma libations offered in the three sac-

A SCENE IN THE HIMALAYAS.

rifices. He then took the thunderbolt and therewith slew the eldest of the Ahis.

"When you killed the eldest of the Ahis, you destroyed the contrivances of the artful contrivers. You cleared the sun and the morning and the sky, and left no enemies behind.

"Indra with his all-destructive thunderbolt slew the darkling Vritra (cloud) and lopped his limbs. Ahi now lies touching the earth like the trunk of a tree felled by the axe.

"The proud Vritra thought that he had no equal, and defied the destroyer and conqueror Indra to combat. But he did not escape destruction, and Indra's foe fell, crushing the clouds in his fall.

"Glad waters are bounding over the prostrate body as rivers flow over fallen banks. Vritra when alive had withheld the water by his power; Ahi now lies prostrate under that water.

"The prostrate body lies concealed and nameless under ceaseless and restless waters, and the waters flow above. Indra's foe sleeps the long sleep."

It would be easy to multiply such legends, but our limits forbid such a course. We will therefore only make a passing mention of the legend of the recovery of light by Indra after the darkness of night. The rays of light are compared to cattle which have been stolen by the powers of darkness, and Indra seeks for them in vain. He sends his messenger Sarama (probably the dawn) after them, and she finds the fortress where the Panis, or powers of darkness, have concealed the cattle. The Panis try to tempt Sarama, but in vain. She returns to Indra, and Indra marches with his forces, destroys the fort, and recovers the cattle; darkness is gone, and the day has dawned. The legend is related in its fullest form in the following hymn:—

The Panis say:—"O Sarama! why hast thou come here? It is a long distance. He who looks back cannot come this way. What have we with us for which thou hast come? How long hast thou travelled? How didst thou cross the Rasa?"

Sarama replies:—"I come as the messenger of Indra. O Panis! it is my object to recover the abundant cattle which you have hidden. The water has helped me; the water felt a fear at my crossing, and thus I crossed the Rasa."

Panis.—"What is that Indra like, whose messenger thou art and for whom thou hast come from a long distance? How does he look? (To one another) Let her come, we will own her as a friend. Let her take and own our cows."

INDRA.
From a modern Hindu drawing.

Sarama.—"I do not see any one who can conquer the Indra whose messenger I am and for whom I have come from a long distance. It is he who conquers everybody. The deep rivers cannot restrain his course. O Panis! you will surely be slain by Indra and will lie down."

Panis.—"O beautiful Sarama! thou hast come from the farthest ends of the sky; we will give thee without any dispute these cows as thou desirest. Who else would have given the cattle without a dispute? We have many sharp weapons with us."

Panis.—"O Sarama! thou hast come here because the god threatened thee and sent thee here. We will accept thee as a sister; do not return. O beautiful Sarama! we will give thee a share of these cows."

Sarama.—"I do not comprehend your words about brothers and sisters. Indra and the powerful sons of Angiras know all. They sent me here to guard the cattle until its recovery. I have come here under their shelter. O Panis! run away far, far from here."

Indra is, in fact, the most vigorous of the Vedic gods, fond of Soma wine, delighting in war, leading his comrades, the Maruts, to fight against drought, leading hosts of the Aryans against the black aborigines, and helping them to win the most fertile spots along the five rivers of the Panjab. The sky and earth gave him birth as a cudgel for their enemies, but when the child went to his mother Aditi for food, he saw Soma wine on her breast and thus drank Soma before he drank his mother's milk.

We now turn to a group of deities who have a more distinctly solar character, some of whom are classed together under the common name of Adityas, or sons of Aditi, the undivided, the unlimited, the eternal.

There is much confusion in the Rig-Veda as to who the Adityas are—the sons of this celestial light. Some lists name Aryaman, Bhaga, Dakṣha, Ansa, Varuna, and Mitra, while elsewhere the Adityas are said to be seven in number, but are not named. We have already seen that Indra is called a son of Aditi. Savitri, the sun, is often described as an Aditya, and so are Pushan and Vishnu, who are also different names of the sun. When, in course of time, the year was divided into twelve months, the number of the Adityas was fixed at twelve, and they became the suns of the twelve months.

Surya and Savitri are the most common names of the sun in the Rig-Veda, and commentators draw a distinction between Savitri, the rising or the unrisen sun, and Surya, the bright sun of day. The golden rays of the sun were naturally compared with arms, until a story found its place in Hindu mythology that Savitri lost his arm at a sacrifice and that it was replaced by a golden arm.

The only extract we will make from the hymns to the sun will be that most celebrated of the many stanzas in the Rig-Veda, the Gayatri, or the morning hymn of the later Brahmans. It is found in the third book and runs as follows:—

SURYA.

Tat savitur varenyam
Bhargo devasya dhīmahi
Dhiyo yo nah prachodayāt.

"We meditate on the desirable light of the divine Savitri who influences our pious rites."

Pushan is the sun as viewed by shepherds in their wanderings in quest of fresh pasture-lands, and the hymns in his honour are all pastoral in their tone. He travels in a chariot yoked with goats, guides men and cattle in their travels and migrations, and knows and protects the flocks. Vishnu has obtained such a prominent place as the Supreme Deity in later Hinduism that there is a natural reluctance among orthodox modern Hindus to accept him in his Vedic character as a mere sun-god. Yet such he is in the Rig-Veda, and he is a very humble deity in the Vedic pantheon, far below Indra or Varuna, Savitri or Agni. It was not till the Puranic times, long after the Christian Era, that Vishnu was considered a Supreme Deity. In the Veda, Vishnu is said to traverse space in three steps, and

A LATE CONCEPTION OF VISHNU.
From Moor's Hindu Pantheon.

is thus to be identified with the sun at dawn, at noon, and at sunset.

Fire was an object of worship in ancient India, where sacrificial fire received the highest regard. As no sacrifice could be performed without fire, Agni, or fire, was called the invoker of the gods. So high was the esteem in which fire was held among the gods of the Rig-Veda, that when the ancient commentator Yaska tried to reduce the number of the Vedic gods to three, he named Agni, or fire, as the god of the earth, Indra or Vayu as the god of the firmament, and the Sun as the god of the sky.

But Agni is not only the terrestrial fire in the Rig-Veda; he is also the fire of the lightning and the sun, and his abode is the invisible heaven. The Bhrigus discovered him there, Matarisvan brought him down, and Atharvan and Angiras, the first sacrificers, first installed him in this world as the protector of men.

AGNI.

Vayu, or the air, has received less consideration from the Vedic bards, and there are but few hymns assigned to him. But the Maruts, or the storm-gods, are oftener invoked, probably because they inspired more terror; and they are considered as the companions of Indra in obtaining rain from the reluctant clouds. The earth trembles as they move in their deer-yoked chariots, and men see the flashing of their arms or the sparkle of their ornaments, the lightning. Yet they are benevolent, and they milk from the udder of their mother Prisni (the storm-cloud) copious showers for the benefit of man.

Rudra, a storm deity, is the father of the Maruts. Like Vishnu, he is a humble deity in the Rig-Veda, and only a few hymns are assigned to him. But like Vishnu, Rudra has attained prominence in later times, and is one of the Hindu Trinity of the Puranic religion, a portion of the Supreme.

Another god who has also changed his character in the Puranas (and very much for the worse!) is Yama, the king of the dead. Whatever the original conception of Yama may be, there is no doubt that in the Rig-Veda he is the king of the departed and the beneficent king of the happy world where the virtuous live and enjoy themselves in after-life. Clothed in a glorious body, they sit by the side of Yama in the realms of light and sparkling waters, they enjoy endless felicity there, and are adored here below under the name of Pitris, or fathers. In the Puranas, on the other hand, Yama, later called the child of the Sun, is the stern avenger of sin and the god of death and hell. The older conception of Yama, whom the Rig-Veda regards as the offspring of Vivasvat (the rising sun) and Saranyu (the dawn), may be illustrated by the stanzas:—

"Worship Yama, the son of Vivasvat, with offerings. All men go to him. He takes men of virtuous deeds to the realm of happiness. He clears the way for many.

"Yama first discovered the path for us. That path will not be destroyed again. All living beings will, according to their acts, follow by the path by which our forefathers have gone."

As a more complete allusion to the future life we may quote here another passage from a hymn to Soma, the juice of a plant made into wine and used as libation in sacrifices:—

"O flowing Soma! take me to that immortal and imperishable abode where light dwells eternal, and which is in heaven. Flow, Soma, for Indra.

"Take me where Yama is king, where there are

the gates of heaven, and where mighty rivers flow. Take me there and make me immortal. Flow, Soma, for Indra.

"Take me where there is the third heaven, where there is the third realm of light above the sky, and where one can wander at his will. Take me there and make me immortal. Flow, Soma, for Indra.

"Take me where every desire is satiated, where Bradhna has his abode, where there is food and contentment. Take me there and make me immortal. Flow, Soma, for Indra.

"Take me where there are pleasures and joys and delights, where every desire of the anxious heart is satiated. Take me there and make me immortal. Flow, Soma, for Indra."

In addition to Yama and his twin sister, Yami, Vivasvat and Saranyu had another pair of twins, the Asvins, who appear in the Rig-Veda as great physicians, healers of the sick and the wounded, and tending many persons with kindness. Long lists of the kind acts of the Asvins are given in several hymns, and the same cures are spoken of over and over again. On their three-wheeled chariot they make the circuit of the world day by day and succour men in their distress.

Brihaspati, or Brahmanaspati, is the lord of hymns, *brahma* in the Rig-Veda meaning hymn. The conception of this deity arose in much the same way as the conception of the deities Fire and Soma. As there is power in the flame and the libation of the sacrifice, so there is power in the prayer uttered; and this power of prayer is personified in the Vedic god Brahmanaspati.

He was a humble god in the Rig-Veda, but in the course of centuries the thinkers of the Upanishads conceived of a Supreme Universal Being and gave him the Vedic name Brahma; and when at last Puranic Hinduism supplanted Buddhism in India, the Puranic thinkers gave the name of Brahmâ to the Supreme Creator of the Universe.

These are the important gods of the Rig-Veda. Of the goddesses there are only two who have any marked individuality, Ushas, the dawn, and Sarasvati, the goddess of the river of that name, who afterwards became the goddess of flowing speech.

There is no lovelier conception in the Rig-Veda than that of the dawn. There are no hymns in the Veda more truly poetical than those dedicated to her, and nothing more charming is to be found in the lyrical poetry of any ancient nation, though here we can make room for only a single extract:—

"She, the young, the white-robed daughter of the sky, the mistress of all earthly treasure, dawns upon us, dissipating darkness! Auspicious Ushas! shine upon us to-day on this spot.

"Following the path of mornings that have passed, to be followed by endless mornings to come, bright Ushas dispels darkness and awakens to life all beings, unconscious like the dead in sleep.

"How long have the Dawns risen? How long will the Dawns arise? The present morning pursues those that are gone, future mornings will pursue this resplendent Ushas.

"Mortals who beheld the pristine Ushas have passed away; we behold her now; and men will come after us who will behold Ushas in the future."

Sarasvati, as her name implies, is the goddess of the river of that name, which was considered holy because of the religious rites performed on its banks and the sacred hymns uttered there. By a natural development of ideas, she was considered the goddess of those hymns, or in other words the goddess of speech, in which character she is worshipped now. She is the only Vedic goddess whose worship continues in India to the present day; all her modern companions, Durga, Kali, Lakshmi, and others, are creations of a later day.

There are no indications in the Rig-Veda of any "temples reared by mortal hands" and consecrated as places of worship. On the contrary, every householder, every patriarch of his family, lighted the sacrificial fire in his own home and poured libations of the Soma-juice and prayed to the gods for happiness to his family, for abundant crops and wealth and cattle, for immunity from sickness, and for victory over the black aborigines. There was no separate priestly caste, and men did not retire into forests and subject themselves to penances in order to meditate on religion and chant these hymns. On the contrary, the old Rishis were worldly men, men with considerable property in crops and in cattle and surrounded by large families, men who in times of danger exchanged the plough for the

Sculptures in the Cave-temple at Karli

One of the most famous cave-temples in India is that of Karli, about midway between Bombay and Poona. The sanctuaries are Buddhist in origin and are of unknown antiquity. The detail and finish of the carvings is marvellous, and the sculptures have fortunately been preserved almost in their original perfection.

spear and the sword, and defended against the black barbarians those blessings of civilization which they solicited from their gods and secured with so much care.

But though each householder was himself the priest, the warrior, and the cultivator, yet we find evidence of kings performing rites on a large scale by help of men specially proficient in the chanting of the hymns and in other religious rites and specially engaged and paid for the purpose. And as we go towards the later hymns of the Rig-Veda, we find this class of professional priests gaining in reputation and in wealth, honoured by chiefs and kings, and rewarded by princely gifts of cattle and chariots. We find mention of particular families specially proficient in the performance of religious rites and ceremonies and in the composition of hymns, and it is more than probable that the existing hymns of the Rig-Veda were composed by members of these families and were

KALI AS WORSHIPPED TO-DAY.
Copyright by Underwood & Underwood, New York.

traditionally learnt by rote and preserved in those families.

It is to these and other venerable houses that the Aryan world owes the preservation of the most ancient compositions of the Aryan race. From century to century the hymns were handed down without break or intermission, and the youths of the priestly houses spent the prime of their life in learning by rote the sacred songs from the lips of their gray-headed sires. It was thus that the inestimable treasure, the Rig-Veda, was preserved for hundreds of years.

In course of time the priests boldly grappled with the deeper mysteries of nature, they speculated about creation and about the future world, and they resolved the nature-gods into the Supreme Deity.

"That all-wise Father saw clearly, and after due reflection created the sky and the earth in their watery form and touching each other. When their boundaries were stretched afar, then the sky and the earth became separated.

"He who is the Creator of all is great; he creates and supports all, he is above all and sees all. He is beyond the seat of the seven Rishis. So the wise men say, and the wise men obtain fulfilment of all their desires.

"He who has given us life, he who is the Creator, he who knows all the places in this universe—he is one, although he bears the names of many gods. Other beings wish to know of him.

"You cannot comprehend him who has created all

this; he is incomprehensible to your mind. People make guesses, being shrouded in a mist; they take their food for the support of their life and utter hymns and wander about."

This sublime hymn teaches us in unmistakable words that the different Vedic gods are but different names of the one incomprehensible Deity. We quote another such hymn:—

"At that time what is, was not, and what is not, was not. The earth was not, and the far-stretching sky was not. What was there that covered? Which place was assigned to what object? Did the inviolate and deep water exist?

"At that time death was not, nor immortality; the distinction between day and night was not. There was only One who lived and breathed without the help of air, supported by himself. Nothing was, excepting Him.

"At first darkness was covered in darkness. All was without demarcation; all was of watery form. The world that was a void was covered by what did not exist and was produced by meditation.

"Desire arose in the mind, the cause of creation was thus produced. Wise men reflect and in their wisdom ascertain the birth of what is from what is not.

"Males with generating seed were produced, and powers were also produced. Their rays extended on both sides and below and above, a self-supporting principle beneath, an energy aloft.

"Who knows truly? Who will describe? When

was all born? Whence were all these created? The gods have been made after the creation. Who knows whence they were made?

"Whence all these were created, from whom they came, whether any one created them or did not create, is known only to Him who lives as Lord in the highest place. If He knows not (no one else knows)."

We will quote here one more hymn, which shows how the later Rishis soared beyond the conception of the nature-gods to the sublime idea of One Deity:—

"In the beginning the Golden Child existed. He was the Lord of all from his birth. He placed this earth and sky in their respective places. Whom shall we worship with offerings?

"Him who has given life and strength, whose will is obeyed by all the gods, whose shadow is immortality and whose slave is death. Whom shall we worship with offerings?

"Him who by his power is the sole king of all the living beings that see and move; him who is the Lord of all bipeds and quadrupeds. Whom shall we worship with offerings?

"Him by whose power these snowy mountains have been made, and whose creations are this earth and its oceans. Him whose arms are these quarters of space. Whom shall we worship with offerings?

"Him who has fixed in their places this sky and this earth; him who has established the heavens and the highest heaven; him who has measured the firmament. Whom shall we worship with offerings?

"Him by whom the sounding sky and earth have been fixed and expanded; him whom the resplendent sky and earth own as Almighty; him by whose support the sun rises and gains its lustre. Whom shall we worship with offerings?

"Mighty waters pervaded the universe, they held in their womb and gave birth to fire. The One Being, who is the life of the gods, appeared. Whom shall we worship with offerings?

"He who by his own prowess controlled the waters which gave birth to energy, he who is the Lord above all gods, he was One. Whom shall we worship with offerings?

"He, the True, who is the creator of this earth, who is the creator of the sky, who is the creator of the glad and mighty waters—may he not do us harm! Whom shall we worship with offerings?

"O Lord of creatures! None but thee has produced all these created things. May the object with which we worship be fulfilled! May we acquire wealth and happiness!"

Thus the religion of the Rig-Veda ascends from nature up to nature's God. The worshipper appreciates the glorious phenomena of nature, and rises from these phenomena to grasp the mysteries of creation and its great Creator.

CHAPTER VIII

THE BRAHMANIC PERIOD AND LITERATURE

WHEN once the Aryan Hindus had reached the Sutlaj, they lost but little time in crossing it and hastening to the valley of the Ganges, so that, in the course of centuries, the entire region as far as the modern Tirhut was the seat of powerful kingdoms and nationalities, who cultivated science and literature in their schools and developed new forms of religion and of civilization widely different from those of the Vedic Period.

Among the nations who flourished in the Ganges valley and left their names in the epic literature of India, the most renowned are the Kurus, who had their kingdom near the modern Delhi; the Panchalas, who settled farther to the southeast, near the present Kanauj; the Kosalas, who occupied the land between the Ganges and the Gandak, or Gunduck, which includes the modern Oudh; the Videhas, who lived beyond the Gandak, in what is now known as Tirhut; and the Kasis, who settled about the modern Benares. These were the most renowned nations of the second period, though other less powerful nationalities also flourished and extended their kingdoms from time to time.

When the Kurus and Panchalas entered the Doab, they gave indications of a vigorous national life, and their internecine wars form the subject of the first National Epic of India, the Mahabharata. And although this work, in its present shape, is the production of a later age, it preserves indications of that rude and sturdy vigour and the warlike jealousy which characterized the early conquerors of the Ganges Valley. The Hindus did not, however, live many centuries in the soft climate of this valley before declining in prowess as they gained in learning and civilization. The royal courts of the Videhas and the Kasis were learned and enlightened, but contemporary literature does not bear witness to their warlike qualities. The Kosalas, too, were a polished nation, but their traditions, preserved in the second National Epic of India, the Ramayana (in its present form a production of later ages), show devotion to social and domestic duties, obedience to priests, and regard for religious forms, rather than the sturdy valour and the fiery jealousies of the Mahabharata.

This gradual enervation of the Hindus was the cause of most important changes in religious and social rules. Religion changed its spirit. The hymns with which the conquerors of the Panjab had invoked the nature-gods scarcely commended themselves to the more effete and more ceremonious Hindus of the Ganges valley. The hymns were still repeated, but lost their meaning and sense, and ceremonials and observances took the place of simple forms. The priestly class increased in number and in influence, until they formed a hereditary caste of their own. The kings and warriors of the valley of the Ganges lived in more splendid courts, and had more gorgeous surroundings than the warriors of the Panjab, and soon separated themselves from the people and formed a caste of their own. The mass of the people—the Vaisyas or Visas of the Rig-Veda—became more feeble than their forefathers in the Panjab, and wore, without a protest, the chains which priests and warriors—the Brahmans and the Kshatriyas—threw around them. And lastly, the aborigines who were subjugated and had adopted the Aryan civilization formed the low caste of Sudras and were declared unfit to perform the Aryan religious rites or to acquire religious knowledge.

TYPE OF THE SUDRA CASTE.

Such was the origin of the caste system in India, in the second period of Hindu history. The system arose out of weakness and lifelessness among the people, and, to a certain extent, it has perpetuated that weakness ever since. At the close of the period, however, there appears to have been a reaction, and the Kshatriyas at last tried to prove their equality with the Brahmans in learning and religious culture. Wearied with the rituals and ceremonials prescribed by priests, the Kshatriyas started new speculations and bold inquiries after the truth. The efforts were unavailing. The priests remained supreme. But the vigorous speculations which the Kshatriyas began are the only redeeming portion of the literature of this period and form the nucleus of the Hindu philosophical systems and religious revolutions of a later day.

It was in this period of Aryan expansion in the Ganges valley that the Rig-Veda and the three other Vedas—Sama, Yajur, and Atharva—were finally arranged and compiled. Then followed another class of compositions known as the Brahmanas, and devoted to sacrificial rites. The custom of retirement from the world into forest life, which was unknown in the earlier ages, then sprang up, and the last portions of the Brahmanas are Aranyakas devoted to forest rites. And lastly, the bold speculations started by the Kshatriyas are known as the Upanishads and form the last portions of the literature of this period, even as they close the so-called Revealed Literature of India formed by the Rig-Veda of the previous period and by the Brahmanas, Aranyakas, and Upanishads, which were written approximately between 1400 and 800 B.C. and which form the literature of the Brahmanic age. This literature alludes constantly to the deeds of the Kurus, the Panchalas, the Kosalas, and the Videhas living in the valley of the Ganges, but it was impossible in the nature of things that hymns like those of the Rig-Veda should be composed after the Hindus had achieved the elaborate civilization and adopted the pompous religious rites of the Brahmanic and Epic Period. Natural phenomena no longer excited the wonder and religious admiration of the cultured and somewhat artificial Aryans of the Ganges valley engaged in solemn rites and elaborate sacrifices. The fervent prayer to the rain-god Indra and the loving address to the dawn-goddess Ushas were almost impossible. The very import and object of the old simple hymns were forgotten, and sacrifices of various descriptions, from simple morning and evening libations to elaborate royal sacrifices lasting for many years, formed the essence of the later religion. The rules of the sacrifices, the import and object of every minute rite, the regulations for each insignificant observance — these constituted the religion of the people, these formed the subjects of discussion between learned kings and royal priests, these formed the bulk of the Brahmana literature.

It was during such a period that the hymns of the Rig-Veda, written in the previous epoch, were compiled, and the same age saw the redaction of the other three Vedas known as the Sama-Veda, the Yajur-Veda (White and Black), and the Atharva-Veda. The reasons which led to the compilation of the Sama-Veda and the Yajur-Veda have been ascertained with a fair degree of certainty. We find mentioned in the hymns of the Rig-Veda different classes of priests who performed different duties at sacrifices. The Adhvaryus were entrusted with the material performance of sacrifice. They measured the ground, built the altar, prepared the sacrificial vessels, fetched wood and water, and immolated animals. The Udgatris, on the other hand, were entrusted with the duty of singing, as according to ancient custom some parts of the sacrifice had to be accompanied by songs. The Hotris had to

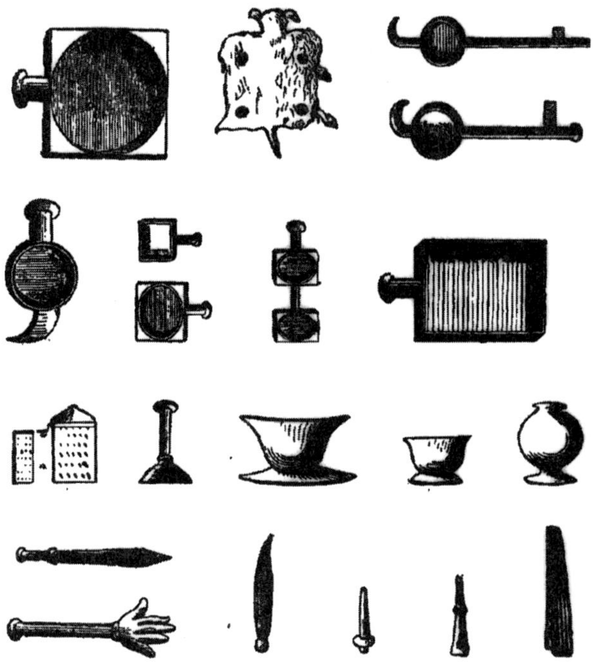

SACRIFICIAL IMPLEMENTS USED IN THE FUNERAL RITES.

recite hymns. And lastly, the Brahmans presided at sacrifices over all the rest.

Of these four classes of priests, neither the Brahman nor the Hotri required any special manual. The Brahman was required to know the entire ceremonial, to be able to superintend the performance of the sacrifice, to advise the other priests on doubtful points, and to correct their mistakes. The Hotri had simply to recite, and if he knew the hymns of the Rig-Veda, he did not require any separate compilation. But the duties of the Adhvaryu and the Udgatri required special training. Special sacrificial formulas must have

UTENSILS FOR RELIGIOUS CEREMONIES.

existed for the former, and a stock of the Rig-Veda hymns, set to music, must also have existed for the latter in the Vedic Period, for we find the names Yajur and Sama in the Rig-Veda hymns. These formulas and chants were, however, separately collected and compiled at a later age, and these separate compilations, in their final form, are the Yajur-Veda and the Sama-Veda as we now have them.

All the verses of the latter Veda, with the exception of a few, are to be found in the Rig-Veda, and it is supposed that these verses, too, must have been contained in some other recension of the Rig-Veda now lost to us. It is clear, therefore, that the Sama-Veda is only a selection from the Rig-Veda set to music for a special purpose.

Of the actual compilers of the Yajur-Veda, on the other hand, we have some information. The more ancient, or Black, Yajur-Veda is called the Taittiriya Samhita, from Tittiri, who probably compiled or promulgated it in its present shape, although in the Anukramani of the Atreya recension of this Veda we are told that it was handed down by Vaisampayana to Yaska Paingi, by Yàska to Tittiri, by Tittiri to Ukha, and by Ukha to Atreya, which would imply that the existing oldest recension of the Yajur-Veda was not the first redaction.

We have fuller information with regard to the more recent White Yajur-Veda. It is called the Vajasaneyi Samhita, from Yajnavalkya Vajasaneya, who held the influential position of chief priest in the court of Janaka, king of the Videhas, so that the promulgation of this new Veda probably proceeded from his royal master's court.

There is a striking difference in arrangement between the White Yajur-Veda and the Black Yajur-Veda. In the latter, the sacrificial formulas are followed by dogmatic explanations, and by accounts of ceremonials belonging to them. In the former, the formulas are found only in the Samhita, the explanation and the ritual being assigned to the Brahmana. It is not improbable, as has been supposed, that it was to improve the old arrangement and to separate the exegetic matter from the formulas, that Yajnavalkya founded the new school known as the Vajasaneyins, and that their labours resulted in a new (Vajasaneyi) Samhita and an entirely separate (Satapatha) Brahmana.

But although the promulgation of the White Yajur-Veda is ascribed to Yajnavalkya, a glance at its contents will show that it is not the compilation of any one man or even of one age. Of its forty chapters only the first eighteen are cited in full and explained in due order in the first nine books of the Satapatha Brahmana, and it is the formulas of these eighteen chapters alone which are found in the older Black Yajur-Veda. These chapters are, therefore, the oldest portion of the White Yajur-Veda, and may have been compiled or promulgated by Yajnavalkya Vajasaneya. The next seven chapters are probably a later addition, while the remaining fifteen chapters are undoubtedly a still later accretion, and are expressly called Parisishta or Khila ("supplement").

Of the Atharva-Veda, we need only state that it was not generally recognized as a Veda till long after the period of which we are speaking, though a class of literature known as the Atharvangiras was growing up during the Brahmanic Period, and is alluded to in the later portions of some of the Brahmanas. Throughout the first three periods of Hindu history, and even in

Manu and other metrical codes, three Vedas are generally recognized. And although the claims of the Atharva were sometimes put forward, still the work was not generally recognized as a fourth Veda till long after the Christian Era. It is only in the Brahmana and Upanishads of the Atharva-Veda itself that we find a uniform recognition of this work as a Veda. It is divided into twenty books, and contains nearly six thousand verses, although a sixth of the collection is in prose. Another sixth is taken from the hymns of the Rig-Veda, mostly from the tenth book. The nineteenth book is a kind of supplement to the previous eighteen, while the twentieth book is made up of extracts from the Rig-Veda.

The Atharva-Veda consists for the most part of formulas intended to protect men against the baneful influences of divine powers, against diseases, noxious animals, and curses of enemies. It knows a host of imps and goblins, and offers homage to them to prevent them from doing harm. The hymns are supposed to bring from the unwilling hands of gods the favours that are wanted. Incantations calculated to procure long life or wealth or recovery from illness, and invocations for good luck in journeys, in gambling, and in intrigue, fill the work. These hymns resemble similar hymns in the last book of the Rig-Veda, except that in the Rig-Veda they are apparently additions made at the time of the compilation, while in the Atharva-Veda they are the natural utterance of the present.

We must now hasten to an account of the compositions called Brahmanas. We have seen that in the Black Yajur-Veda the texts are, as a rule, followed by their dogmatic explanations. These explanations were supposed to elucidate the texts and to explain their hidden meanings, and they contain the speculations of generations of priests. A single discourse

A LAKE SCENE IN INDIA.

of this kind was called a Brahmana; and in later times collections of such discourses were called Brahmanas.

The Rig-Veda has two Brahmanas, the Aitareya and the Kaushitaki. The composition of the former is attributed to Mahidasa Aitareya, son of Itara. In the Kaushitaki Brahmana, on the other hand, special regard is paid to the sage Kaushitaki, whose authority is considered to be final. These two Brahmanas, however, seem to be only two recensions of the same work, used by the Aitareyins and the Kaushitakins respectively, and they agree with each other in many respects, except that the last ten chapters of the Aitareya are not found in the Kaushitaki and probably belong to a later age.

The Sama-Veda has the Tandya, or Panchavinsa, Brahmana, the Shadvinsa Brahmana, the Mantra Brahmana, and the better known Chhandogya.

The Black Yajur-Veda, or Taittiriya Samhita, has its Taittiriya Brahmana, and the White Yajur-Veda, or Vajasaneyi Samhita, has its voluminous Satapatha Brahmana. We have already stated that the Satapatha Brahmana is attributed to Yajnavalkya, though it is more likely the text-book of the school he founded, as he is often quoted in the work. Nor does the work belong entirely to one school or to one age. On the contrary, both in the case of the White Yajur-Veda Samhita and in the case of its Brahmana, there is reason to think that the work belongs to different periods. The first eighteen chapters of the Samhita are the oldest part of the work, and the first nine books of the Brahmana, which comment on these eighteen chapters, are the oldest part of the Brahmana. The remaining five books are later than the first nine.

The Atharva-Veda has its Gopatha Brahmana, a comparatively recent production, the contents of which are a medley, derived to a large extent from other sources.

Next after the Brahmanas come the Aranyakas, which may indeed be considered the last portions of the Brahmanas. They were so designated because they had to be read in the forest, while the Brahmanas were

OVERLOOKING INDRAPAT, THE ANCIENT PANDU CAPITAL.

for use in sacrifices performed by householders in their homes.

The Rig-Veda has its Kaushitaki Aranyaka and its Aitareya Aranyaka, the latter ascribed to Mahidasa Aitareya. The Black Yajur-Veda has its Taittiriya Aranyaka, and the last book of the Satapatha Brahmana is called its Aranyaka. The Sama-Veda and the Atharva-Veda have no Aranyakas.

What gives these Aranyakas a special importance, however, is that they are the proper repositories of those celebrated religious speculations known as the Upanishads. The Upanishads that are the best known and that are undoubtedly ancient are the Aitareya and the Kaushitaki, found in the Aranyakas of those names and belonging to the Rig-Veda; the Chhandogya and the Talavakara (or Kena), belonging to the Sama-Veda; the Vajasaneyi (or Isa) and the Brihadaranyaka, belonging to the White Yajur-Veda; the Taittiriya and Katha and Svetasvatara, belonging to the Black Yajur-Veda; and the Mundaka and Prasna and Mandukya, belonging to the Atharva-Veda. But when the Upanishads had once come to be considered sacred and authoritative works, new compositions of the class began to be added, until the total number reaches two hundred or more. Some of the later Upanishads, which are generally known as the Atharva Upanishads, are as late as the Puranic times, and are sectarian in tendency, instead of being devoted to an inquiry into the nature of Brahma, or the Supreme Spirit, like the old Upanishads. Others still were written long subsequent to the Mohammedan Conquest of India, and the idea of a universal religion which was cherished by the great emperor Akbar finds expression in an Upanishad called the Allah Upanishad.

With the ancient Upanishads the Brahmanic Period ends. Other classes of works, besides those named herein, undoubtedly existed during this epoch, but they have now been lost to us or more frequently replaced by newer works, so that only a fragment of the vast literature of the Brahmanic age has survived to the present day.

॥ अथ श्रीमहाभारतस्य अनुक्रमणिकाप्रारंभः ॥

THE OPENING PAGE OF THE BOMBAY EDITION OF THE MAHABHARATA, REDUCED.

CHAPTER IX

THE EPIC AGE—THE MAHABHARATA

THE tide of Aryan conquests rolled onward. If the reader will refer to a map of India, he will find that from the banks of the Sutlaj to the banks of the Jumna and the Ganges, there is not a very wide strip of country to cross. The Aryans, who had colonized the whole of the Panjab, were not likely to remain inactive on the banks of the Sutlaj or of the Sarasvati. Already in the Vedic Period bands of enterprising colonists had crossed those rivers and explored the distant shores of the Jumna and the Ganges, and those noble streams, though alluded to in the hymns as on the very horizon of the Hindu world, were not unknown. In course of time the emigrants to the fertile banks of the two rivers must have increased in number, until they founded a powerful kingdom of their own in the country near the modern Delhi—the kingdom of the Kurus.

These colonists were no others than the Bharatas renowned in the wars of Sudas, but their kings belonged to the house of Kuru, and hence the tribe went by both names, Bharatas and Kurus. From what part of the Panjab the Kurus came, is a question still involved in obscurity. In the Aitareya Brahmana it is stated that the Uttara Kurus and the Uttara Madras lived beyond the Himalaya, perhaps in Kashmir, but in the epics of the Mahabharata and the Ramayana, the land of the Uttara Kurus became a mythical country, although it is identified with the Ottorakorrha of Ptolemy and placed somewhere east of the modern Kashgar; but we would place the Uttara Kuru alluded to in the Aitareya Brahmana somewhere north of the Sub-Himalayan range, *i. e.* in Kashmir. We assume that the colony of the Kurus on the Ganges rose to prowess and fame about 1400 B. C.

When the Hindus had once begun to settle on the fertile banks of the Jumna and the Ganges, other colonists descended these streams and soon occupied the whole of the Doab, the tract of country between the two rivers. While we find the Kurus or Bharatas occupying the country near the modern Delhi, another adventurous tribe, the Panchalas, seized the tract of country near the modern Kanouj. The original seat of the Panchalas is still less known than that of the Kurus, and it has been supposed that they also came from the northern hills, like the Kurus.

The Panchala kingdom probably rose to distinction about the same time as the kingdom of the Kurus, and the Brahmana literature frequently refers to these allied tribes as forming the very centre of the Hindu world and as renowned by their valour, their learning, and their civilization. Centuries had elapsed since the Aryans had first settled on the banks of the Indus, and the centuries had done their work in progress and civilization. Manners had changed, society had become more refined and polished, learning and art had made considerable progress. Kings invited wise men to their courts, held learned controversies with their priests, performed elaborate sacrifices according to the rules of the age, led trained armies to the field, appointed qualified men to collect taxes and to administer justice, and performed all the duties of civilized administrators. The relations and friends of the king and the warriors of the nation practised archery and driving the war-chariot from their early youth, and also learned the Vedas and all the sacred lore that was handed down from generation to generation. The priests multiplied religious rites and observances, preserved the traditional learning of the land, and instructed and helped the people in their religious duties. And the people lived in their towns and villages, cherished the sacrificial fire in their houses, cultivated the arts of peace, trained their boys from early youth in the Vedas and in their social and religious duties, and gradually developed those social customs which in India have the force of laws. Women had their legitimate influence in society and moved without restriction or restraint.

Civilization, however, does not necessarily put a stop to wars and dissensions; and the only reminiscences we possess of the political history of the Kurus and the Panchalas are those of a sanguinary war in which many neighbouring tribes took part, and which forms the subject of one of the two great epics of India. The incidents of the war described in the Mahabharata are undoubtedly legendary, but nevertheless the great epic is based on the recollections of an actual war of the great Bharatas and faithfully describes the manners and customs of the ancient Hindus in the Brahmanic and Epic Period, as the Iliad describes the manners of the ancient Greeks.

The capital of the Kurus at the time of which we are speaking was the city of Hastinapura, the supposed ruins of which have been discovered on the upper course of the Ganges, about sixty-five miles to the northeast of Delhi. Santanu, the aged King of Hastinapura, died, leaving two sons, Bhishma, who had taken a vow of celibacy, and a younger prince, who became king. This young prince died in his turn, leaving two sons, Dhritarashtra, who was blind, and Pandu, who ascended the throne.

Pandu died, leaving five sons who are the heroes of the epic. Dhritarashtra virtually remained king during the minority of the five Pandavas and of his own children, while Dhritarashtra's uncle, Bhishma, remained the chief councillor and friend of the state.

The account of the martial training of the young Pandavas and the sons of Dhritarashtra throws much light on the manners of royal houses. Drona was a Brahman and a renowned warrior, for caste had not yet completely formed itself, Kshatriyas had not yet obtained the monopoly of the use of arms, nor Brahmans of religious learning. He had been insulted by his former friend, the King of the Panchalas, and had

THE FIVE PANDUS AND DRAUPADI.

retired in disgust to the court of the Kurus, where he educated the princes in the art of war.

Yudhisthira, the eldest of the Pandavas, never became much of a warrior, but was versed in the religious learning of the age, and is the most righteous character in the epic. Bhima, the second, learned to use the club, was renowned for his gigantic size and giant strength, and is indeed the Ajax of the poem. The third, Arjuna, excelled all other princes in the skill of arms and aroused the jealousy and hatred of the sons of

Dhritarashtra, even in their boyhood, Nakula, the fourth, learned to tame horses, and Sahadeva, the fifth, became proficient in astronomy. Duryodhana, the eldest son of Dhritarashtra, was proficient in the use of the club and was a rival to Bhima.

At last the day came for a public exhibition of the proficiency which the princes had acquired in the use of arms. A spacious area was enclosed. Seats were arranged all round for warriors and aged chieftains, for ladies and courtiers, while the whole population of Kuru-land flocked to see the skill of their young princes.

There was shooting of arrows at a target and there was fighting with swords and bucklers and clubs. Duryodhana and Bhima soon began to fight in earnest, and rushed toward each other like mad elephants. Shouts ascended to the sky, and soon the fight threatened to have a tragic end, but at last the infuriated young men were parted, and peace was restored.

Then the young Arjuna entered the lists in golden mail, with his wondrous bow. His splendid archery surprised his most passionate admirers and thrilled the heart of his mother with joy, while shouts of admiration rose from the multitude like the roar of the ocean. He played with his sword, which flashed like lightning, and also with his sharp-edged quoit, or chakra, and never missed his mark. Lastly, he brought down horses and deer to the ground by the noose and concluded by doing obeisance to his worthy preceptor Drona, amidst the ringing cheers of the assembled multitude.

The dark cloud of jealousy lowered on the brow of Dhritarashtra's sons, and soon they brought to the field an unknown warrior, Karna, who was a match for Arjuna in archery. Kings' sons could fight only with their peers, like the knights of old, and Dhritarashtra therefore knighted the unknown warrior, or rather made him a king on the spot, so that Arjuna might have no excuse for declining the fight. To awkward questions which were put to him, the haughty Karna replied that rivers and warriors knew not of their origin and birth—their prowess was their genealogy; but the Pàndavas declined the fight, and Karna retired in silence and in rage.

Drona now demanded the reward of his tuition. Like doughty warriors of old, he held revenge to be the dearest joy of a warrior, and for his reward he asked the help of the Kurus to be revenged on Drupada, king of the Panchalas, who had insulted him. The demand could not be refused. Drona marched against Drupada, conquered him, and wrested from him half his kingdom. Drupada swore to be avenged.

Dark clouds now arose on the horizon of Kuru-land. The time had come for Dhritarashtra to name a Yuvaraja, or prince who would reign during his old age. The claim of Yudhisthira to the throne of his father could not be gainsaid, and he was appointed Yuvaràja. But the proud Duryodhana rebelled against the arrangement, and the old monarch had to yield, and sent the five Pandavas in exile to Varanavata, perhaps the modern Barnawa, not far from Delhi, and then the very frontier of Hindu settlements. The vengeance of Duryodhana pursued them there, and the house where the Pandavas lived was burnt to ashes. The Pandavas and their mother escaped by an underground passage and for a long time roamed about disguised as Brahmans.

Heralds now went from country to country and proclaimed in all lands that the daughter of Drupada,

WINNING THE HAND OF THE PRINCESS.

king of the Panchalas, was to choose for herself a husband among the most skilful warriors of the time. The trial was a severe one, for a heavy bow of great size must be bent, and an arrow shot through a whirling chakra, or quoit, into the eye of a golden fish set high on the top of a pole!

Not only princes and warriors, but multitudes of spectators flocked from all parts of the country to Kampilya, the capital of the Panchalas. The princes thronged the seats, and Brahmans filled the place with Vedic hymns. Then appeared Draupadi with the garland in her hand which she was to offer to the victor of the day. By her side stood her brother Dhrishtadyumna, who proclaimed the feat which was to be performed.

Kings rose and tried to bend the bow, one after another, but in vain. The proud and skilful Karna stepped forth to do the feat, but was prevented.

A Brahman suddenly rose and drew the bow, shooting the arrow through the whirling chakra into the eye of the golden fish. A shout of acclamation arose. And Draupadi, the Kshatriya princess, threw the garland round the neck of the brave Brahman, who led her away as his bride. But murmurs of discontent arose like the sound of troubled waters from the Kshatriya ranks at this victory of a Brahman, who, technically, had no right to the use of arms; and they gathered round the bride's father and threatened violence. The Pandavas now threw off their disguise, and the victor of the day proclaimed himself to be Arjuna, a true-born Kshatriya!

Then follows the strange myth that the Pandavas went back to their mother and said that a great prize had been won. Their mother, not knowing what the prize was, told her sons to share it among them, and as a mother's mandate cannot be disregarded, the five brothers wedded Draupadi as their wife. The Pandavas now formed an alliance with the powerful king of the Panchalas, and forced the blind King Dhritarashtra to divide the Kuru country between his sons and the Pandavas. The division, however, was unequal;

the fertile tract between the Ganges and the Jumna was retained by the sons of Dhritarashtra, while the uncleared jungle in the west was given to the Pandavas. The jungle Khandava Prastha was soon cleared by fire, and a new capital called Indraprastha was built, the supposed ruins of which are shown to every modern visitor to Delhi. The Pandavas, according to the Mahabharata, now undertook various military campaigns

THE ILL-FATED GAMBLING-MATCH.

extending to Bengal and even to Ceylon, but the accounts of these distant expeditions are thought to be later interpolations in the poem.

Now Yudhishthira, as Yuvaraja, was to celebrate the Rajasuya, or coronation ceremony, and all the princes of the land, including his kinsmen of Hastinapura, were invited. The place of honour was given to Krishna, chief of the Yadavas of Gujarat. Sisupala of Chedi violently protested, and Krishna killed him on the spot. The tumult finally subsided, however, and the consecrated water was sprinkled on the newly created monarch, while Brahmans went away laden with presents.

But the newly created king was not long to enjoy his realm. With all his righteousness, Yudhishthira had a weakness for gambling like the other chiefs of the time, and the unforgiving and jealous Duryodhana challenged him to a game. Kingdom, wealth, himself and his brothers, and even his wife were staked and lost, and the five brothers and Draupadi became the slaves of Duryodhana. The proud Draupadi refused to submit to her position, but Duhsasana dragged her to the assembly-room by her hair, and Duryodhana compelled her to sit on his knee in the sight of the stupefied assembly. The blood of the Pandavas was rising, when the old Dhritarashtra was led to the assembly-room and stopped a tumult. It was decided that the Pandavas had lost their kingdom, but should not be slaves. They agreed to go into exile for twelve years, after which they should remain concealed for a year. If the sons of Dhritarashtra failed to discover them during the year, they would get back their kingdom.

THE REPUTED BIRTHPLACE OF KRISHNA AT MATHURA.

Thus the Pandavas again went into exile; and after twelve years of wanderings in various places, disguised themselves in the thirteenth year and took service under the King of Virata. Yudhishthira was to teach the king gambling; Bhima was the head cook; Arjuna was to teach dancing and music to the king's daughter; Nakula and Sahadeva were to be master of horse and master of cattle respectively, and Draupadi was to be the queen's handmaid. A difficulty arose. The queen's brother was enamoured of the new handmaid of superb beauty and insulted her and was resolved to possess her. Bhima interfered and killed the ruffian in secret.

DRAUPADI DRAGGED INTO THE ASSEMBLY.
From Oman's Indian Epics.

Cattle-lifting was not uncommon among the princes of those days, and the princes of Hastinapura carried away some cattle from Virata. Arjuna, the dancing-master, could stand this no longer; he put on his armour, drove out in chariot, and recovered the cattle, but was discovered. The question whether the year of secret exile had quite expired was never settled.

And now the Pandavas sent an envoy to Hastinapura to claim back their kingdom. The claim was refused, and both parties prepared for a war, the like of which had never been seen in India. All the princes of note joined one side or the other, and the battle which was fought in the plains of Kurukshetra, north

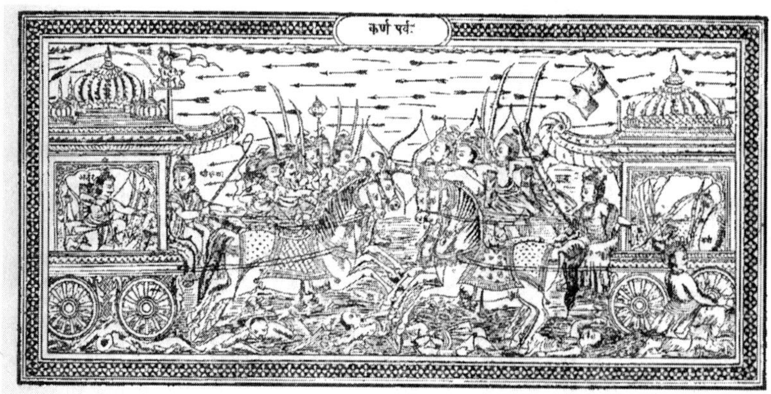

THE PANDUS AND KURUS IN BATTLE.

of Delhi, lasted for eighteen days, ending in fearful slaughter and carnage.

The long story of the battle with its endless episodes need not detain us. Arjuna killed the aged Bhishma unfairly, after that chief was forced to cease from fighting. Drona, with his impenetrable "squares" or phalanxes, slew his old rival Drupada, but Drupada's son revenged his father's death and killed Drona unfairly. Bhima met Duhsasana, who had insulted Draupadi in the gambling-room, cut off his head, and in fierce vindictiveness drank his blood. Lastly, there was the crowning contest between Karna and Arjuna, who had hated each other through life; and Arjuna killed Karna unfairly when his chariot wheels had sunk in the earth and he could not move or fight. On the last or eighteenth day, Duryodhana fled from Bhima, but was compelled by taunts and rebukes to turn and fight, and Bhima by a foul blow (because struck below the waist)

AFTER THE BATTLE OF EIGHTEEN DAYS.

broke the knee to which Duryodhana had once dragged Draupadi. The wounded warrior was left to die, but the bloodshed was not yet over, for Drona's son made a midnight raid on the enemy's camp, killed Drupada's son, and finally quenched the ancient feud in blood. The Pandavas then went to Hastinapura, and Yudhishthira became king. He is said to have subdued every monarch in Aryan India, and at last celebrated the Asvamedha ceremony, or great horse-sacrifice, by letting loose a horse which wandered for a year at will and which no king dared to stop; thus betokening the submission of all the surrounding monarchs, since all the land traversed by the consecrated steed became the domain of the king who had sent it forth.

Such is the story of India's great epic divested of its numerous legends and episodes, its supernatural incidents and digressions; but it is clear, even from this brief account, that the first Hindu colonists of the Ganges valley had not yet lost the sturdy valour and the stubborn warlike determination of the Vedic Age. How imperfectly the caste system flourished among these sturdy races is shown by many facts which still loom out in bold outline amidst the interpolations and additions of later writers. Santanu, the ancient king of Hastinapura, had a brother Devapi, who was a priest; the most learned character in the epic, Yudhishthira, was a Kshatriya; and the most skilful warrior, Drona, was a Brahman.

॥ इति सटीकं श्रीमहाभारतं समाप्तम् ॥

THE CLOSING PAGE OF THE BOMBAY EDITION OF THE MAHABHARATA, REDUCED.

CHAPTER X

THE EPIC AGE—THE RAMAYANA

THE tide of Aryan conquests rolled onward. When the country between the Jumna and the Ganges had been completely conquered, peopled, and Hinduized, new bands of adventurous settlers crossed the Ganges and marched further eastward to found new colonies and new Hindu kingdoms. Stream after stream was crossed, forest after forest was explored and cleared, region after region was slowly conquered, peopled, and Hinduized in this onward march towards the unknown east. The history of the long struggles and the gradual development of the Hindu power in these regions has been lost to us; and we only see, in the literature which has been preserved, the establishment of powerful and civilized Hindu kingdoms east of the Ganges—the kingdom of the Kosalas in the country now known as Oudh, that of the Videhas in North Behar, and that of the Kasis round the modern Benares.

Some recollection of the eastern march of the Videhas has been preserved in a stray passage in the first book of the Satapatha Brahmana.

In legendary form the story is told how King Madhava followed the course of the sacred fire from the

A PLACE HALLOWED BY RAMA.

banks of the Sarasvati eastward to the river which flows from the northern mountains, or the Himalayas, and is called Sadanira, the modern Gandak. That river formed the boundary between the two kingdoms; the

Kosalas lived to the west of it, and the Videhas to the east of it.

In course of years, probably of centuries, the kingdom of the Videhas rose in power and in civilization, until it became the most prominent kingdom in Northern India, and Janaka, King of the Videhas, is probably the most important figure in the history of the Brahmanic and Epic Period in India, for he not only established his power in the farthest confines of the Hindu dominions, but also gathered round him the most learned men of his time, entered into discussion with them, and instructed them in holy truths about the Universal Being. But Janaka has a still higher claim to our respect and admiration. While the priestly caste was multiplying rituals and supplying dogmatic explanations for each rite, the royal caste seems to have felt some impatience at this course, and learned Kshatriyas, while still conforming to the rites laid down by priests, began to inquire about the destination of the soul and the nature of the Supreme Being. So bold, so healthy, and so vigorous were these new and earnest speculations, that the priestly classes at last felt their inferiority and came to Kshatriyas to learn something of the wisdom of the new school. The Upanishads contain these speculations of the warrior caste, and King Janaka of Videha is honoured and respected more than any other king of the time as one of those who inspired the Upanishads, the culmination, in many ways, of the philosophy of India.

These are real claims of Janaka, King of the Videhas, to the admiration and gratitude of posterity, but, curiously enough, posterity remembers him, as well

SCENE IN CEYLON.

as the Videhas and the Kosalas, rather through a myth which has become associated with their names, and relates to the Aryan conquest of Southern India, the Ramayana, the second great epic of India, being devoted to the conquest of Ceylon by a king of the Kosalas who had married the daughter of Janaka, King of the Videhas. This poem, like the Mahabharata, is utterly valueless as a narrative of historical events and incidents. In both the heroes are myths pure and simple.

Sita, the field furrow, had received divine honours from the time of the Rig-Veda and had been worshipped as a goddess. When cultivation gradually spread in Southern India, it was not difficult to invent a poetical myth that Sita was carried to the south. And when this goddess and woman had acquired a distinct and lovely individuality, she was naturally described as the daughter of the holiest and most learned king on record, Janaka of the Videhas.

But who is Rama, described in the epic as Sita's husband and the King of the Kosalas? The later Puranas tell us that he was an incarnation of Vishnu, but Vishnu himself had not risen to prominence at the time of which we are speaking. Indra was still the chief of the gods of the Brahmanic and Epic Period, and in the Sutra literature we learn that Sita, the furrow goddess, is the wife of Indra; it seems, therefore, that Rama, the hero of the Ramayana, is, in his original conception, only a new form of Indra battling with the demons of drought. Myth is thus mixed with the epic which describes the historic conquest of Southern India.

But though the Ramayana is utterly valueless as a narrative of events, still, like the Mahabharata, it throws side-lights on the state of ancient society in India, and the story of the epic therefore needs to be briefly told. In the Ramayana we miss the fiery valour and the proud self-assertion of the Kshatriyas of the Mahabharata, and the subordination of the people to the priestly caste is more complete. Janaka himself is not described as the proud assertor of Kshatriya learning and dignity that he was, but as a humble servant of priests, and Rama himself, the hero of the epic, though he encounters and defeats a Brahman warrior, Parasurama, does so with many apologies and due submission! The story of Parasurama probably conceals a great historic truth. He is said to have fought against the Kshatriyas and exterminated the caste; and then he was conquered by the Kshatriya Rama, the hero of the epic. It would seem that this story indicates the real rivalry and hostilities between the priestly and warrior castes, indications of which we have found in a literary form in the Upanishads.

For the rest, one feels on reading the Ramayana that the real heroic age of India had passed, and that centuries of residence in the valley of the Ganges had produced an enervating effect on the Aryans. We miss the heroic, if somewhat rude and sturdy, manners and incidents which mark the Mahabharata. We miss characters distinguished by real valour and battles fought with real obstinacy and determination. We miss men of flesh and blood, of pride and determination, like Karna and Duryodhana and Bhima; and the best-developed characters in the Ramayana are women like the proud and scheming Kaikeyi or the gentle and ever suffering Sita.

The heroes of the Ramayana are somewhat tame and commonplace personages, very respectful to priests, very anxious to conform to the rules of decorum and duty, doing a vast amount of fighting work mechanic-

TEMPLE DEDICATED TO RAMA AT PUSHKAR NEAR AJMERE.

ally, but without the determination, the persistence of real fighters. A change had come over the spirit of the nation; princes and men had become more polished and law-abiding, but they had become less sturdy and heroic.

Turning to the story of the Ramayana, we find that Dasaratha, a distinguished king of the Kosalas, had his capital in Ayodhya, or Oudh, whose ruins are still shown to travellers in some shapeless mounds. King Dasaratha had three queens honoured above the rest, of whom Kausalya bore him his eldest son Rama, while Kaikeyi was the mother of Bharata, and Sumitra of Lakshmana and Satrughna. Dasaratha in his old age decided on making Rama the Yuvaraja, or reigning prince, but Kaikeyi insisted that her son should be Yuvaraja, and the feeble old king yielded to the determined will of his wife.

SACRED TANK OF RAMA AT NASIK.

Before this Rama had won Sita, the daughter of Janaka, King of the Videhas, at a *svayamvara*, or court of love, in which the bride chooses her husband. Kings and princes had assembled there, but Rama alone could lift the heavy bow and bend it till it broke in twain. But now, when Ayodhya was still ringing with acclamation at the prospect of Rama's installation as Yuvaraja, it was decided in Queen Kaikeyi's chambers that Bharata must be the Yuvaraja and that Rama must go into exile for fourteen years.

Rama was too obedient and dutiful to resist or even to resent this decision. His faithful half-brother Lakshmana accompanied him, and the gentle Sita would not hear of parting from her lord. Amidst the tears and lamentations of the people of Ayodhya, Rama and Sita and Lakshmana went from Kosala's capital.

The exiles first found their way to the hermitage of Bharadvaja in Prayaga, or Allahabad, and then to that of Valmiki in Chitrakuta, somewhere in modern Bundelkhand. Valmiki is reputed to be the author of the epic Ramayana, just as Krishna Dvaipayana Vyasa, the compiler of the Vedas, is said to be the author of the Mahabharata.

Dasaratha died of grief for Rama. The youthful Bharata proceeded at once to Chitrakuta, informed Rama of their father's death, and implored him to return. But Rama felt himself bound by the promise he had made, and it was agreed that he should return after fourteen years and then ascend the throne. Bharata hastened back to Ayodhya, and leaving Chitrakuta, Rama wandered for thirteen years in the Dandaka forest and toward the sources of the Godavari among jungles and non-Aryan tribes, for Southern India had not yet been colonized by the Aryans.

Meanwhile Ravana, the monster King of Lanka, or Ceylon, and of Southern India, heard of the beauty of Sita, who now dwelt in the jungles, and in the absence of Rama he stole her away from their hut and carried her off to Ceylon. Rama, after a long search, obtained a clue of her, made an alliance with the non-Aryan tribes of Southern India, who are described as monkeys and bears, and made preparations for crossing over to Ceylon to recover his wife.

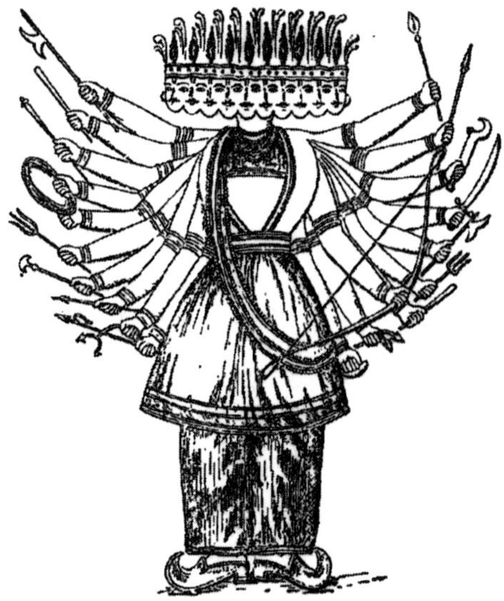

RAVANA.

Vali was a great king among the non-Aryans, but his brother Sugriva thirsted after his kingdom and his wife. Rama fought and killed Vali, helped Sugriva to win the kingdom and Vali's widow, and Sugriva then marched his army to Lanka.

Hanuman, the commander-in-chief of the non-Aryan army, led the way. He leaped over the strait of sixty miles which separates India from Ceylon, found Sita, and returned to Rama.

A causeway was then built across the strait by means of boulders and stones. The reader is aware that a natural causeway runs nearly across the strait, and there is no doubt that the physical aspect of this locality suggested to the poet the idea that the causeway was built by the superhuman labours of Rama's army. The whole army then crossed over and laid siege to the capital of Ravana.

The account of the war which follows, though full of poetical incidents and stirring description, is unnatural and tedious. Chief after chief was sent out by Ravana to beat back the invaders, but they all fell

ABDUCTION OF SITA.
From Oman's Indian Epics.

before the supernatural weapons and mystic mantras of Rama. Indrajit, the proud son of Ravana, battled from the clouds, but Lakshmana killed him. Ravana came out in rage and killed Lakshmana, but the dead hero revived under the influence of some medicine brought by the faithful Hanuman. One of Ravana's brothers, Vibhishana, had left his brother and had joined Rama, and told him the secret by which each warrior could be killed, and thus chief after chief of Ravana's proud host fell. At last Ravana himself came out, and was killed by Rama. Sita was recovered, but she had to prove her purity by throwing herself into a lighted pyre and then coming out of it uninjured.

The fourteenth year of exile having now expired,

HANUMAN.

Rama and Sita returned to Ayodhya and ascended the throne. But the suspicions of the people fell on Sita, who had been in Ravana's house and could not, they thought, have returned unstained. And Rama, as weak as his father had been, obediently exiled his wife.

Valmiki received her at Chitrakuta, and there her two sons, Lava and Kusa, were born. Valmiki composed the poem of the Ramayana and taught the boys to repeat it, and thus years were passed.

Then Rama decided to celebrate the Asvamedha sacrifice, and sent out the horse. The animal came as far as Valmiki's hermitage, and the boys playfully caught it and detained it. Rama's troops tried in vain

HANUMAN AND THE VANARS REJOICING AT THE RESTORATION OF SITA.
Reduced from Moor's "Hindu Pantheon."

to recover the animal. At last Rama himself saw the princely boys, but did not know who they were; he heard the poem Ramayana chanted by them, and it was in a passion of grief and regret that he at last knew them and embraced them as his own.

But there was no joy in store for Sita. The people's suspicions could not be allayed, and Rama was too weak to act against his people. The earth, which had given

Sita birth, opened and received its long-suffering child. The Vedic conception of Sita, as the field furrow, manifests itself in the epic in this incident; but to millions of Hindus, Sita is a real human character, a pattern of female virtue and female self-abnegation. There are few Hindu women throughout the length and breadth of India to whom the story of Sita is not known, and to whom her character is not a model to strive after and to imitate. And Rama, too, though scarcely equal to Sita in worth of character, has been a pattern to men for his truth, his obedience, and his piety. And thus the epic has been for the millions of India a means of moral education, the value of which can hardly be overestimated.

RAMA WITH SITA, LAKSHMANA, AND HANUMAN.

From a native painting.

CHAPTER XI

ARYANS AND NON-ARYANS

THE great river systems of Northern India determined the course of Aryan conquests; when we survey the course of these rivers, we comprehend the history of Aryan conquests during ten centuries. And when we have traced the course of the Indus and its tributaries, and of the Ganges and the Jumna as far as Benares and North Behar, we have seen the whole extent of the Indo-Aryan world as it existed at the close of the Brahmanic and Epic Period, or about 1000 B.C. Beyond this wide tract of Hindu kingdoms, South Behar, Malwa, and a portion of the Deccan and the regions to the south of the Rajputana desert formed a wide semicircular belt of country, as yet not Hinduized, but becoming gradually known to the Hindus and therefore finding occasional mention in the latest works of the Brahmana literature. We can imagine hardy colonists penetrating into this encircling belt of unknown and uncivilized regions, obtaining a mastery over the aborigines wherever they went, establishing some isolated settlements on the banks of fertile rivers, and presenting to the astonished barbarians some of the results of civilized administration and civilized life. We can also imagine saintly anchorites retiring into these wild jungles and fringing the tops of hills or fertile valleys with their holy hermitages, which were the seats of learning and of sanctity. And lastly, adventurous royal huntsmen not infrequently penetrated into these jungles, and unhappy princes exiled by their more powerful rivals often chose to retire from the world and take up their abode in these solitudes.

There is a passage in the last book of the Aitareya Brahmana which, along with an account of the principal Hindu kingdoms of the time, makes some mention of aboriginal races in the south and southwest, and the passage deserves to be quoted:—

"The Vasavas then inaugurated him (Indra) in the eastern direction during thirty-one days by these three Rig verses, the Yajur verse, and the great words ('earth, ether, sky'), for the sake of obtaining universal sovereignty. Hence all kings of eastern nations are inaugurated to universal sovereignty and called Samraj ('universal sovereign') after this precedent made by the gods.

"Then the Rudras inaugurated Indra in the southern region during thirty-one days, with the three Rig verses, the Yajur, and the great words, for obtaining enjoyment of pleasures. Hence all kings of living creatures in the southern region are inaugurated for the enjoyment of pleasures and called Bhoja ('the enjoyer').

"Then the divine Adityas inaugurated him in the western region during thirty-one days, with those three Rig verses, that Yajur verse, and those great words for obtaining independent rule. Hence all kings of the Nichyas and Apachyas in the western countries are inaugurated to independent rule and called 'independent rulers.'

"Then the Visvedevas inaugurated him during thirty-one days in the northern region by those three Rig verses, that Yajur verse, and those great words, for distinguished rule. Hence all people living in northern countries beyond the Himalaya, such as the Uttara Kurus and Uttara Madras, are inaugurated for living without a king and called Viraj ('without a king').

"Then the divine Sadhyas and Aptyas inaugurated Indra during thirty-one days in the middle region, which is a firmly established footing ('the immovable centre') to the kingship. Hence the kings of the Kuru Panchalas, with the Vasas and Usinaras, are inaugurated to kingship and called 'kings.'"

This passage shows us at a glance the whole of the Hindu world as it existed at the close of the Epic Period. To the farthest east lived the Videhas and the Kasis and the Kosalas, as we have seen before, and those newest and youngest of the Hindu colonists excelled in learning and reputation their elder brethren in the west.

In the south, some bands of Aryan settlers must

have worked their way up the valley of the Chambal and become acquainted with the aboriginal tribes inhabiting the country now known as Malwa. We note, however, that the kingdoms in this direction were already called Bhoja, which was in later times the name of the same region, lying immediately to the north of the Vindhya chain and along the valley of the Chambal.

Westwards from this place surged the waves of

HINDUS OF WESTERN DECCAN.

Aryan settlers or adventurers, until the invaders came to the shores of the Arabian Sea and could proceed no farther. The aboriginal tribes in these distant tracts were regarded with contempt by the civilized colonists or invaders, yet these races, dimly known at the very close of the Epic Period, were the ancestors of the proudest and most warlike Hindu tribe of later times, the Maharattas.

To the north the Uttara Kurus and the Uttara Madras and other tribes seem to have lived in the valleys of the Himalayas. To the present day men in these hills live in independent primitive communities, and have very little concern with chief or king, and it is no wonder that in ancient times they should be known as peoples without kings.

And then, in the very centre of the Hindu world, along the valley of the Ganges, lived the powerful tribes of the Kurus and the Panchalas, and the less known tribes, the Vasas and the Usinaras.

In the west, the deserts of Rajputana were wholly unexplored by the Aryans, and the Bhil aborigines of those deserts and mountains were left undisturbed until new and hardy tribes of invaders entered India after the Christian era.

In the far east, South Behar was not yet Hinduized. A passage in the Atharva-Veda which shows that the people of South Behar did not yet belong to the Hindu confederation alludes in terms of enmity to the Angas and the Magadhas. Bengal proper was as yet unknown.

The whole of India south of the Vindhya range was as yet unoccupied by the Hindus, but the Aitareya Brahmana gives the names of certain degraded barbarous tribes, including the Andhras, who in the Philosophic Period rose to be a great civilized Hindu power in the Deccan.

We have now spoken of all the principal Aryan races and kingdoms which flourished in the Epic Period, and of the non-Aryan kingdoms, which formed a semicircular belt in the south of the Hindu world. But before we take leave of kings, we must make some mention of the great coronation ceremony, as described in the Aitareya Brahmana:—

"He spreads the tiger-skin on the throne in such a manner that the hairs come outside and that part

A RAJPUT DESCENDANT OF THE KSHATRIYA CASTE.

which covered the neck is turned eastward. The king, when taking his seat on the throne, approaches it from behind, turning his face eastwards, kneels down with crossed legs, so that his right knee touches the earth, and taking hold of the throne with his hands, prays over it an appropriate mantra.

"The priest then pours the holy water over the king's head and repeats the following: 'With these waters, which are happy, which cure everything, and increase the royal power, the immortal Prajapati sprinkled Indra, Soma sprinkled the royal Varuna, and Yama sprinkled Manu; with the same sprinkle I thee! Be the ruler over kings in this world!' And the ceremony concludes with a drink of the Soma wine which the priest gives to the king."

We are then told that with this ceremony priests invested a number of kings whose names are already known to us. Tura, the son of Kavasha, thus inaugurated Janamejaya, the son of Parikshit. "Thence Janamejaya went everywhere, conquering the earth up to its ends, and sacrificed the sacrificial horse." Parvata and Narada thus invested Yudhamsraushti, the son of Ugrasena. Vasishtha invested Sudas, the great conqueror of the Rig-Veda hymns; and Dirghatamas invested Bharata, the son of Duhshanta, with this ceremony. All these allusions have some historic value.

We have another excellent account of the coronation rite in the White Yajur-Veda, from which we quote a remarkable passage in which the priest blesses the newly crowned king: "May God who rules the world bestow on you the power to rule your subjects. May fire, worshipped by householders, bestow on you supremacy over the householders. May Soma, the lord of trees, bestow on you supremacy over forests. May Brihaspati, the god of speech, bestow on you supremacy in speech. May Indra, the highest among gods, bestow on you the highest supremacy. May Rudra, the cherisher of animals, bestow on you supremacy over animals. May Mitra, who is truth, make you supreme in truth. May Varuna, who cherishes holy works, make you supreme in holy acts."

And in the same Veda is found the sum total of all kingly ethics and kingly duty in the noble verse:—

"If thou shalt be a ruler, then from this day judge the strong and the weak with equal justice, resolve on doing good continually to the people, and protect the country from all calamities."

CHAPTER XII

CASTE IN THE BRAHMANIC AND EPIC AGE

FOUR or five centuries of peaceful residence in a genial climate in the fertile basin of the Ganges and the Jumna enabled the Hindus to found civilized kingdoms, to cultivate philosophy, science, and arts, and to develop their religious and social institutions; but it was under the same gentle but enervating influences that they divided themselves into those separate social classes known as "castes."

We have seen that about the close of the Vedic Period the priests had already formed themselves into a separate profession, and sons stepped forward to take up the duties of their fathers. When religious rites became more elaborate in the Brahmanic and Epic Period, when with the founding of new kingdoms along the fertile Doab kings prided themselves on the performance of vast sacrifices with endless rites and observances, it is easy to understand that the priests who alone could undertake such complicated rites rose in the estimation of the people, until they were naturally regarded as aloof from the ordinary people, as a distinct and superior race—as a caste. They devoted

The Monkey Temple at Benares

This temple, erected in honour of the dread goddess Durga by the Queen of Natre in the eighteenth century, derives its name from the myriads of monkeys which throng it and live on the offerings of food given them by those who visit the shrine.

their lifetime to learning these rites, they alone were able to perform them in all their details, and the natural inference in the popular mind was that they alone were worthy of the holy task.

The very same causes led to the rise of a royal caste. Royalty had not assumed a very high dignity among the Panjab Hindus. Warlike chiefs led clans from conquests to conquests, and the greatest of them were regarded rather as leaders of men and protectors of clans than as mighty kings. Far different was the state of things with the Hindus along the Ganges. Probably in the early days of the martial Kurus and Panchalas caste distinctions had not yet been fully matured. But later, the kings of the peaceful Kosalas and Videhas, surrounded by all the pomp and circumstance of royalty, were looked upon by the humble and lowly people as more than human.

Although the simple origin of caste was obscured in later Hindu literature by strange myths and legends, later Hindu writers never completely lost sight of the fact that it was originally only a distinction based on professions, and this account of its genesis often occurs in the same Puranic works which elsewhere delight in marvellous legends concerning its beginnings.

In the Vayu Purana we are told that in the first, or Krita, Age there were no castes, and that subsequently Brahma established divisions among men according to their works. "Those who were suited for command and prone to deeds of violence, he appointed to be Kshatriyas, from their protecting others. Those disinterested men who attended upon them, spoke the truth, and declared the Veda aright, were Brahmans. Those of them who formerly were feeble, engaged in the work of husbandmen, tillers of the earth, and industrious, were Vaisyas, cultivators and providers of subsistence. Those who were cleansers and ran about on service, and had little vigour or strength, were called Sudras." Accounts more or less similar to this occur in the other Puranas as well.

The Ramayana in its present shape is, as we have seen before, the work of later ages. In its closing sections we are told that in the Krita Age Brahmans alone practised austerities; that in the Treta Age Kshatriyas were born, and then was established the modern system of four castes. Reduced from mythical to historical language, this implies that in the Vedic Age the Hindu Aryans were a united body and practised Hindu rites, but in the Epic Age priests and kings separated themselves as distinct castes, and the people also formed themselves into the lower orders, the Vaisyas and the Sudras.

The Mahabharata also is, in its present shape, a work of later ages, yet there we read that "red-limbed twice-born men who were fond of sensual pleasure, fiery, irascible, daring, and forgetful of their sacrificial duties, fell into the caste of Kshatriyas. Yellow twice-born men, who derived their livelihood from cows and agriculture, and did not practise religious performances, fell into the caste of Vaisyas. Black twice-born men who were impure and addicted to violence and lying, and were covetous and subsisted by all kinds of works, fell into the caste of Sudras. Being thus separated by these their works, the twice-born men became of different castes."

Throughout the Epic Period, and throughout the

SHOP OF A MERCHANT OF THE VAISYA CASTE.

succeeding periods almost to the time of the Mohammedan conquest, the great body of the Aryan people were Vaisyas, although they followed numerous professions. Along with the Brahmans and the Kshatriyas, they formed the Aryan nation, and were entitled to all the rights and privileges and the literary and religious heritages of the nation. The conquered aborigines, who formed the Sudra caste, were alone debarred from the heritage of the Aryans.

This is the cardinal distinction between the ancient caste-system and the caste-system of the present age. Caste reserved some privileges for priests, and some privileges for warriors, in ancient times; but never divided and disunited the Aryan people. Priests and warriors and citizens, though following their hereditary professions from generation to generation, felt that they were one nation and one race, received the same religious instructions, attended the same schools of learning, possessed the same literature and traditions, ate and drank together, intermarried and intermixed in all respects, and were proud to call themselves the Aryan race.

There are numerous passages in the Brahmana literature which show that the distinctions between the castes were by no means so rigid in the early times as at a later period. A remarkable passage, for instance, occurs in the Aitareya Brahmana. When a Kshatriya eats at a sacrifice the portion assigned for Brahmans, his progeny has the characteristics of a Brahman, "ready to take gifts, thirsty after drinking Soma, hungry of eating food, and ready to roam about everywhere according to pleasure." And "in the second or third generation he is capable of entering completely into Brahmanship." When he eats the share of Vaisyas, his "offspring will be born with the characteristic of Vaisyas, paying taxes to another king"; "and in the second or third degree they are capable of entering the caste of Vaisyas." When he takes the share of Sudras, his progeny "will have the characteristics of Sudras; they are to serve the three higher castes, to be expelled and beaten according to the pleasure of their masters." And "in the second or third degree, he is capable of entering the condition of Sudras."

In the same Brahmana we are told of Kavasha, the son of Ilusha, whom the other Rishis expelled from a sacrificial session, saying, "How should the son of a slave girl, a gamester, who is no Brahman, remain among us and become initiated!" But Kavasha knew the gods and all the gods knew him, and he was admitted as a Rishi. Similarly, in the beautiful legend of Satyakama Jabala in the Chhandogya Upanishad, is exemplified the fact that truth and learning opened out in those days a path to the highest honour and to the highest caste. The legend is so beautiful in its simplicity and its poetry, that we feel no hesitation in quoting a portion of it:—

"Satyakama, the son of Jabala, addressed his mother and said: 'I wish to become a Brahmachari (religious student), mother. Of what family am I?'

"She said to him: 'I do not know, my child, of what family thou art. In my youth, when I had to move about much as a servant, I conceived thee. I do not know of what family thou art. I am Jabala by name, thou art Satyakama; say that thou art Satyakama Jabala.'

"He, going to Gautama Haridrumata, said to him:

'I wish to become a Brahmachari with you, sir. May I come to you, sir?'

"He said to him: 'Of what family are you, my friend?' He replied: 'I do not know, sir, of what family I am. I asked my mother, and she answered, "In my youth, when I had to move about much as a

BRAHMAN TYPES.

servant, I conceived thee. I do not know of what family thou art. I am Jabalà by name, thou art Satyakama." I am therefore Satyakama Jabala, sir.'

"He said to him: 'No one but a true Brahman would thus speak out. Go and fetch fuel, friend; I shall initiate you. You have not swerved from the truth.'"

And this truth-loving young man was initiated, and,

according to the custom of the times, went out to tend his teacher's cattle. In time he learnt the great truths which nature, and even the brute creation, teach those whose minds are open to instruction. He gained wisdom even from the herd that he was tending, from the fire that he had lighted, and from a flamingo and a diver-bird which flew near him, when in the evening he had penned his cows and laid wood on the evening fire, and sat behind it. Then the young student came back to his teacher, and his teacher said: "Friend, you shine like one who knows Brahma: who then has taught you?" "Not men," was the young student's reply. And the truth which the young student had learnt, though clothed in the fanciful style of the period, was that the four quarters of heaven, and the earth, the sky, the ocean, the sun, the moon, the lightning, and the fire, and the organs and minds of living beings were none other than Brahma, or God.

This legend shows that the rules of caste had not yet become rigid when such legends were composed. We find in the legend that the son of a servant girl, who did not know his own father, became a religious student simply through his love of truth, learnt the lessons which nature and the learned men of the time could teach him, and subsequently became classed among the wisest religious teachers of the time. Surely the caste of that ancient time must have been freedom itself compared to the system of later times, when the Kshatriya, the Vaisya, and the Sudra were doomed throughout their lives never to rise above the station in which they had been born, though they might sink to the lowest Pariahs if they disobeyed the laws of caste.

CHAPTER XIII

SOCIAL LIFE IN BRAHMANIC AND EPIC TIMES

THE great distinction between the society of Vedic times and the society of the Brahmanic and Epic Periods was, as we have seen, that caste was unknown in the former, and had developed in the latter. But this was not the only distinction. Centuries of culture and progress had had their influence on society, and the Hindus of the period of which we are now speaking had attained a high degree of refinement and civilization, and had developed minute rules to regulate their domestic and social duties. Royal courts were the seats of learning, and sages of all nations were invited, honoured, and rewarded. Justice was officially administered, and law regulated every duty of life. Cities were multiplied throughout India, and had their judges, their executive officers, and their police. Agriculture was fostered, and the king's officers looked to the collection of taxes and the comforts of cultivators.

To such courts as those of the Videhas, the Kasis, and the Kuru-Panchalas learned priests were attached for the performance of sacrifices, and also for the cultivation of learning; and many of the Brahmanas which have been handed down to us were composed in the schools which these priests founded. On great occasions men of learning came from distant towns and villages, and discussions were held not only on ritualistic matters, but on such subjects as the human soul, the future world, the nature of the gods, and the different orders of being, and lastly, on the nature of the Universal Being.

But learning was not confined to royal courts. There were Parishads, or Brahmanic establishments for the cultivation of learning, to which young men went to acquire learning. According to modern writers, a Parishad ought to consist of twenty-one Brahmans well versed in philosophy, theology, and law; but these rules are laid down in later law books, and do not describe the character of the Parishads of earlier days, when four, or even three, Brahmans in a village, who knew the Veda and kept the sacrificial fire, might form a Parishad.

Besides these Parishads, individual teachers often gathered round themselves students from various parts of the country. These students lived with their teachers, served them in a menial capacity during the time of their studentship, and, after twelve years or more, made suitable presents to their teachers and returned to their homes and their relatives. Learned Brahmans too, who retired to forests in their old age, frequently attracted students, and much of the boldest speculation of this period proceeded from these sylvan seats of sanctity and learning.

When students had thus acquired the traditional learning of the age either in Parishads or under private teachers, they returned to their homes, married, and settled down as householders. With marriage began their duties as householders, and the first duty

A HINDU YOUTH.

of a householder was to light the sacrificial fire under an auspicious constellation, to offer libations of milk to the fire both morning and evening, to perform other religious and domestic rites, and, above all, to offer hospitality to strangers. The essence of a Hindu's duties are inculcated in passages like the following:—

"Say what is true! Do thy duty! Do not neglect the study of the Veda! After having brought to thy teacher the proper reward, do not cut off the lives of children! Do not swerve from the truth! Do not swerve from duty! Do not neglect what is useful! Do not neglect greatness! Do not neglect to teach the Veda!

"Do not neglect the works due to the gods and fathers! Let thy mother be to thee like unto a god! Let thy father be to thee like unto a god! Let thy teacher be to thee like unto a god! Whatever actions are blameless, those should be regarded, not others. Whatever good works have been performed by us, those should be observed by thee."

Pleasing pictures of a happy state of society are presented in many passages which we meet with in the literature of the period: "May the Brahmans in our kingdom," says the priest at a horse-sacrifice, "live in piety; may our warriors be skilled in arms and mighty; may our cows yield us profuse milk, our bullocks carry their weights, and our horses be swift; may our women defend their homes, and our warriors be victorious; may our youths be refined in their manners. . . . May Parjanya shower rain in every home and in every region; may our crops yield grains and ripen, and we attain our wishes and live in bliss."

In the Brahmanic age wealth consisted of gold and silver and jewels; of chariots; horses, cows, mules, and slaves; of houses and fertile fields, and even of elephants. Many metals besides gold and silver were known, as is clear from a passage of the Chhandogya Upanishad which describes gold as soldered by means of borax, and silver by means of gold, and tin by means of silver, and lead by means of tin, and iron by means

HINDU WOMEN BATHING IN A POOL.

From a painting by Edwin Lord Weeks. Copyright, 1895, by Harper & Brothers.

of lead, and wood by means of iron, and also by means of leather.

Here and there in the towns and villages were pools that collected rain-water to serve the varied needs of the people. In these pools they washed their clothes, and in their waters they often found relief from the oppressive heat of midday.

As in the Vedic Period, the food of the people consisted of various kinds of grain as well as the meat of animals. In the Brihadaranyaka Upanishad, ten kinds of seeds are mentioned, rice and barley, sesamum and kidney beans, millet and panic seed, wheat, lentils, pulse, and vetches, while the White Yajur-Veda also mentions green gram, wild rice, and shamalo-grass. Grains were ground and sprinkled with curds, honey, and clarified butter, and made into different kinds of cake. Milk and its various preparations have ever been a favourite food in India.

A COUNTRY BULLOCK-CART.

Animal food was in use in the Brahmanic and Epic Period, and the cow and the bull were often laid under requisition. The Aitareya Brahmana states that an ox or a cow was killed when a king or an honoured guest was received; and an honoured guest is called, even in comparatively modern Sanskrit, a cow-killer.

In the Brahmana of the Black Yajur-Veda, the kind and character of the cattle which should be slaughtered in minor sacrifices, for the gratification of particular divinities, are laid down in detail, and the same Brahmana lays down instructions for carving, while the Gopatha Brahmana tells who received the different portions. The priests got the tongue, the neck, the shoulder, the rump, and the legs, while the master of the house appropriated to himself the sirloin, and his wife had to content herself with the pelvis. Plentiful libations of Soma were taken to wash down the meat.

In the Satapatha Brahmana there is an amusing discussion as to the propriety of eating the meat of an ox or a cow, but the conclusion is not very definite: "Let him (the priest) not eat the flesh of the cow and the ox." Nevertheless Yajnavalkya said (taking apparently a very practical view of the matter), "I, for one, eat it, provided it is tender," yet he could scarcely have contemplated the wonderful effects of vegetable and animal diets respectively, as laid down in the following passage in the Brihadaranyaka Upanishad:—

"If a man wishes that a learned daughter should be born to him, and that she should live to her full age, then after having prepared boiled rice with sesamum and butter they (the husband and wife) should both eat, being fit to have offspring.

"And if a man wishes that a learned son should be born to him, famous, a public man, a popular speaker, that he should know all the Vedas, and that he should live to his full age, then, after having prepared boiled rice with meat and butter, they (the husband and wife) should both eat, being fit to have offspring. The meat should be of a young or of an old bull."

And now let our readers construct for themselves a picture of the social life which the Hindus of the Brahmanic and Epic Period—the citizens of Hastinapura and Kampilya and Ayodhya and Mithila—lived three thousand years ago. The towns were surrounded by walls, beautified by edifices, and laid out in streets. The king's palace was always the centre of the town, and was frequented by boisterous courtiers and a rude soldiery, as well as by holy saints and learned priests. The people flocked to the palace on every great occasion, loved, respected, and worshipped the king, and had no higher faith than loyalty to the king. Householders and citizens had their possessions and wealth in gold, silver, and jewels; in chariots, horses, mules, and slaves; and in the fields surrounding the town. They kept the sacred fire in every respectable household, honoured guests, lived according to the law of the land, offered sacrifices with the help of Brahmans, and honoured knowledge. Every Aryan boy was sent to school at an early age. Brahmans and Kshatriyas and Vaisyas were educated together, learned the same lessons and the same religion, and returned home, married, and settled down as householders. Priests and soldiers were a portion of the people, intermarried with the people, and ate and drank with the people. Various classes of manufacturers supplied the various wants of a civilized society, and followed their ancestral professions from generation to generation, but were not cut up into separate castes. Agriculturists lived with their herds and their ploughs in their own villages, and, according to the ancient custom of India, Hindu village communities managed and settled their own village concerns.

We have seen that the absolute seclusion of women was unknown in ancient India. Hindu women held an honoured place in society from the dawn of Hindu civilization four thousand years ago; they inherited and possessed property; they took a share in sacrifices and religious duties; they attended great assemblies on state occasions; they openly frequented public places; they often distinguished themselves in science and in the learning of their times; and they even had their legitimate influence on politics and administration. And although they never mixed so freely in the society of men as women do in modern Europe, yet absolute seclusion and restraint were not Hindu customs; they were unknown in India till the Mohammedan times, and are to this day unknown in parts of India like the Maharashtra, where the rule of the Moslems was brief.

Innumerable passages might be quoted from the Brahmana literature, showing the high esteem in which women were held, but we will content ourselves with one or two. The first is the celebrated conversation between Yajnavalkya and his learned wife Maitreyi on the eve of his retirement to the forest:—

"Now when Yajnavalkya was going to enter upon another state, he said: 'Maitreyi, verily I am going away from this my house. Forsooth let me make a settlement between thee and Katyayani.'"

"Maitreyi said: 'My lord, if this whole earth full of wealth belonged to me, tell me, should I be immortal by it?' 'No,' replied Yajnavalkya; 'like the life of rich people will be thy life. But there is no hope of immortality by wealth.'

"And Maitreyi said: 'What should I do with that by which I do not become immortal? What my lord knoweth of immortality, tell that to me.'

"Yajnavalkya replied: 'Thou who art truly dear to me, thou speakest dear words. Come, sit down, I will explain it to thee, and mark well what I say.'"

And then he explained the principle which is so often and so impressively taught in the Upanishads, that the Universal Soul dwells in the husband, in the wife, in the sons, and in wealth; in the Brahmans and Kshatriyas, and in all the worlds; in the Devas, in all living creatures, and in all the universe. Maitreyi received and grasped this great truth, and valued it more than the wealth of all the world.

Our next quotation, which is also from the Brihadaranyaka Upanishad, relates to a great assembly of learned men in the court of Janaka, King of the Videhas:—

"Janaka Videha sacrificed with a sacrifice at which many presents were offered to the priests. Brahmans of the Kurus and the Panchalas had come thither, and Janaka wished to know which of those Brahmans was the best read. So he enclosed a thousand cows, and ten padas of gold were fastened to each pair of horns.

"And Janaka spoke to them: 'Ye venerable Brahmans, he who among you is the wisest, let him drive away these cows.' Then those Brahmans durst not, but Yajnavalkya said to his pupil, 'Drive them away!' He replied, 'O glory of the Sama!' and drove them away."

On this the Brahmans became angry, and plied Yajnavalkya with questions, but he was a match for them all, and the sages, one by one, held their peace.

There was one in the great assembly who was not deficient in the learning and the priestly lore of those times, and that one was a woman, who rose in the open assembly, and said: "O Yajnavalkya, as the son of a warrior from the Kasis or Videhas might string his loosened bow and take two pointed foe-piercing arrows in his hand and rise to battle, I have risen to fight thee with two questions. Answer me these questions." The questions were put and were answered, and Gargi Vachaknavi was silent.

A TYPE OF BRAHMAN WOMAN.

These passages and many others like them show that women were honoured in ancient India and considered the intellectual companions of their husbands, their affectionate helpers in the journey of life, and the inseparable partners of their religious duties. Hindu wives received the honour and respect due to their position, in addition to having rights to property and to inheritance. In return Hindu wives have ever been honourably distinguished for their fidelity, and feminine unfaithfulness is comparatively rare.

Early marriage and child-marriage were still unknown in the Brahmanic and Epic Periods, and we have numerous allusions to the marriage of girls after they had reached maturity. Widow-marriage was not only not prohibited, but there is distinct sanction for it; and the rites which the widow had to perform before she entered into the married state again are distinctly laid down. As caste was still a pliable institution, men belonging to one caste frequently married widows of another, and Brahmans married widows of other castes without any scruple.

Polygamy was allowed among the Hindus as among many other ancient nations, but was practically confined to kings and wealthy lords. Polyandry, we need hardly say, was unknown in Aryan India, so that the Aitareya Brahmana declares: "For one man has many wives, but one wife has not many husbands at the same time."

There is in the Satapatha Brahmana a curious passage prohibiting marriages among blood-relations to the third or fourth generation: "For now kinsfolk live sporting and rejoicing together, saying, 'in the fourth or third generation we unite,'" and the rule of prohibition became still more strict in later times.

CHAPTER XIV

LAW, ASTRONOMY, AND LEARNING

THE punishment of criminals and the proper administration of laws are foundations on which all civilized societies are built, and no nobler concept of the law has ever been discovered than that formulated by the Brihadaranyaka Upanishad in the words: "Law is the power of the kingdom, nor is there aught higher than the law. Therefore even a weak man rules a stronger with the help of the law as with the help of a king. Thus the law is what is called the true. And if a man declares what is true, they say he declares the law; and if he declares the law, they say he declares what is true. Thus both are the same."

The judicial procedure was still crude, however, and, as among other ancient nations, criminals were often tried by the ordeal of fire.

"They bring a man hither whom they have taken by the hand, and they say: 'He has taken something, he has committed theft.' (When he denies, they say) 'Heat the hatchet for him.' If he committed the theft, then he grasps the heated hatchet, he is burnt, and he is killed. But if he did not commit the theft, then he grasps the heated hatchet, he is not burnt, and he is delivered." Murder, theft, drunkenness, and adultery were considered the most heinous offences.

We will now turn to astronomy. The first elementary knowledge of the astronomical science is discern-

THE ASTRONOMICAL OBSERVATORY, YANTRA SAMANTRA, AT DELHI.

ible in the Rig-Veda itself. The year was divided into twelve lunar months, and a thirteenth, or intercalary, month was added to adjust the lunar with the solar year. The six seasons of the year were named Madhu, Madhava, Sukra, Suchi, Nabha, and Nabhasya, and each was sacred to an individual god. The different phases of the moon were observed and were personified as deities. The position of the moon with regard to the Nakshatras, or the lunar mansions, is also recognized, and some of the constellations of the lunar mansions are named. It would appear from this that the Nakshatras were observed and named in the Vedic Age, but it was in the later period that the lunar zodiac was finally settled.

As might be expected, considerable progress was made in the Brahmanic Period. Astronomy had now come to be regarded as a distinct science, and astronomers by profession were called Nakshatra Darsa and Ganaka. The twenty-eight lunar mansions are also enumerated in the Black Yajur-Veda, and a second and later enumeration occurs in the Atharva Samhita and in the Taittiriya Brahmana, while sacrificial rites were regulated by the position of the moon with reference to these lunar asterisms.

Besides astronomy, other branches of learning were also cultivated in the Brahmanic and Epic Period. Thus in the Chhandogya Upanishad we find Nàrada saying to Sanatkumara, "I know the Rig-Veda, sir, the Yajur-Veda, the Sama-Veda, as the fourth the Atharvana, as the fifth the Itihàsa Purana, the Veda of the Vedas (grammar); the Pitrya (rules for sacrifices for the ancestors); the Rasi (the science of numbers); the Daiva (the science of portents); the Nidhi (the science of time); the Vakovàkya (logic); the Ekayana (ethics); the Deva Vidya (etymology); the Brahma Vidya (pronunciation, prosody, and similar subjects); the Bhuta Vidya (the science of demons); the Kshatra Vidya (the science of weapons); the Nakshatra Vidya (astronomy); the Sarpa Devanjana Vidya (the science of serpents and of genii). All this I know, sir."

In the Brihadaranyaka we are told that "Rig-Veda, Yajur-Veda, Sama-Veda, Atharvangirasas, Itihasa (legends), Purana (cosmogonies), Vidya (knowledge), the Upanishads, Slokas (verses), Sutras (prose rules), Anuvyakhyanas (glosses), and Vyakhyanas (commentaries) have all been breathed forth from the Supreme Being"; while in the eleventh book of the Satapatha Brahmana, we have mention of the three Vedas, the Atharvangirasas, the Anusasanas, the Vidyas, the Vakovakya, the Itihasa Purana, the Narasansis and the Gathas.

It is true that these names do not necessarily imply distinct works which existed in the Epic Period, and which have since been lost to us, and many of these names merely imply the different subjects which are still found in the Brahmanas. It was at a later age, in the Philosophic Period, that these different subjects which we find interwoven in the Brahmanas and Upanishads were developed into separate subjects of study, and were taught in the separate Sutra works and compositions which have come down to us. At the same time, many of these subjects could scarcely have been taught properly and handed down from teacher to pupil without the help of special works on those subjects. We therefore believe that such separate works existed in the Epic Period, and have been lost, only to be replaced by more elaborate and scientific works of a later age on the same subjects.

RAIL IN THE GAUTAMIPUTRA CAVE, NASIK.

CHAPTER XV

THE SACRIFICIAL RITES OF THE BRAHMANAS

THE main feature which distinguishes the religion of the Brahmanic and Epic Period from that of the preceding age is the great importance which came to be attached to sacrifice. In the earlier portion of the Vedic age, men composed hymns in praise of the most imposing manifestations of nature; they deified these various natural phenomena, and they worshipped these deities under the name of Indra or Varuna, of Agni or the Maruts. And the worship took the shape of sacrifice, the offering of milk or grain, as well as of animals or of libations of Soma-juice to the gods.

A gradual change, however, is perceptible towards the close of the Vedic Age, and in the Brahmanic and Epic Age the sacrifice as such, the mere forms and ceremonials and offerings, had acquired such an abnormal importance that everything else was lost in it. This was inevitable when the priests formed a caste. They multiplied ceremonials, and attached the utmost importance to every minute rite, until both they and the worshippers almost lost sight of the deities they worshipped in the voluminous rites they performed.

Sacrifices were generally accompanied by gifts of cattle, gold, garments, and food, and by the offering of animals as victims, and there is a curious passage in the Satapatha Brahmana about animal sacrifice, which deserves to be quoted:—

"At first the gods offered up a man as a victim. When he was offered up, the sacrificial essence went out of him. It entered into the horse. They offered up the horse. When it was offered, the sacrificial essence went out of it. It entered into the ox. When it was offered up, the sacrificial essence went out of it. It entered into the sheep. They offered up the sheep. When it was offered up, the sacrificial essence went out of it. It entered into the goat. They offered up the goat. When it was offered up, the sacrificial essence went out of it. It entered into this earth. They searched for it by digging. They found it in the shape of those two substances, the rice and barley: therefore even now they obtain those two by digging; and as much efficacy as all those sacrificed animal victims would have for him, so much efficacy has this oblation for him who knows this."

If, however, human sacrifice actually prevailed in India either before or during the Vedic Period, we should certainly have found far more frequent allusions to it in the hymns themselves than we find in the later Brahmana literature. But in the Rig-Veda we find no

Sacred Tank of the Temple at Madura.
From a Photograph.

such allusions, for the story of Sunahsepha is no evidence of human sacrifice, and there is absolutely nothing else in the Rig-Veda which can be so construed. It is impossible, on the other hand, to suppose that such a custom should have existed and gradually fallen into disuse without leaving the slightest trace in the Vedic

CEREMONIAL BATHING IN THE GANGES.

hymns, some of which have come down from a very ancient date.

Where, then, do we find allusions to human sacrifice in the literature of the Brahmanic Period? The Sama-Veda is compiled from the Vedic hymns, and of course there is no mention of human sacrifice in this Veda, nor are there allusions to it in the Black Yajur-Veda, or the early portions of the White Yajur-Veda. It is in the very latest compositions of the Brahmanic

Period, in the *khila* or supplementary portion of the White Yajur-Veda, in the Brahmana of the Black Yajur-Veda, in the Aitareya Brahmana of the Rig-Veda, and the last book but one of the Satapatha Brahmana, that we have accounts of human sacrifice. Is it possible to postulate the existence of a custom in India which had passed from the memory of men before the composition and compilation of the Rig-Veda, in the Sama-Veda, in the Black or White Yajur-Veda, but which suddenly revived after a thousand years in the supplements and Brahmanas of the Vedas? Is it not far more natural to suppose that all the allusions to human sacrifice in the later compositions of the Epic Period are the speculations of priests, just as there are speculations about the sacrifice of the Supreme Being himself? If the priests needed any suggestion, the customs of the non-Aryan tribes with whom they became familiar in the Epic Period would give them their cue.

We will now give a brief account of the principal sacrifices which were performed in this ancient age, especially since we know from the Yajur-Veda what these sacrifices were.

The Darsa-purnamasa was performed on the first day after the full and new moon, and Hindus down to the present time consider these days as sacred. The Pindapitri-yajna was a sacrifice to the departed ancestors and is one of the few ancient sacrifices which are performed to this day. The Agnihotra was the daily libation of milk to the sacred fire, performed morning and evening, and the Chaturmasya was a sacrifice which was performed only once every four months. The Agnishtoma was a Soma sacrifice, and the Sautramani was originally an expiation for overindulgence in Soma. The Rajasuya was the imperial coronation sacrifice which was performed by great kings after they had established their prowess and fame by conquests, and the Asvamedha was the celebrated horse-sacrifice which was also performed after great wars and conquests. Humbler than these, but far more important for our purpose, was the Agnyadhana, or setting up of the sacrificial fires, which had an important bearing on the life of every Hindu, and which deserves a few words in explanation.

The monarch Asvapati boasted that in his kingdom there was no thief, no miser, no drunkard, no ignorant person, no adulterer or adulteress, and "no man without an altar in his house." In those days, to keep the sacred fire in the altar was a duty incumbent on every householder, and the breach of this rule was regarded as the deepest impiety. The student who had returned home from his teacher or his Parishad married in due time and then set up the sacrificial fires. This was generally done on the first day of the waxing moon, but sometimes also at full moon, probably to enable the newly married couple to enter on the sacred duties as early as possible. The performance of the Agnyadhana, or the establishment of the sacred fires, generally required two days. The sacrificer chose his four priests, the Brahman, the Hotri, the Adhvaryu, and the Agnidhra, and erected two sheds or fire-houses, for the

Garhapatya and the Ahavaniya fires respectively. A circle was marked for the Garhapatya fire, and a square for the Ahavaniya; while if a southern, or Dakshinagni, fire was required, a semicircular area was marked to the south of the space between the other two.

The Adhvaryu then procured a temporary fire, either

CREMATION ON THE BANKS OF THE GANGES AT BENARES.

producing it by friction, or obtaining it from certain specified sources in the village, and after the usual five-fold lustration of the Garhapatya fireplace, he placed the fire upon it. Towards sunset the sacrificer invoked the gods and manes. He and his wife then entered the Garhapatya house, and the Adhvaryu handed him two pieces of wood, the Arani, for the production of the Ahavaniya fire on the next morning. The sacrificer and his wife laid them on their laps, performed propitiatory ceremonies, and remained awake the whole night and kept up the fire. In the morning the Adhvaryu extinguished the fire, or if there was to be a Dakshinagni, he kept it till that fire was kindled. Such, in brief, is the ceremony of the Agnyadhana, or the setting up of sacrificial fires, which formed an important duty in the life of every Hindu householder in ancient days, when the gods were worshipped by each man on his hearth, and when temples and idols were unknown.

In ancient ages burial was practised by the Hindus. In the Epic Period, however, the custom of burying had ceased altogether; the dead were burnt, and the ashes were buried. According to the account in the White Yajur-Veda, the bones of the dead were collected in a vessel and buried in the ground near a stream, and a mound was raised as high as the knee and covered with grass. The relatives then bathed and changed their clothes and left the funeral ground. The same ceremony is more fully described in the Aranyaka of the Black Yajur-Veda. It is scarcely necessary to add that the custom which now prevails among the Hindus is simple cremation, without the burial of the ashes, and probably began early in the Christian Era.

Another important rite which deserves some explanation is the Pindapitri-yajna, or the gift of cakes to the departed ancestors. The cakes were offered to Fire and to Soma, and the Fathers were invoked to receive their shares. Then followed an address to the Fathers with reference to the six seasons of the year. The worshipper then looked at his wife and said: "Fathers! you have made us domestic men—we have brought these gifts to you according to our power." Then, offering a thread or wool or hair, he said: "Fathers! this is your apparel, wear it." The wife then ate a cake with a desire to have children, and said: "Fathers! let a male be born in me in this season. Do you protect the son in this womb from all sickness." Departed spirits, according to the Hindu religion, receive offerings from their living descendants, and get none when the family is extinct. Hence the extreme fear of Hindus of dying without male issue, so that the birth or adoption of a son is a part of their religion.

We do not purpose to give an account of the other sacrificial rites; what we have already said will convey a general idea as to how sacrifices were performed. We will now turn to some of the legends of the Brahmanas, which are curious and interesting. A most remarkable legend is told of Manu, who in the Vedic hymns is mentioned as the ancient progenitor of man, and who introduced cultivation and worship by fire. The legend of Manu in the Satapatha Brahmana gives the Hindu version of the story of the Flood. As Manu was washing his hands, a fish came unto him and said: "Rear me, I will save thee." Manu reared it, and in time it told him: "In such and such a year that flood will come. Thou shalt then attend to me by preparing a ship." The flood came, and Manu entered into the ship which he had built in time, and the fish swam up to him and carried the ship beyond the northern mountain. There the ship was fastened to a tree, and as the flood subsided, Manu gradually descended. "The flood then swept away all these creatures, and Manu alone remained here."

THE FISH AVATAR OF VISHNU.

The legends relating to the creation of the world are also interesting. There is a beautiful Vedic simile in which the Sun pursuing the Dawn is compared to a lover pursuing a maiden. This gave rise to the legend which is found in the Brahmanas, that Prajapati, the supreme god, felt a passion for his daughter, and this was the origin of creation. This legend in the Brahmanas was further developed in the Puranas, where Brahma is represented as enamoured of his daughter, and all these myths arose from a simple metaphor in the Rig-Veda about the Sun following the Dawn. That such is the origin of the Puranic fables was known to Hindu thinkers and commentators, as will appear from the following well-known argument of Kumarila, the great opponent of Buddhism and the predecessor of Sankaracharya:—

"It is fabled that Prajapati, the Lord of Creation, did violence to his daughter. But what does it mean?

Prajapati, the Lord of Creation, is a name of the sun; and he is so called because he protects all creatures. His daughter Ushas is the dawn. And when it is said that he was in love with her, this only means that at sunrise the sun runs after the dawn, the dawn being at the same time called the daughter of the sun because she rises when he approaches. In the same manner it is said that Indra was the seducer of Ahalya. This does not imply that the god Indra committed such a crime; but Indra means the sun, and Ahalya the night; and as the night is seduced and ruined by the sun of the morning, Indra is called the paramour of Ahalya."

There is another legend of creation in the Taittiriya Brahmana. In the beginning there was nothing except water and a lotus leaf standing out of it. Prajapati dived in the shape of a boar and brought up some earth and spread it out and fastened it down by pebbles. This was the earth.

A similar story is told in the Satapatha Brahmana that, after the creation, the gods and demons both sprang from Prajapati, and the earth trembled like a lotus leaf when the gods and their foes contended for mastery.

Another account of the creation is given in the same Brahmana: "Verily in the beginning Prajapati alone existed here." He created living beings and birds and reptiles and snakes, but they all passed away for want of food. He then made the breasts in the fore part of their body teem with milk, and so the living creatures survived. And thus the world was originally peopled.

While legends and sacrificial rites thus multiplied in the Brahmanic Period, religion was still the same as in the Vedic Period. The gods of the Rig-Veda were still worshipped, and the hymns of the Rig, Sama, or Yajur were still uttered as texts, but the veneration with which the gods were looked up to in the Vedic Period was now merged in the veneration for the sacrificial ceremonies.

New gods, however, were slowly finding a place in the Hindu pantheon. Arjuna was another name of Indra, even in the Satapatha Brahmana. In the White Yajur-Veda we find Rudra already assuming his more modern Puranic names, and acquiring a more distinct individuality, while in the Rig-Veda, as we have already seen, Rudra is the father of the storms, and typifies the thunder. In the White Yajur-Veda he is also described as the thunder-cloud, although his chief aspect is that of a god of destruction and the deity of thieves and criminals. Among his epithets are Girisha (because clouds rest on mountains), Tamra, Aruna, Babhru (from the colour of the clouds), Nilakantha, or blue-necked (for the same reason), Kapardin, or the long-haired, Pasupati, or the nourisher of animals, Sankara, or the benefactor, and Siva, or the beneficent. Yet nowhere in Brahmana literature do we find Rudra represented as the Puranic Siva, the consort of Durga or Kali. In the Kaushitaki Brahmana we find great importance attached in one passage to Isana, or Mahadeva, and the Satapatha Brahmana contains the remarkable passage: "This is thy share, O Rudra! Graciously accept it, together with thy sister Ambika!" In a celebrated passage in the Mundaka Upanishad, an Upanishad of the Atharva-Veda, we find Kali, Karali, Manojava, Sulohita, Sudhumarvarna, Sphulingini, and Visvarupi as the names of the seven tongues of fire. Finally, in the Satapatha Brahmana we are told of a sacrifice being performed by Daksha Parvati, and in the Kena Upanishad we find mention of a woman named Uma Haimavati, who appeared before Indra and explained to Indra the nature of Brahma. These are a few specimens of the scattered materials in the Brahmana literature, from which the gorgeous Puranic legend of Siva and his consort was developed.

SIVA SLAYING KAMADEVA, OR CUPID.

In the Aitareya Brahmana and in the Satapatha Brahmana we are told the story of the gods obtaining from the Asuras the part of the world which Vishnu could stride over or cover, and thus they managed to get the whole world. It is in the concluding book of this latter Brahmana that Vishnu obtains a sort of supremacy among gods, and his head is then struck off by Indra. Krishna, the son of Devaki, is not yet a deity; he is a pupil of Ghora Angirasa in the Chhandogya Upanishad.

While in these scattered allusions we detect materials for the construction of the Puranic mythology of a later day, we also find in the Brahmanic and Epic Period occasional traces of that disbelief in rites and creeds which broke out at a later day in the Buddhist revolution. The Tandya Brahmana of the Sama-Veda contains the Vratya-stomas, by which the Vratyas, or Aryans not living according to the Brahmanical system, could get admission into that community, and some of these heretics are thus described: "They drive in open chariots of war, carry bows and lances, wear turbans, robes bordered with red and having fluttering ends, shoes, and sheepskins folded double; their leaders are distinguished by brown robes and silver neck-ornaments; they pursue neither agriculture nor commerce; their laws are in a state of confusion; they speak the same language as those who have received Brahmanical consecration, but nevertheless call what is easily spoken hard to pronounce."

VISHNU.

CHAPTER XVI

THE RELIGIOUS DOCTRINES OF THE UPANISHADS

FROM the ritual and legends of the Brahmanas the mind of India passed to the more vigorous speculations of the Upanishads. Some impatience appears to have been felt with the elaborate but unmeaning rites, the dogmatic but childish explanations, and the mystic but grotesque reasoning which fill the voluminous Brahmanas; and thinking men asked themselves if this was all that religion could teach. While still conforming to the rites laid down in the older texts, they began to speculate on the destination of the Soul and on the nature of the Supreme Being, and even after the lapse of nearly three thousand years, we must marvel still at the vigour, the earnestness, and the philosophy which characterize the Upanishads, whose most important doctrines are the universal soul, creation, transmigration, and final beatitude.

We begin with the doctrine of a universal soul, an all-pervading Breath, which is the keystone of the philosophy and thought of the Upanishads. This idea is somewhat different from monotheism as it is now understood, for monotheism generally recognizes a Creator as distinct from his creation, but the monotheism of the Upanishads, which has been the monotheism of the Hindu religion ever since, recognizes God as the Universal Being: all things else have emanated from him, are a part of him, and will mingle in him, so as to have no separate existence. This is the great idea which is taught in the Upanishads in a hundred similes, stories, and legends, that impart to them their unique value in the literature of the world. In this spirit the Chhandogya Upanishad declares:—

"All this is Brahma (the Universal Being). Let a man meditate on the visible world as beginning, ending, and breathing in Brahma.

"His body is spirit, his form is light, his thoughts are true, his nature is like ether (omnipresent and invisible), from him all works, all desires, all sweet odours and tastes proceed; he it is who embraces all this, who never speaks and is never surprised.

"He is my self within the heart, smaller than a corn of rice, smaller than a corn of barley, smaller than a mustard seed, smaller than a canary seed or the kernel of a canary seed. He also is my self within the heart, greater than the earth, greater than the sky, greater than heaven, greater than all these worlds.

"He from whom all works, all desires, all sweet odours and tastes proceed, who embraces all this, who never speaks and is never surprised, he—my self within the heart—is that Brahma. When I shall have departed from hence, I shall obtain him."

Such is the sublime language in which the ancient

Hindus expressed their sublime conception of the minute but all-pervading and Universal Being whom they called Brahma, or God.

In the same Upanishad is told the beautiful story of Svetaketu, who stayed with his teacher from his twelfth year to his twenty-fourth, and then returned home, " having then studied all the Vedas, conceited, considering himself well read, and stern." But he had yet things to learn which were not ordinarily taught in the schools of the age, and his father Uddalaka Aruneya taught him the true nature of the Universal Being in such similes as these:—

" As the bees, my son, make honey by collecting the juices of distant trees, and reduce the juice into one form; and as these juices have no discrimination, so that they might say, ' I am the juice of this tree or that,' in the same manner, my son, all these creatures, when they have become merged in the True, know not that they are merged in the True.

" These rivers, my son, run, the eastern (like the Ganges) towards the east, the western (like the Indus) towards the west. They go from sea to sea (*i. e.* the clouds lift up the water from the sea to the sky and send it back as rain to the sea). They become indeed sea. And as those rivers, when they are in the sea, do not know, ' I am this or that river,' in the same manner, my son, all these creatures, proceeding from the True, know not that they have proceeded from the True.

" ' Place this salt in water and then wait on me in the morning.'

" The son did as he was commanded. The father said to him: 'Bring me the salt which you placed in the water last night.' The son, having looked for it, found it not, for, of course, it was dissolved.

" The father said: 'Taste it from the surface of the water. How is it?' The son replied: 'It is salt.' 'Taste it from the middle. How is it?' The son replied: 'It is salt.' 'Taste it from the bottom. How is it?' The son replied: 'It is salt.' The father said: 'Throw it away and then wait on me.'

" The son waited on the father, and the father explained to his son that the Universal Being, though invisible, dwells in us, as the salt is in the water."

These extracts from the Chhandogya bring home to us the Hindu idea of a Universal Being. We will now quote one or two passages from the Kena and the Isa Upanishads:—

" At whose wish does the mind, sent forth, proceed on its errand?" asks the pupil. "At whose command does the first breath go forth? At whose wish do we utter this speech? What god directs the eye or the ear?"

The teacher replies: "It is the ear of the ear, the mind of the mind, the speech of the speech, the breath of the breath, and the eye of the eye.

" That which is not expressed by speech, and by which speech is expressed; that which does not think by mind, and by which mind is thought; that which does not see by the eye, and by which one sees; that which does not hear by the ear, and by which the ear is heard; that which does not breathe by breath, and by which breath is drawn—that alone know as Brahma —not that which people here adore."

And the joy of him who has comprehended, however feebly, the incomprehensible God, has been well described:—

"He who beholds all beings in the Self, and Self in all beings, he never turns away from it.

"When, to a man who understands, the Self has become all things, what sorrow, what trouble can there be to him who once beheld that unity?

"He, the Self, encircled all, bright, incorporeal, scatheless, without muscles, pure, untouched by evil, a seer, wise, omnipresent, self-existent, he disposed all things aright for eternal years."

Lastly, in the Brihadaranyaka Upanishad we are told that all gods are the manifestation of Self, or Purusha, "for he is all gods"; and likewise that he exists in all men, in the Brahman, the Kshatriya, the Vaisya, and the Sudra.

Our extracts on this subject have been somewhat lengthy, but the reader will not regret it. For the doctrine of a Universal Soul is the very keystone of the Hindu religion, and it is necessary to know how this idea was first developed in India in the Upanishads. We will now pass on to another important teaching, the doctrine of creation.

The creation of the world was still a mystery to those early thinkers, and the attempts to solve it were necessarily fanciful. A few passages may be quoted:—

"In the beginning the universe was non-existent. It became existent as it grew. It turned into an egg.

AN INDIAN SCENE.

The egg lay for the time of a year. The egg broke open. The two halves were one of silver, the other of gold.

"The silver one became this earth, the golden one the sky, the thick membrane (of the white) the mountains, the thin membrane (of the yolk) the mist with the clouds, the small veins the rivers, the fluid the sea.

"And what was born from it was Aditya, the Sun. When he was born shouts of joy arose, and all beings arose, and all things which they desired."

A different account is given in the same Chhandogya Upanishad, where we are told that "in the beginning there was that only, which is, One only, without a second." And that sent forth fire, and fire sent forth water, and the water sent forth the earth.

The Aitareya Aranyaka describes how Prana, the Universal Breath, created the world, and then discusses the question of the material cause out of which the world was created. As in the Rig-Veda, and as in the Biblical account of creation, water is said to be the first material cause.

"Was it water really? Was it water? Yes, all this was water indeed. The water was the root, the world was the shoot. He (the person) is the father, they (earth, fire, and other elements) are the sons." And elsewhere in the same Upanishad the following account of Creation is given:—

"Verily in the beginning all this was Self—one only. There was nothing else whatsoever." And that Self sent forth the water (above the heaven), the lights which are the sky, the mortal which is the earth, and the waters under the earth. He then formed the Purusha, and the universe was produced from the Purusha.

Some of these extracts clearly recognize an original

Creator—the Breath or the Soul or the Self—and also a material cause, water or fire. We shall see hereafter how this doctrine of a Primal Soul and Primal Matter is developed in later Hindu Philosophy. We must now turn to the most important doctrine of the transmigration of souls. It is to the Hindus what the doctrine of Resurrection is to Christians. And while the Christians believe that our souls will live in another sphere after death, the Hindus believe that our souls have lived in other spheres before, and will live again in other spheres after death.

The central idea is that which has been adopted as the cardinal principle of the Hindu religion, that good acts lead to their rewards in future existences, but only true knowledge leads to union with the Universal Spirit. "As here on earth whatever has been acquired by exertion perishes, so perishes whatever is acquired for the next world by sacrifices and other good actions performed on earth. Those who depart from hence without having discovered the Self and those true desires, for them there is no freedom in all the worlds."

The doctrine of transmigration of souls is explained as follows in the Brihadaranyaka Upanishad:—

"As a caterpillar, after having reached the end of a blade of grass, and after having made another approach to another blade, draws itself together towards it, thus does the Self, after having thrown off this body and dispelled all ignorance, and after making another approach to another body, draw itself together towards it.

"And as a goldsmith, taking a piece of gold, turns it into another newer and more beautiful shape, so does the Self, after having thrown off this body and dispelled

GOLD WIRE-DRAWERS.

all ignorance, make unto himself another newer and more beautiful shape, whether it be like the Fathers, or like the Gandharvas, or like the Devas, or like Prajapati, or like Brahma, or like other beings.

"So much for the man who desires. But as to the

man who does not desire; who, not desiring, free from desires, is satisfied in his desires, or desires the Self only, his vital spirits do not depart elsewhere; being Brahma, he goes to Brahma.

"And as the slough of a snake lies on an ant-hill, dead and cast away, thus lies the body; but that disembodied immortal spirit is Brahma only, is only light."

And this brings us to the doctrine of final beatitude and salvation. There is nothing more sublime in the literature of the ancient Hindus than the passages in which they fervently recorded their hope and faith that the disembodied soul, purified from all stains and all sins, will at last be received in the Universal Soul, even as light mingles with light. We quote another passage from the Brihadaranyaka Upanishad:—

"He, therefore, that knows, after having become quiet, subdued, satisfied, patient, and collected, sees self in Self, sees all in Self. Evil does not overcome him, he overcomes all evil. Evil does not burn him, he burns all evil. Free from evil, free from spots, free from doubt, he becomes a true Brahman—enters the Brahma world."

It was this doctrine of final beatitude which Death explained to Nachiketas in that beautiful idyl of an Upanishad called Katha, and our chapter may find a fitting close in an extract from that beautiful creation of fancy and of piety.

Nachiketas was given by his father unto Death and entered the abode of Yama Vaivasvata, whom he asked for three boons, the last of which was this:—

"There is that doubt, when a man is dead; some saying, he is; others, he is not. This I should like to know, taught by thee; this is the third of my boons."

But Death was unwilling to reveal his secrets, and told Nachiketas to ask for other boons.

"Choose sons and grandsons who shall live a hundred years, herds of cattle, elephants, gold, horses. Choose the wide abode of the earth, and live thyself as many harvests as thou desirest.

"If thou canst think of any boon equal to that, choose wealth and long life. Be king, Nachiketas, on the whole earth. I make thee the enjoyer of all desires.

"Whatever desires are difficult to attain among mortals, ask for them, anything to thy wish; these fair maidens with their chariots and musical instruments —such indeed are not to be obtained by men; be waited on by them whom I give thee, but ask not me about dying."

Nachiketas said: "These things last till to-morrow, O Death, for they wear out this vigour of all the senses. Even the whole of life is short. Keep thou thy horses, keep dance and song for thyself."

Pressed by the pious inquirer, Death at last revealed the great secret, which is the principle of the Upanishads and the principle of the Hindu religion:—

"The sage who, by means of meditation on himself, recognizes the Ancient, who is difficult to be seen, who has entered into the dark, who has hidden in the cave, who dwells in the abyss, as God—he indeed leaves joy and sorrow far behind.

"A mortal who has heard this and embraced it, who has separated from it all qualities, and has thus reached the subtle Being, rejoices because he has obtained what is a cause for rejoicing. The house of Brahma is open, I believe, O Nachiketas!"

BRAHMA.

Who can, even in the present day, peruse these pious inquiries and fervent thoughts of a long-buried past, without feeling a new emotion in his heart, without seeing a new light before his eyes? The mysteries of the unknown future will never be solved by human intellect or by human science; but the first recorded attempts of India to solve them in a pious, fervent, philosophical spirit will ever have an abiding interest for every patriotic Hindu and for every thoughtful man.

By no other has this truth been recognized more fully or felt more deeply than by Schopenhauer when he wrote: "From every sentence deep, original, and sublime thoughts arise, and the whole is pervaded by a high and holy and earnest spirit. Indian air surrounds us, and original thoughts of kindred spirits. In the whole world there is no study so beneficial and so elevating as that of the Upanishads. It has been the solace of my life; it will be the solace of my death."

CHAPTER XVII

THE AGE OF LAWS AND PHILOSOPHY

THE age of laws, rationalism, and philosophy is, in many respects, the most brilliant epoch of India's history, for it was in this period that the Aryans spread forth from the valley of the Ganges and established Hindu kingdoms with Hindu civilization as far as the southernmost boundaries of the peninsula. Magadha, or South Behar, already known to the Hindus of the Brahmanic period, was now completely Hinduized, and the young and powerful kingdom founded there soon eclipsed all the ancient realms of the Ganges valley. Buddhism spread from Magadha to surrounding dominions, and Aryan colonists penetrated to Bengal and introduced Hindu religion and culture among the aborigines. The kingdoms established in the south won still greater distinction. The Andhras founded a powerful dominion in the Deccan and developed great schools of learning, while further south the Aryans came in contact with the ancient Dravidian civilization. The more perfect Hindu culture prevailed, and the Dravidians were Hinduized and founded kingdoms which became distinguished for learning and power. The three sister kingdoms of the Cholas, the Cheras, and the Pandyas made their mark before the third century B. C., and Kanchi (Conjevaram), the capital of the Cholas, distinguished itself as the seat of Hindu learning at a later day. In the west the Saurashtras (including Gujarat and the Maharatta country) received Hindu civilization; and in this period

SCULPTURE FROM THE BUDDHIST TOPE NEAR BENARES.

Ceylon was discovered, and formed a great resort of Hindu traders.

The practical and enterprising spirit of the age showed itself in literature as well as in territorial conquests.

All learning, all sciences, and all religious teachings were reduced to concise practical manuals called Sutras, whose characteristic is brevity, as verbosity is of the Brahmanas. One main reason which led to this extreme conciseness was that young Hindu students were expected to place themselves under some teacher at the early age of eight or ten or twelve, and for twelve years or more to remain in their teacher's house, doing menial service under him, begging alms for him, and learning the ancestral religion by rote. The diffuse details of the Brahmanas were therefore compressed into short treatises in order that they might be imparted and learnt with ease, and a separate body of Sutras was thus composed for each Sutra-charana or school. The names of the authors of many of these compositions have been handed down to us, and while the Vedas and the Brahmanas are declared to be revealed, no such claim is put forward for the Sutras, which are admitted to be human compositions. The so-called revealed literature of India closes, therefore, with the Upanishads, which form the last portions of the Brahmanas.

When the composition of Sutras had once begun, the system spread rapidly all over India, and Sutra schools multiplied. The Charanyavyuha names five Charanas of the Rig-Veda, twenty-seven of the Black Yajur-Veda, fifteen of the White Yajur-Veda, twelve of the Sama-Veda, and nine of the Atharva-Veda. A vast mass of Sutra literature thus gradually sprang up in India, but of the Sutras which must have been composed and taught in these numerous Sutra-charanas comparatively few have survived. The Sutra literature falls into three great classes, dealing respectively with religion (Srauta Sutras), law (Dharma Sutras), and domestic life (Grihya Sutras). Of these the earliest were the Sutras connected with religion and consisting

पञ्चाशद्ब्राह्मणो दण्ड्यः क्षत्रियस्याभिशंसने ।
वैश्ये स्यादर्धपञ्चाशच्छूद्रे द्वादशको दमः ॥ २६८ ॥
समवर्णे द्विजातीनां द्वादशैव व्यतिक्रमे ।
वादेष्ववचनीयेषु तदेव द्विगुणं भवेत् ॥ २६९ ॥
एकजातिर्द्विजातींस्तु वाचा दारुणया क्षिपन् ।
जिह्वायाः प्राप्नुयाच्छेदं जघन्यप्रभवो हि सः ॥ २७० ॥
नामजातिग्रहं त्वेषामभिद्रोहेण कुर्वतः ।
निक्षेप्यो ऽयोमयः शङ्कुर्ज्वलन्नास्ये दशाङ्गुलः ॥ २७१ ॥
धर्मोपदेशं दर्पेण विप्राणामस्य कुर्वतः ।
तप्तमासेचयेत्तैलं वक्त्रे श्रोत्रे च पार्थिवः ॥ २७२ ॥
श्रुतं देशं च जातिं च कर्म शारीरमेव च ।
वितथेन ब्रुवन्दर्पाद्दाप्यः स्याद्द्विशतं दमम् ॥ २७३ ॥
काणं वाप्यथवा खञ्जमन्यं वापि तथाविधम् ।
तथ्येनापि ब्रुवन्दाप्यो दण्डं कार्षापणावरम् ॥ २७४ ॥
मातरं पितरं जायां भ्रातरं तनयं गुरुम् ।
आक्षारयञ्छतं दाप्यः पन्थानं चाददद्गुरोः ॥ २७५ ॥
ब्राह्मणक्षत्रियाभ्यां तु दण्डः कार्यो विजानता ।
ब्राह्मणे साहसः पूर्वः क्षत्रिये त्वेव मध्यमः ॥ २७६ ॥
विट्शूद्रयोरेवमेव स्वजातिं प्रति तत्त्वतः ।
छेदवर्जं प्रणयनं दण्डस्येति विनिश्चयः ॥ २७७ ॥

LAW CODE OF MANU—A PAGE OF THE TEXT.

of concise manuals of the details of Vedic sacrifices. Two collections of these Srauta Sutras belonging to the Rig-Veda, called Asvalayana and Sankhayana; three belonging to the Sama-Veda, and called Masaka, Latyayana, and Drahyayana; four belonging to the Black Yajur-Veda, and called Baudhayana, Bharadvaja, Apastamba, and Hiranyakesin; and one belonging to the White Yajur-Veda, and called Katyayana, have been left entire. To the general reader the Srauta Sutras are but dreary and tedious reading, and we therefore turn with pleasure to the Dharma Sutras, which present to us the customs and manners and laws of the times, and are far more valuable for our historical purpose. In the Srauta Sutras we see the Hindus as sacrificers; in the Dharma Sutras we see them as citizens. But the Dharma Sutras of this ancient period have a deeper claim to our attention, because they were modified and put into verse at a later age, and transformed into those law-books with which modern Hindus are familiar, such as Manu and Yajnavalkya. In their original Sutra form (often in prose, sometimes in prose and verse, but never in continuous verse like the later codes), they were composed, just as the Srauta Sutras, by the founders of the Sutra-charanas, and were learned by rote by young Hindus, so that they might, in later life, never forget their duties as citizens and as members of society.

Among the Dharma Sutras which are lost and have not yet been recovered, was the Manava Sutra, or Sutra of Manu, from which the later metrical Code of Manu was compiled, and which was held in high esteem in the Sutra Period, just as the metrical Code of Manu is honoured at the present day.

Among the Dharma Sutras still extant, the Vasishtha belonging to the Rig-Veda, the Gautama belonging to the Sama-Veda, and the Baudhayana and Apastamba belonging to the Black Yajur-Veda are accessible in English translations.

In point of time Gautama is the oldest, and we find Baudhayana transferring a whole chapter of Gautama's into his Sutra, while Vasishtha, in his turn, borrowed the same chapter from Baudhayana.

We have spoken of the Srauta Sutras which treat of the duties of a worshipper, and of the Dharma Sutras, which define the duties of a citizen. But man has other responsibilities beyond those of a worshipper and a citizen. As a son, a husband, and a father, he has duties to perform towards the members of his family. He has rites to perform in connection with domestic occurrences, which are quite different from the elaborate ceremonials taught in the Srauta Sutras. A distinct class of rules was necessary to fix the details of the domestic rites, and these regulations are given in the Grihya Sutras.

Much interest attaches to these simple domestic rites performed at the domestic fireside, and not at the hearths which had to be specially lighted at great sacrifices. The domestic fire was kindled by each householder on his marriage, and the simple rites, the

Paka-yajnas, were easily performed. Gautama enumerates seven Paka sacrifices: Astaka, performed in the four winter months; Parvana, at full and new moon; Sraddha, or monthly funeral oblations; Sravani, Agrahayani, Chaitri, and Asvayuji, performed on the days of full moon in the months from which the rites have been named. The account of these rites contained in the Grihya Sutras is deeply interesting, because after a lapse of over two thousand years the Hindus still practise the same rites, sometimes under the same name, and often under a different name and in a somewhat different way. The Grihya Sutras also contain accounts of social ceremonies performed at marriage, at the birth of a child, at his first feeding, at his assuming the life of a student, and at other important periods in his life, and thus we get a complete idea of domestic life among the ancient Hindus from these Grihya Sutras.

The Srauta Sutra, the Dharma Sutra, and the Grihya Sutra go collectively under the name of Kalpa Sutra. Indeed, each Sutra-charana is supposed to have had a complete body of Kalpa Sutra, including the divisions mentioned above, but much of what once existed has been lost, and we have only fragments of the Sutra literature left. The entire Kalpa Sutra of Apastamba still exists, and is divided into thirty prasnas or sections. The first twenty-four of these treat of Srauta sacrifices; the twenty-fifth contains the rules of interpretation; the twenty-sixth and twenty-seventh treat of the Grihya rites; the twenty-eighth and twenty-ninth contain the Dharma Sutra, and the thirtieth section, the Sulva Sutra, teaches the geometrical principles according to which the altars for the sacrifices had to be constructed. In addition to the Sutras, ancient writers enumerate five other Vedangas, or departments of Vedic study, which may be briefly enumerated here.

Siksha, or Phonetics, is the science of pronunciation, and there is reason to believe that rules on the subject were formerly embodied in the Aranyakas and even in the Brahmanas, but that they have disappeared in consequence of the appearance of more scientific works on the same subject in the Philosophic Period. These works are called Pratisakhyas, since they were collections of phonetic rules applicable to each Sakha, or recension, of each Veda.

Many of the Pratisakhyas, however, have been lost, and only one Pratisakhya for each Veda (except the Sama-Veda) has been preserved to us. The Pratisakhya of the Rig-Veda is ascribed to the renowned Saunaka. Similarly, a Pratisakhya of the White Yajur-Veda is also extant and is ascribed to Katyayana. A Pratisakhya of the Black Yajur-Veda and one of the Atharva-Veda are also extant, but the names of the authors are forgotten.

Chhandas, or Metre, is mentioned in the Vedas, and whole chapters in the Aranyakas and Upanishads are devoted to it. But as in the case of Siksha, so in the case of Chhandas, we have a clear scientific treatment of the subject for the first time in the Sutra literature.

Vyakarana, or Grammar, was a product of this age, and the deservedly great fame of Panini, perhaps the foremost grammarian of the world, has eclipsed all other grammarians of the period. We will not enter here into the controversy of the date of this great scholar, who is thought by some to have lived in the fourth century B. C., but in our own opinion it seems not improbable that his date is to be placed before the rise of Buddhism. Whatever may be the fact, it is acknowledged that his grammatical rules affected the entire classical language of the Sanskrit and exercised an influence even on the modern science of language, which owes its existence to the opening of Sanskrit to Europe within little more than a century. Second only to Panini in ancient philological work is Yaska in the kindred department of etymology (Nirukta).

The object of Jyotisha, or Astronomy, which should likewise be mentioned here, was to give a knowledge of the heavenly bodies necessary for fixing the time for sacrifices, and to establish a sacred calendar.

Besides the six Vedangas detailed above, there is another class of works called the Anukramani, or Index to the Vedas, which also belongs to Sutra literature. The Anukramani of the Rig-Veda is ascribed to Katyayana and gives the first words of each hymn, the number of verses, the name of the poet, the metre, and the deity; and although there were older Anukramanis of the Rig-Veda, all have been superseded by Katyayana's fuller work.

The Yajur-Veda has three Anukramanis, one for

the Atreya recension of the Black Yajur-Veda, one for the recension of the Charakas, and the third for the Madhyamdina recension of the White Yajur-Veda.

Of the Sama-Veda we have an ancient index in the Arsheya Brahmana, and others among the Parisishtas, or supplementary works; while one of the Atharva-Veda exists in manuscript in the British Museum.

It is appropriate to draw attention, furthermore, to a science which belongs to the Age of Philosophy. It is the science of geometry, which, like grammar, astronomy, and other sciences, owes its origin to India, and has its roots in religion, for geometry was developed in India from the rules for the construction of the altars. It should be remembered that the world owes its first lessons in geometry not to Greece, but to India, even if the Greeks of a later age cultivated the science with greater success than the Hindus. The system of decimal notation is also of Indian origin, as the Arabs first learned it from the Hindus and introduced it into Europe. All science must therefore recognize an obligation to India in this respect.

We have still to refer to the most important product of the Hindu mind in this Philosophic and Rationalistic Period. The inquiries started at the close of the Brahmanic and Epic Period in the Upanishads led to those deeper investigations and profound researches which are known as the six schools of Hindu Philosophy. The most abstruse problems of matter and spirit, of creation and future existence, were considered by the Sankhya Philosophy, not as by the Upanishads in guesses and speculations, but with the strictest method and most relentless logic. Other schools of philosophy followed the lead of the Sankhya system, and boldly inquired into the mysteries of soul and mind, of creation and of the Creator.

Orthodox Hindus became alarmed at the spread of skeptical ideas, and a reaction set in. The result is the Vedanta system of philosophy, which re-asserts the great doctrines of the Upanishads, and which forms to this day the basis of Hindu beliefs and religious convictions. In the meantime, however, a far mightier movement than that caused by philosophical opinions had been set on foot, when, in the sixth century before Christ, Gautama Buddha was born and proclaimed to the poor and the lowly that Vedic rites were useless, that a holy and tranquil and benevolent life is the essence of religion, and that caste distinctions do not exist among those who strive after holiness and purity. Thousands responded to his appeal, and thus a catholic religion began to spread in India, which has since become the religion of Asia.

From this brief account of the age given by way of introduction, the reader will have some idea of the intellectual activity of this most brilliant period of Hindu civilization. Religious rights and duties were laid down lucidly and concisely for householders; civil and criminal laws were compiled; phonetics, metre, and grammar were dealt with with scientific accuracy; geometry and mathematics were cultivated; mental philosophy and logic were studied and developed with marvellous success; and a noble religion was proclaimed which is now the faith of a third of the human race.

CHAPTER XVIII

EXPANSION OF THE HINDUS

THE history of India received a new light in the Age of Laws, or Philosophic Period, when the Greeks visited India and also compiled accounts of it from report. The first two epochs of Hindu history receive no light, therefore, from Greek literature, but in this third era India began to be known to Greece. Not to mention the philosopher Pythagoras, who is supposed by some scholars to have come under Indian influence, we may refer to the allusions to India in Herodotus, the Father of History, who lived in the fifth century before Christ.

Herodotus never visited India, but he gives from report valuable accounts of the Hindus, although he mingles them with legends and stories, and often confounds Hindu customs with those of the uncivilized aborigines who still inhabited large tracts in India. He tells us that the Indians were the greatest nation of the age, that they were divided into various tribes and spoke different tongues, that they procured great quantities of gold in their country, that India abounded in animals larger than those of any other country, and produced wild trees which bore wool (cotton) from which the Indians made their clothing. He also mentions the fact, which is probably historically true, that Darius, King of Persia, subjugated a part of India, and that his ships sailed down the Indus to the sea.

And lastly, Megasthenes came to India in the fourth century before Christ, and lived in the court of Chandragupta in Pataliputra, or ancient Patna, writing an account of India which still survives in fragments preserved by subsequent authors, although his original work is lost.

We have seen that by the end of the Brāhmanic and Epic Periods the whole of the valley of the Ganges and Jumna from Delhi to North Behar had been conquered, peopled, and Hinduized, and we also know that towards the close of this period Hindu settlers and colonists left the valley of the Ganges and penetrated into remote unknown lands, into Southern Behar, Malwa, the Deccan, and Gujarat. Thus these non-Aryan provinces were becoming gradually known to the Hindus, and were slowly coming under Hindu influence and power when the Epic Period closed and the Philosophic Period began.

The waves of Hindu conquests rolled onwards, and the aborigines submitted themselves to a higher civilization and a nobler creed. Rivers were crossed, forests were cleared, lands were reclaimed, wide wastes were peopled, and new countries hitherto aboriginal witnessed the rise of Hindu power and of Hindu religion.

Where a few scanty settlers had penetrated at first, powerful colonies grew; where religious teachers had retired in seclusion, quiet villages and towns arose. Where a handful of merchants had made their way by

TRAVELLING IN THE NILGIRI HILLS.

some unknown river, boats plied up and down with valuable cargoes for a civilized population. Where hardy warriors or scions of royal houses had dwelt in exile or by the chase, powerful monarchs reigned over a conquered, civilized, and Hinduized aboriginal population. And where foresters had felled trees and cleared small tracts of land, smiling fields covered with waving corn spread for miles around, betokening the spread of civilization and of the civilized arts of life.

Such was the history of Aryan conquests from generation to generation and from century to century in the Philosophic Period, and each succeeding Sutra work shows that the circle of civilization spread wider, and that the zone of unreclaimed barbarism receded farther and farther. And long before the close of this period, in the fourth century B. C., the entire peninsula had been reclaimed, civilized, and Hinduized, and primitive barbarians dwelt only in rocks, forests, and deserts which the Aryans disdained to conquer. It is not merely a story of conquests, which would have little interest for the philosophical reader. It is a story of the spread of Hindu civilization among hitherto unknown countries and aboriginal nations. It was the acceptance, by the Andhras of the Deccan and the Ṣaurashtras of Gujarat, by the Cholas, Cheras, and Pandyas of Southern India, by the Magadhas, the Angas, the Vangas, and the Kalingas of Eastern India, of that superior religion and language and civilization which the Hindu Aryans offered to them. The gift was accepted and cherished, and henceforth the Dravidian and other tribes of Southern and Eastern India were Aryans in religion, language, and civilization. This was the great work and result of the Philosophic Period.

Baudhayana lived probably in the sixth century before Christ, and was one of the earliest of the Sutrakaras. In his time the zone of Hindu kingdoms and civilization extended as far south as Kalinga, or the eastern seaboard, stretching from modern Orissa southward to the mouth of the Krishna. The passage which we quote is interesting, because it shows that the ancient Aryan region along the Ganges and the Jumna was still regarded as the suitable home of the Aryans, while tracts of country in which the non-Aryan tribes had been recently Hinduized were regarded with some degree of contempt.

"The country of the Aryas (Aryavarta) lies to the east of the region where the River (Sarasvati) disappears, to the west of the Black Forest (Kalakavana), to the north of the Paripatra (Vindhya mountains), and to the south of the Himalaya. The rule of conduct which prevails there is authoritative.

"Some declare the country between the Yamuna and Ganga (to be the Aryavarta).

"Now the Bhallavins quote also the following verse:

"In the west the boundary river, in the east the region where the sun rises, as far as the black antelopes wander, so far spiritual pre-eminence is found.

"The inhabitants of Avanti (Malwa), of Anga (East Behar), of Magadha (South Behar), of Saurashtra (Gujarat), of the Deccan, of Upavrit, of Sindh, and the Sauviras (South Panjab) are of mixed origin.

"He who has visited the Arattas (in the Panjab), Karaskaras (in South India), Pundras (in North Bengal), Sauviras (in the Panjab), Vangas (in Eastern Bengal), Kalingas (in Orissa), or Pranunas shall offer a Punastoma or a Sarvaprishtha sacrifice"—such was the extreme limit of the Hindu world about the sixth century before Christ.

That portions of Southern India had not only been colonized by this date, but had become the seats of Hindu kingdoms and of distinct schools of laws and learning, is proved by the writings of Baudhayana. Baudhayana himself may have been a southerner, at any rate he takes care to mention the peculiar laws and customs of Southern India. We will cite one passage:—

"There is a dispute regarding five practices, in the south and in the north.

"We will explain those peculiar to the south.

"They are to eat in the company of an uninitiated person, to eat in the company of one's wife, to eat stale food, to marry the daughter of a maternal uncle or of a paternal aunt.

"Now the customs peculiar to the north are: to deal in wool, to drink rum, to sell animals that have teeth in the upper and in the lower jaws, to follow the trade of arms, and to go to sea.

"He who follows these practices in any other country than where they prevail commits sin.

"For each of these customs the rule of the country should be the authority."

Let us now take leave of Baudhayana and come to the next Sutrakara of India. If Baudhayana be supposed to have flourished in the sixth century before Christ, Apastamba probably flourished in the fifth. There can be little doubt that Apastamba lived and taught in the Andhra country, and the limits of that great monarchy embraced all the districts between the Godavari and the Krishna, the capital apparently being situated near the modern Amaravati on the lower Krishna. It was the Andhra text of the Taittiriya Aranyaka which Apastamba recognized and followed, and his teachings are to this day held in regard by the Apastambiya Brahmanas of Nasik, Puna, Ahmadabad, Satara, Sholapur, Kolhapur, and other places in the Deccan.

CAPITAL OF HALF COLUMN FROM A TEMPLE IN ORISSA.

Thus we find that the conquest of Southern India which was commenced at the close of the Epic Period went on through succeeding centuries; that by the sixth century, Bengal, Orissa, Gujarat, and the Deccan had been conquered and Aryanized; and that by the fifth century the Deccan as far south as the Krishna River was the seat of a powerful Hindu Empire. By the fourth century B. C. the whole of Southern India south of the Krishna River had been Hinduized, and three great Hindu kingdoms, those of the Cholas, the Cheras, and the Pandyas had been founded, stretching as far south as Cape Comorin; and Ceylon, too, had been discovered. And when we come towards the close of this century, we issue now from the obscurity of isolated passages in the Sutra works into the sunlight of Greek accounts of India. For it was in this century that Megasthenes, the ambassador of Seleucus, came to India and resided in the royal court of Chandragupta in Pataliputra, or ancient Patna, between 317 and 312 B. C.

The account of the races and kingdoms in India given by Megasthenes is full and intelligible, and gives us a clear idea of the state of the country at the close of the Philosophic Period.

The Prachyas, by which name we are now to understand the Magadhas, had become the most powerful and foremost nation in India in the fourth century B. C., as the Kurus, the Panchalas, the Videhas and the Kosalas had been in the Epic Period. They had their capital at Pataliputra, a flourishing town described as eighty stadia, or nine miles, long and fifteen stadia, or nearly two miles, wide. It was a parallelogram in shape, girded with a wooden wall pierced with loopholes for the discharge of arrows, and defended by a ditch in front.

It would seem that the whole of Northern India was now included in the powerful and extensive empire of Chandragupta, for the Jumna, flowing through Mathura and Caresbora, was said to run through the kingdom of Pataliputra. The nation surpassed in power and glory every other people in India, and their king Chandragupta had a standing army of 600,000 foot soldiers, 30,000 cavalry, and 9,000 elephants.

Speaking of South Bengal, Megasthenes mentions

the Kalingoi living nearest the sea, the Mandu and the Malli living higher up, the Gangerides, near the mouths of the Ganges, and the Modo-Galingoi in an island in the Ganges. It is impossible not to recognize in the first and last of these names the ancient name of Kalinga, which included Orissa and the sea-coast of Bengal.

Megasthenes describes Parthalis as the capital of the Kalingoi. The powerful king of this place had 60,000 foot-soldiers, 1,000 horse, and 700 elephants. A large island in the Ganges is said to have been inhabited by the Modo-Galingoi (Madhya-Kalinga), and beyond them several powerful tribes lived under a king who had 50,000 foot-soldiers, 4,000 cavalry, and 400 elephants. Beyond them again lived the Andaroi, in whom it is impossible not to recognize the Andhras of Southern India. The Andhras were a great and powerful nation who had settled originally between the Godavari and the Krishna, but who before the time of Megasthenes had extended their kingdom as far north as the Narmada. Megasthenes writes that they were a powerful race, possessed numerous villages and thirty walled towns, and supplied their king with 100,000 infantry, 2,000 cavalry, and 1,000 elephants.

In the extreme northwest, Megasthenes speaks of the Isari, the Cosyri, and other tribes located probably in Kashmir or its neighbourhood. The Indus is said to skirt the frontiers of the Prachyas, by which we understand that the powerful and extensive empire of Magadha extended as far as the frontiers of the Panjab, and embraced all Northern India.

In the time of Megasthenes a great portion of modern Rajputana was still the home of aboriginal tribes, of men who lived in woods, among tigers noted for their ferocity. He speaks of the tribes who lived in the fertile tracts surrounded by deserts, and of tribes who inhabited the hills, which ran in an unbroken chain parallel to the shores of the ocean. He also speaks of the tribes who lived enclosed by the loftiest mountain, Capitalia, which has been identified with Abu. He speaks further on of the Horatoi, who were undoubtedly the Saurashtras. They had a capital on the coast, which was a noble emporium of trade, and their king was the master of 1,600 elephants, 150,000 foot, and 5,000 horse.

"Next come the Pandoi, the only race in India ruled by women. They say that Hercules had but one daughter, who was on that account all the more beloved, and that he endowed her with a noble kingdom. Her descendants rule over 300 cities and command an army of 150,000 foot and 500 elephants."

Such is the half-mythical account which Megasthenes gives us of the Pandyas, who were the ruling nation in the extreme south of India. These Pandyas have a history which is remarkable.

The Yadavas, who, under the leadership of Krishna, left Mathura and settled in Dwarka in Gujarat, did not flourish there long. They fell fighting among themselves, and the remainder left Dwarka by sea. It is believed that they came to Southern India, where they founded a new kingdom. They probably called themselves Pandyas because they pretended to be of the same race with the Pandavas, and they named their new southern capital Mathura, or Madura, as the town is called to the present day. Megasthenes no doubt refers to Krishna under the name of Hercules, and he had probably heard some legend which was then current in India, about the foundation of the southern kingdom by Krishna for his daughter.

And lastly, the island of Ceylon was known in the time of Megasthenes. It was conquered by Vijaya, a prince of Magadha who had been exiled by his father for his misdeeds in the fifth century before Christ. When Megasthenes came to India, Ceylon was already a Hindu kingdom. The island was called Taprobane by the Greeks, the name being slightly altered from the Pali name Tambapanni, which corresponds to the Sanskrit Tamraparni, or the copper-leaved. Megasthenes says that the island was separated from the mainland by a river, and that the country was productive of gold and large pearls, and elephants much larger than the Indian breeds. Ælian, who wrote long after Megasthenes, but got much of his information about India from the account of Megasthenes, states that Taprobane was a large mountainous island full of palm groves, that the inhabitants dwelt in huts of reeds, and that they transported their elephants in boats which they constructed for the purpose, and sold them to the King of Kalinga.

CHAPTER XIX

ADMINISTRATION, AGRICULTURE, AND ARTS

AN account of the system of administration which prevailed in India over two thousand years ago will naturally interest our readers, and fortunately both Hindu Sutrakaras and Greek writers furnish us with reliable information on the subject. We will begin our account with some extracts from Sutra works. The king is directed to build a royal town and a palace for himself, looking towards the south:—

"The palace shall stand in the heart of the town.

"In front of that there shall be a hall. That is called the hall of invitation.

"At a little distance from the town to the south he shall cause to be built an assembly house with doors on the south and on the north sides, so that one can see what passes inside and outside."

Fires shall burn constantly and oblations shall be offered in these fires, and—

"In the hall he shall entertain his guests, at least those who are skilled in the Vedas.

"Rooms, a couch, meat, and drink should be given to them according to their good qualities."

A table with dice should also be provided, and Brahmans, Vaisyas, and Sudras may be allowed to play there. Assaults of arms, dancing, singing, and music are allowed in the houses of the king's servants;

AN INDIAN SCENE.

and the king shall constantly take care of his subjects:—

"That king only takes care of the welfare of his subjects in whose dominions, be it in villages or forests, there is no danger from thieves."

Both Vasishtha and Baudhayana declare that the king is entitled to a sixth portion of the income of his subjects as taxes, but they exempt many classes who are unable to pay, while Gautama details the taxes thus:—

"Cultivators pay to the king a tax amounting to one-tenth, one-eighth, or one-sixth (of the produce).

"Some declare that the tax on cattle and gold amounts to one-fiftieth (of the stock).

"In the case of merchandise one-twentieth (must be paid by the seller) as duty.

"Of roots, fruits, flowers, medicinal herbs, honey, meat, grass, and fire-wood, one-sixtieth.

"Each artisan shall monthly do one day's work (for the king).

"Hereby the taxes payable by those who support themselves by personal labour have been explained.

"And those payable by owners of ships and carts.

"He must feed these persons while they work for him."

Megasthenes gives us a valuable account of the manner in which the work of administration was actually carried on, and the following passages from McCrindle's translation will be read with interest:—

"Those who have charge of the city are divided into six bodies of five each. The members of the first look after everything relating to the industrial arts. Those of the second attend to the entertainment of foreigners. To these they assign lodgings, and they keep watch over their modes of life by means of those persons whom they give to them for assistants. They escort them on the way when they leave the country, or in the event of their dying, forward their property to their relatives. They take care of them when they are sick, and if they die bury them. The third body consists of those who inquire when and how births and deaths occur, with the view not only of levying a tax, but also in order that births and deaths among both high and low may not escape the cognizance of government. The fourth class superintends trade and commerce. Its members have charge of weights and measures, and see that the products in their season are sold by public notice. No one is allowed to deal in more than one kind of commodity unless he pays a double tax. The fifth class supervises manufactured articles, which are sold by public notice. What is new is sold separately from what is old, and there is a fine for mixing the two together. The sixth and last class consists of those who collect the tenths of the prices of the articles sold."

The military officers "also consist of six divisions with five members to each. One division is appointed to co-operate with the admiral of the fleet; another with the superintendent of the bullock trains which are used for transporting engines of war, food for the soldiers, provender for the cattle, and other military requisites. The third division has charge of the foot-soldiers, the fourth of the horses, the fifth of the war-chariots, and the sixth of the elephants."

Besides the municipal officers and military officers, there was yet a third class of officers who superintended agriculture, irrigation, forests, and generally the work of administration in rural tracts. "Some superintend the rivers, measure the land, as is done in Egypt, and inspect the sluices by which water is let out from the main canals into their branches, so that every one may have an equal supply of it. The same officers have charge also of the huntsmen, and are entrusted with the power of rewarding or punishing them according to their deserts. They collect the taxes and superintend the occupations connected with land, as those of the wood-cutters, the carpenters, the blacksmiths, and the miners. They construct roads, and at every ten stadia set up a pillar to show the by-roads and distances."

BHIL WOMEN OF KATHIAWAR.

Of the personal habits and occupations of kings, Megasthenes has given us a picture which agrees in the main with the picture given in Sanskrit literature. The care of the king's person was entrusted to female slaves, who were bought from their parents, and the guards and the rest of the soldiery were stationed outside the gates. The king attended the court every day and remained there during the day without allow-ing the business to be interrupted. The only other occasions on which he left the palace were when he performed sacrifices or went out for the chase. Crowds of women surrounded him when he went out for the chase, and outside this circle the spearmen were ranged. Armed women attended the king in chariots, on horses, or on elephants, when he hunted in the open grounds from the back of an elephant. Sometimes he shot arrows from a platform inside an enclosure, and two or three armed women stood by him on the platform. These accounts show that the sturdy and warlike manners of the Kurus and the Panchalas of the Epic Age had already been replaced by more luxurious and effeminate habits in the Philosophic Age. The age of chivalry had gone, and that of luxury had come.

Arrian gives an account of the way in which the Hindus equipped themselves for war: "The foot-soldiers carry a bow made of equal length with the man who bears it. This they rest upon the ground, and pressing against it with their left foot, thus discharge the arrow, having drawn the string far backwards; for the shaft they use is little short of being three yards long, and there is nothing which can resist an Indian archer's shot — neither shield nor breastplate, nor any stronger defence, if such there be. In their left hand they carry bucklers made of undressed ox-hide, which are not so broad as those who carry them, but are about as long. Some are equipped with javelins instead of bows, but wear a sword, which is broad in the blade, but not longer than three cubits; and this, when they engage in close fight (which they do with reluctance), they wield with both hands to fetch down a lustier blow. The horsemen are equipped with two lances like the lances called *Saunia*, and with a shorter buckler than that carried by the foot-soldiers. For they do not put saddles on their horses; nor do they curb them with bits in use among the Greeks or the Kelts, but they fit on round the extremity of the horse's mouth a circular piece of stitched raw ox-hide studded with pricks of iron or brass pointing inwards, but not very sharp; if a man is rich he uses pricks made of ivory."

The laws of war were more humane among the Hindus than among other nations in the world, and Apastamba declares that "the Aryans forbid the slaughter of those who have laid down their arms, of those who beg for mercy with flying hair or joined hands, and of fugitives," while Baudhayana says: "Let him not fight with those who are in fear, intoxicated, insane, or out of their minds, nor with those who have lost their armour, nor with women, infants, aged men, and Brahmans." Megasthenes also vouches for the humane laws of war among the Hindus. "For whereas among other nations it is usual in the contests of war to ravage the soil and thus to reduce it to an uncultivated waste, among the Indians, on the contrary, by whom husbandmen are regarded as a class that is sacred and inviolable, the tillers of the soil, even when battle is raging in their neighbourhood, are undisturbed by any sense of danger; for the combatants on either side, in waging the conflict, make carnage of each other, but allow those engaged in husbandry to remain quite unmolested. Besides, they neither ravage an enemy's land with fire, nor cut down its trees."

Megasthenes tells us that the Indian tribes numbered 118 in all. On the north of India and beyond the Himalaya the country "is inhabitated by those Scythians who are called the Sakai." Such is the brief mention made of that powerful tribe which hung like an ominous cloud on the northern slopes of the Himalaya in the fourth century before Christ, but which in the course of a few centuries burst like a hurricane on the plains of Western India.

Of the peaceful and law-abiding people in India, Megasthenes gives an account which is well-nigh Utopian:—"They live happily enough, being simple in their manners and frugal. They never drink wine, except at sacrifices. Their beverage is a liquor prepared from rice instead of barley, and their food is principally a rice pottage. The simplicity of their laws and their contracts is proved by the fact that they seldom go to law. They have no suits about pledges and deposits, nor do they require either seals or witnesses, but make their deposits and confide in each other. Their houses and property they generally leave unguarded. These things indicate that they possess sober sense. Truth and virtue they hold alike in esteem. Hence they accord no special privileges to the old unless they possess superior wisdom."

Megasthenes further states that the Indians did "not even use aliens as slaves, and much less a countryman of their own," that thefts were very rare among them, that their laws were administered from memory, and even that they were ignorant of the art of writing. We have the evidence of Nearchos, however, that writing was known in India in the Philosophic Period, and the statement of Megasthenes only shows that writing was in very little use, either in schools, where boys received their learning and their religious lessons by rote, or even in courts of justice, where the Dharma Sutras were administered by learned judges entirely from memory.

Arrian quotes a passage from Nearchos, and says that the Indians "wear an under-garment of cotton which reaches below the knee half-way down to the ankles, and also an upper garment which they throw partly over their shoulders and partly twist in folds round their head. They wear shoes made of white leather, and these are elaborately trimmed, while the soles are variegated, and made of great thickness." And the great mass of the "people of India live upon grain and are tillers of the soil, but we must except the hillmen, who eat the flesh of beasts of chase."

Our faithful guide Megasthenes also gives us an account of cultivation in Ancient India which, on the whole, corresponds with the system of cultivation prevalent at the present time. He speaks of a double rainfall in the year, considering the winter showers as a regular rainfall. He speaks of "many vast plains of great fertility, more or less beautiful, but all alike intersected by a multitude of rivers. The greater part of the soil, moreover, is under irrigation and consequently bears two crops in the course of the year. It teems at the same time with animals of all sorts, beasts of the field and fowl of the air, of all different degrees of strength and size. It is prolific, besides, in elephants which are of monstrous bulk. In addition

FRESCO IN THE SHEESH MAHAL, AT RAJGARH.

to cereals, there grows throughout India much millet, which is kept well watered by the profusion of river streams, and much pulse of different sorts, and rice also, and what is called *bosporum*, as well as many other plants useful for food, of which most grow spontaneously. The soil yields, moreover, not a few other edible products fit for the subsistence of animals about which it would be tedious to write. It is accordingly affirmed that famine has never visited India, and that there has never been a general scarcity in the supply of nourishing food. For since there is a double rainfall in the course of each year — one in the winter season, when the sowing of wheat takes place as in other countries, and the second at the time of the summer solstice, which is the proper season for sowing rice and *bosporum*, as well as sesamum and millet— the inhabitants of India almost always gather two harvests annually; and even should one of the sowings prove more or less abortive, they are always sure of the other crop. The fruits, moreover, of spontaneous growth, and the esculent roots, which grow in marshy places and are of varied sweetness, afford abundant sustenance for man."

The excellent manufactures of India were known to the traders of Phœnicia and in the markets of Western Asia and Egypt long before the Christian era. Megasthenes naïvely says that the Indians were "well skilled in the arts, as might be expected of men who inhale a pure air and drink the very finest water." The soil, too, has "under ground numerous veins of all sorts of metals, for it contains much gold and silver, and copper and iron in no small quantity, and even tin and other metals, which are employed in making articles of use and ornament, as well as the implements and accoutrements of war."

With regard to finery and ornament, Megasthenes says that "in contrast to the general simplicity of their style, they love finery and ornament. Their robes are worked in gold and ornamented with precious stones, and they also wear flowered garments of the finest muslin. Attendants walking behind hold up umbrellas over them, for they have a high regard for beauty and avail themselves of every device to improve their looks."

GANESA.

CHAPTER XX

LAWS

IN India, as throughout the ancient world, legal equality was unknown. There was one law for the Brahman and another for the Sudra; the former was treated with undue leniency, the latter with cruel severity. If a Brahman committed one of the four or five heinous crimes enumerated in the law-books,. that is, if he slew a Brāhman, violated his guru's bed, stole the gold of a Brahman, or drank spirituous liquor, the king branded him on the forehead with a heated iron and banished him from his realm. If a man of a lower caste slew a Brāhman, he was punished with death and the confiscation of his property, while if he slew a man of equal or lower caste, other suitable punishments were meted out to him.

Adultery has always been looked upon in India not only as a criminal offence, but as an offence of a heinous nature; but here again punishment for the offence was regulated by the caste of the offender. A man of the first three castes who committed adultery with a Sudra woman was banished; but a Sudra who committed adultery with a woman of the first three castes suffered capital punishment.

Indeed, Brahman legislators have painted themselves worse than they really were. In order to point out the vast distinction between themselves and the Sudras, they prescribed monstrous punishments for the latter, which, it is safe to assert, always remained an empty threat, and were meant as a threat only. If a Sudra spoke evil of a virtuous person belonging to one of the first three castes, his tongue was to be cut out, and a Sudra who assumed an equal position with those castes was to be flogged. Similarly we are told that a Sudra who reviled a twice-born man or assaulted him with blows should lose the limb with which he offended; that if he listened to a recitation of the Veda, his ears should be stopped with molten lac or tin; that if he recited the Veda, his tongue should be cut out; and if he remembered Vedic texts, his body should be split in twain. .

A Kshatriya abusing a Brahman must pay 100 karshapanas, and one beating a Brahman pays 200 karshapanas. A Vaisya abusing a Brahman is fined 150 karshapanas, and we suppose pays 300 for beating him. But a Brahman has to pay only 50 karshapanas for abusing a Kshatriya, 25 for abusing a Vaisya, and for abusing a Sudra—nothing!

Death or corporal punishment seems to have been the punishment for theft, at least in some cases; and the thief is directed to appear before the king with dishevelled hair, holding a club in his hand, and proclaiming his deed. If the king pardons him and does not slay him or strike him, the guilt falls on the king.

The prerogative of mercy was the king's alone, but a guru, a priest, a learned householder, or a prince could intercede for an offender, except in the case of a capital offence.

The lawgiver Vasishtha reserves the right of self-defence in the case of a person attacked by an Atatayi, a class of criminals including incendiaries, poisoners, those ready to kill with weapons in their hands, robbers, and those who take away another's land or abduct another's wife.

Agriculture and trade were the means of the people's subsistence, and crimes relating to a cultivator's land or to an artisan's trade were punished with the utmost severity. We have seen that defence of land was one of the cases in which the right of self-protection was allowed, and false evidence given about land was regarded with the utmost detestation. By giving false evidence concerning small cattle, a witness commits the sin of killing ten men; by false evidence concerning cows, horses, and men, he commits the sin of killing a hundred, a thousand, and ten thousand men respectively; but by false evidence concerning land, he commits the sin of killing the whole human race.

A severe penance is ordained for the man who attempts suicide, and the relations of a suicide are prohibited from performing funeral rites for him. Such was the criminal law of the Hindus over two thousand years ago.

We now turn to the more complicated subject of civil law, which may be conveniently treated under five heads, the law of agriculture and pasture, the law of property, usury laws, the law of inheritance, and the law of partition. We begin with the law of agriculture and pasture. According to Apastamba:—

"If a person who has taken a lease of land does not exert himself, and hence the land bears no crop, he shall, if he be rich, be made to pay the value of the crop that ought to have been grown.

"A servant in tillage who abandons his work shall be flogged.

"The same punishment shall be awarded to a herdsman who leaves his work.

"And the flock entrusted to him shall be taken away.

"If cattle, leaving their stable, eat crops, the owner of the crops may make them lean (by impounding them); but shall not exceed that.

"If a herdsman who has taken cattle under his care allows them to perish or loses them, he shall replace them to the owners.

"If (the king's forester) sees cattle that have been sent into the forest through negligence, he shall lead them back to the village and restore them to their owners."

Again Gautama says:—

"If damage is done by cattle, the responsibility falls on the owner.

"But if the cattle were attended by a herdsman, it falls on the latter.

"If the damage was done in an unenclosed field

near the road, the responsibility falls on the herdsman and on the owner of the field."

As in the present day, unenclosed fields were used as common property for grazing cattle and for obtaining firewood.

Some equitable provisions are laid down by Vasish-

WATER SCENE IN INDIA.

tha about the right of way and about the evidence necessary in disputes about immovable property.

"It is declared in the Smriti that there are three kinds of proof which give a title to property, documents, witnesses, and possession; thereby an owner may recover property which formerly belonged to him.

"From fields through which there is a right of way a space sufficient for the road must be set apart, likewise a space for turning a cart.

"Near new-built houses and other things of the same description, there shall be a passage three feet broad.

"In a dispute about a house or a field, reliance must be placed on the depositions of neighbours.

"If the statements of the neighbours disagree, documents may be taken as proof.

"If conflicting documents are produced, reliance must be placed on the statements of aged inhabitants of the village or town, and on those of guilds and corporations of artisans or traders."

This brings us to the law of property. Property is divided into eight classes, thus:—

"Property inherited from a father, a thing bought, a pledge, property given to a wife after marriage by her husband's family, a gift, property obtained for performing a sacrifice, the property of re-united copartners, and wages as the eighth.

"Whatever belonging to these eight kinds of property has been enjoyed by another person for ten years continuously is lost to the owner.

"A pledge, a boundary, the property of minors, an open deposit, a sealed deposit, women, the property of a king, and the wealth of a Srotriya, are not lost by being enjoyed by others.

"Property entirely given up by its owner goes to the king."

Women and females here mean female slaves. With regard to minors and widows, there are provisions to the effect that the king shall administer their property and shall restore it in the case of a minor when he comes of age.

We next turn to the usury laws of Ancient India. According to Vasishtha and Gautama, the interest for a money-lender was five mashas for twenty (karshapanas) every month.

The commentator Hara Datta reckons 20 mashas to the karshapana, so that the rate of interest comes to $1\frac{1}{4}$ per cent. per month, or fifteen per cent. per annum; and Krishna Pandita correctly states that this rate of interest applies to loans for which security is given. Gautama also says that after the principal has been doubled, interest ceases, and when the object pledged is an object used by the creditor, the money lent bears no interest at all.

Other articles might be lent at a much higher percentage of interest, apparently when no security was given, as is clear from the following rules:—

" Gold may be lent, taking double its value on repayment, and grain trebling the original price.

" The case of flavouring substances has been explained by the rule regarding grain.

" As also the case of flowers, roots, and fruit.

" He may lend what is sold by weight, taking eight times the original value on repayment " ; and Gautama says: " The interest on products of animals, on wool, on the produce of a field, and on beasts of burden, shall not increase more than fivefold the value of the object lent."

Gautama likewise names no less than six different

forms of interest, compound, periodical, stipulated, corporal, and daily, in addition to the use of a pledge. He lays down the rule that the heirs shall pay the debts of the dead, but provides that money due by a surety, a commercial debt, a fee due to the parents of the bride, immoral debts, and fines shall not devolve on the sons of the debtor.

We thus come to the most important portion of the civil law, the law of inheritance.

To leave male issue was considered a religious duty by the ancient Hindus, and in the older law-books several kinds of sons are recognized, some of whom were legitimate or quasi-legitimate, and might therefore inherit, while others were considered unlawful and were debarred from all rights to their fathers' estates. At an early time, however, a reaction appears to have set in against the recognition of sons legitimate and illegitimate, even to escape the torments of hell after death. Apastamba, who lived a century or more after Baudhayana, protests against the recognition of heirs and sons of various kinds, and explains away ancient customs by stating that what had been allowed in ancient times could not be permitted among the sinful men of the present time. He made a clear sweep, moreover, not only of *niyoga*, or the appointment of a wife to raise issue, but also of the adoption or the purchase of a son, and modern Hindus recognize no kinds of sons except legitimate sons, or those adopted in the absence of legitimate issue.

Lastly, we come to the subject of the law of partition. The law of primogeniture never obtained in India, but so long as the joint family system remained in vogue, the property of the father was inherited by the eldest son, who supported the rest as a father. It would seem, however, that to live in a joint family under the eldest brother was never the universal custom in India, and even Gautama, the earliest of the Sutrakaras whose works are extant, considers a partition among brothers preferable. According to Gautama, the eldest son got as an additional share a twentieth part of the estate, some animals, and a carriage; the middlemost son received some poor animals, and the youngest obtained sheep, grain, utensils, a house, a cart, and some animals; while the remaining property was divided equally. As an alternative, he allowed the eldest two shares, and the remaining sons one share each; or he would permit each to take one kind of property by choice, according to seniority; or the special shares might be adjusted according to their mothers.

Vasishtha permitted the eldest brother to take a double share and a little of the kine and horses; he allowed the youngest to take the goats, sheep, and house; while the middlemost received utensils and furniture. If a Brahman had sons by Brahman, Kshatriya, and Vaisya wives, the first obtained three shares, the second two, and the third one.

Baudhayana allowed all the children to receive equal shares, or the eldest son might take one-tenth more than his brothers. Where there were sons born of wives of different castes, the sons were to receive four, three, two, and one shares respectively, according to the order of the castes.

Apastamba differed in this respect from his predecessors, and protested against the unequal division of property, declaring that all sons who were virtuous should inherit, but that he who spent money unrighteously should be disinherited, though he were the eldest son.

The separate property of a wife, that is, her nuptial presents and ornaments, was inherited by her daughters.

Such were the laws of the Philosophic Age. They show unmistakably the vast distance of time between this and the Epic Period, and show also the culture, the training, and the practical method of dealing with intricate subjects which were the peculiar features of this epoch. Criminal offences and civil cases were no longer tried according to the vague and varying opinions and feelings of learned men and priests, but were arranged, condensed, and codified into bodies of laws which learned men were called upon to administer.

CHAPTER XXI

CASTE IN THE AGE OF LAWS AND PHILOSOPHY

IN trying to reduce the caste-system into a code of rigid rules, the Sutrakaras of the period met with difficulty from the very first. They firmly believed that there were originally but four castes among men, Brahmans, Kshatriyas, Vaisyas, and Sudras; but they actually found around them various other castes, formed by tribes of non-Aryans, who had gradually entered into the Hindu fold and formed low Hindu castes. Believing that all mankind was originally divided into only four castes, the Sutrakaras tried to evolve the new castes from the four parent castes. The fiction was then conceived that the new castes were formed by intermarriages among the parent castes. Thus Vasishtha, from whom other Sanskrit authorities vary but in detail, says:—

"The offspring of a Sudra and a Brahman woman becomes a Chandala.

"That of a Sudra and Kshatriya woman, a Vaina.

"That of a Sudra and Vaisya woman, an Antyavasayi.

"The son begotten by a Vaisya on a Brahman woman becomes a Ramaka.

"The son begotten by a Vaisya on a Kshatriya woman, a Paulkasa.

"The son begotten by a Kshatriya on a Brahman woman becomes a Suta.

"Children begotten by Brahmans, Kshatriyas, and Vaisyas on women of the next lower, second lower, and third lower castes become respectively Ambashthas, Ugras, and Nishadas.

"The son of a Brahman and a Sudra woman is a Parasava."

Here we have an authoritative statement which may well stagger the most faithful believer. Magadhas and Vaidehas, who were different races, Chandalas and Paulkasas, who were undoubtedly non-Aryan tribes, and even Yavanas, who were Bactrian Greeks and foreigners, were all treated by the same general and rigid law which recognized no exception, and were all declared to be descended from

WOMAN CARRYING WATER.

the four parent castes. And as the Hindus came to know other foreign nations later on, the elastic theory was stretched, and Manu derived those nations, too, from the same Hindu parent castes.

It is remarkable, however, that the castes or races named above were nearly all aboriginal tribes or foreigners, or Aryans who had incurred odium by their partiality for skepticism and Buddhism. We do not find names of profession-castes, answering to the Kayasthas, the Vaidyas, the goldsmiths, the blacksmiths, the potters, the weavers, and other artisans of Modern India, for the great and yet undivided Vaisya caste of the Philosophic Period still embraced all those different professions which in modern times have been divided and disunited into castes. The Aryan Vaisyas followed different trades and professions in Ancient India without forming separate castes; they were scribes and physicians, goldsmiths and blacksmiths, potters and weavers, while still belonging to the same caste. Thus the great body of the Aryan population was still united, and was still entitled to religious knowledge and learning.

The study of the Veda, the performance of sacrifices, and the gift of alms were prescribed for all twice-born men, *i. e.* for Brahmans, Kshatriyas, and Vaisyas. The special and additional occupations of the Brahman were the performance of sacrifice for others and the receiving of alms, and agriculture and trade were also allowed to him provided he did not work himself. Yet the abuses begotten of the privileges of caste had already commenced as early as the Philosophic Period, and Brahmans, relieved of manual labour, had already commenced to feed on the resources of the industrious classes, without acquiring that learning which alone would justify their exemption from labour. Vasishtha felt the injustice keenly and protested against it in language which could only be indited while Hinduism was still a living nation's religion, when he wrote:—

"(Brahmans) who neither study nor teach the Veda nor keep sacred fires become equal to Sudras.

"The king shall punish that village where Brahmans, unobservant of their sacred duties and ignorant of the Veda, subsist by begging, for it feeds robbers.

"The sin that dunces, perplexed by ignorance, and unacquainted with the sacred law, declare to be duty, shall fall, increased a hundredfold, on those who propound it.

"An elephant made of wood, an antelope made of leather, and a Brahman ignorant of the Veda, those three have nothing but the name of their kind."

The additional occupations of the Kshatriya were to govern and fight and make conquests, to learn the management of chariots and the use of the bow, and to stand firm in battle and not to turn back. The special duties of the Vaisya were trade, agriculture, tending cattle, lending money, and labour for gain. Sudras were to serve the other three castes, but were also allowed to labour for gain, and there can be no doubt that they traded and earned money by independent work to a large extent in the Philosophic Period as in all succeeding periods. Religious knowledge was, however, forbidden to them.

It is evident that the seven castes described by Megasthenes are virtually the four castes spoken of above. His philosophers and counsellors were the Brahmans, those who engaged in religious study, and those who took employment under the state respectively. His husbandmen, shepherds, and artisans were the Vaisyas and Sudras, who engaged in cultivation, in pasture, and in manufacture. And his soldiers were the Kshatriyas; while his overseers were only special servants, spies of the king.

Megasthenes further subdivides the philosophers into Brahmans or householders, and Sramans or ascetics. Of the former he says that "the children are under the care of one person after another, and as they advance in age, each succeeding master is more accomplished than his predecessor. The philosophers have their abode in a grove in front of the city within a moderate-sized enclosure. They live in a simple style, and lie on beds of rushes or skins. They abstain from animal food and sensual pleasures, and spend their time listening to religious discourse and in imparting their knowledge to such as will listen to them. After living in this manner for seven and thirty years, each individual retires to his own property, where he lives for the rest of his days in ease and security. They then array themselves in fine muslin, and wear a few trinkets of gold on their fingers and in their ears. They eat flesh, but not that of animals employed in labour. They abstain from hot and highly seasoned food. They marry as many wives as they please, with a view to having numerous children, for by having many wives greater

SYLVAN SCENE.

advantages are enjoyed, and since they have no slaves, they have more need to have children around them to attend to their wants."

Of the Sramans, or ascetics, Megasthenes tells us that "they live in the wood, where they subsist on leaves of trees and wild fruits, and wear garments made from the bark of trees. They communicate with the kings, who consult them by messengers, regarding the causes of things, and who through them worship and supplicate the deity." Some of them practised medicine, and Megasthenes writes: "They effect cures rather by regulating diet than by the use of medicines. The remedies most esteemed are ointments and plasters." We learn from this account, as we learn from other sources, that sects of ascetics, subsisting on roots and wild fruits, lived in Ancient India, bearing the name of Sramanas, before and after the time of Gautama Buddha. And when that great reformer preached a holy life and retirement from the world as the essence of his religion, his followers, who retired from the world, were called Sakyaputriya Sramans, or ascetics who followed the Sakya, to distinguish them from other sects of ascetics.

Elsewhere Megasthenes says of the philosopher-caste that they, " being exempted from all public duties, are neither the masters nor the servants of others. They are, however, engaged by private persons to offer the sacrifices due in lifetime and to celebrate the obsequies of the dead. They forewarn assembled multitudes about droughts and wet weather, and also about propitious winds and diseases."

Of the military class, or the Kshatriya caste, Megasthenes gives a very brief sketch. The soldiers were organized and equipped for war, but in times of peace gave themselves up to idleness and amusements.

Of the husbandmen, shepherds, and artisans, Megasthenes gives us a more interesting and lifelike sketch. Being exempted from fighting and other public services, the husbandmen " devote the whole of their time to tillage; nor would an enemy, coming upon a husbandman at work on his land, do him any harm, for men of this class, being regarded as public benefactors, are protected from all injury. The land thus remaining unravaged, and producing heavy crops, supplies the inhabitants with all that is requisite to make life very enjoyable. They pay a land tribute to the king, because all India is the property of the crown, and no private person is permitted to own land. Besides the land tribute, they pay into the royal treasury a fourth part of the produce of the soil. The shepherds neither settle in towns nor in villages, but live in tents. By hunting and trapping they clear the country of noxious birds and wild beasts. Of the artisans some are armourers, while others make the implements which husbandmen and others find useful in their different callings. This class is not only exempted from paying taxes, but even receives maintenance from the royal exchequer."

CHAPTER XXII

SOCIAL LIFE IN THE AGE OF PHILOSOPHY

IT is in the Sutras that we first find mention of the different forms of marriage with which we are familiar from the later metrical codes of law. Vasishtha mentions six forms:—

Brahma marriage; the father pours out a libation of water and gives his daughter to a suitor, a student.

Daiva marriage; the father decks his daughter with ornaments and gives her to an officiating priest, while a sacrifice is performed.

Arsha marriage; the father gives his daughter in exchange for a cow or a bull.

Gandharva marriage; the lover takes and weds a loving maiden.

Kshatra (or Rakshasa) marriage; the bridegroom forcibly takes a maiden, destroying her relatives by force of arms.

Manusha (or Asura) marriage; the suitor purchases a damsel from her father.

The lawgiver Apastamba recognizes only these six forms of marriage; but the older writers, Gautama and Baudhayana, sanction eight forms of marriage, adding to these six forms one rite, Prajapatya, which was considered praiseworthy, and another form, Paisacha, which was sinful. In the Prajapatya form the father merely gave away his daughter to the suitor, saying, "Fulfil ye the law conjointly." The Paisacha form was simply a rape of an unconscious woman.

Marriages among kinsfolk were rigorously prohibited in the Philosophic Period. Vasishtha prohibits marriage between a man and a woman of the same *gotra* or *pravara*, or who are related within four degrees on the mother's side, or within six degrees on the father's side. Apastamba forbids wedlock between men and women of the same *gotra*, or who are related (within six degrees) on the mother's (or father's) side, but Baudhayana allows a man to marry the daughter of a maternal uncle or a paternal aunt.

The marriage of girls at a tender age was not yet prevalent in the Philosophic Period. Vasishtha says:—

"A maiden who has attained puberty shall wait for three years.

"After three years, she may take a husband of equal caste."

The marriage of widows, which was a prevalent custom in the Vedic and Brahmanic Periods, continued to prevail in the Philosophic Period, but was not looked upon with favour except in the case of child-widows, and the son of a remarried widow was often classed with adopted sons, or sons by an appointed wife or daughter.

The first great event in a boy's life seems to have

been his initiation as a student. A Brahman boy was initiated between eight and sixteen, a Kshatriya between eleven and twenty-two, and a Vaisya between twelve and twenty-four. The initiated boy then lived as a religious student in the house of his teacher for twelve, twenty-four, thirty-six, or forty-eight years, according as he wished to master one, two, three, or the four Vedas. During this period of his life he avoided all spiced food, perfumes, and articles of luxury; he tied his hair in a knot, he bore a staff and a girdle, and a cloth of flax or hemp, or even only a skin. Avoiding all places of amusement and of pleasure, restraining his senses, modest and humble, the young student went out every morning with his staff to beg for food from charitable householders in the neighbouring villages, and all that he obtained in the course of the day he placed before his teacher, tasting food only after his teacher had done with his meals. He went to the forest to fetch fuel, and evening and morning he brought water for household use. Every morning he swept and cleaned the altar, kindled the fire, and placed the sacred fuel on it; and every evening he washed his teacher's feet and rubbed him and put him to bed, before he retired to rest. Such was the humble and simple life which ancient Hindu students led, when they devoted all the energies of their mind to the acquisition of the sacred learning of their forefathers.

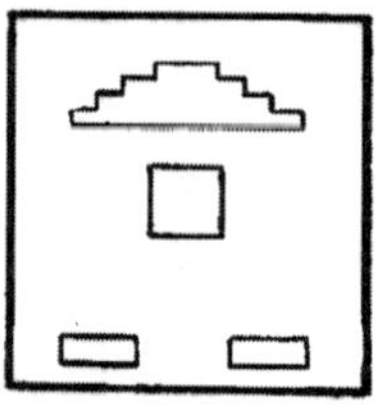

THE VEDI, OR MARRIAGE ALTAR.

Instruction, it is needless to repeat, was imparted by rote. The student respectfully held the hand of his teacher, and fixed his mind on the teacher and said, "Venerable sir, recite," and the Savitri (the well-known Gayatri verse of the Rig-Veda) was recited, and learned as the introduction to the study of the Vedas. From day to day new lessons were recited and learned, the student dividing his day's work between his lessons and the household work of his teacher.

When, after years of study, often under different teachers, the student at last returned to his home, he made a handsome gift to his instructors, married, and settled down as a householder. The Sutrakaras are never tired of impressing on householders the paramount duty of courtesy and hospitality towards guests, for the reception of guests is an everlasting sacrifice offered by the householder to God.

Besides the order of the student and that of the householder, there were two other orders of life, those of the ascetic (*bhikshu*), and the hermit (*vaikhānasa*). We learn from later Sanskrit literature that a typical or perfect life was the life of a man who belonged to these four orders in the successive periods of his life. But this was not the original idea, and in early times a man might have chosen to spend the whole of his life in one of these four orders. It is needless here to dwell on rules laid down for an ascetic and a hermit respectively. It will suffice to state that an ascetic shaved his head, had no property or home, practised austerities, fasted or lived on alms, wore a single garment or a skin, slept on the bare ground, wandered about from place to place, and discontinued the performance of all religious ceremonies, but never ceased to study the Veda or to meditate upon the Universal Soul. A hermit, on the other hand, though dwelling in woods, living on roots and fruits, and leading a chaste

ASCETIC AT BENARES.

life, kindled the sacred fire and offered the morning and evening libations.

We now return to the householders, who formed the nation. For them no less than forty sacraments were prescribed, and an account of them will give us a glimpse into the religious and domestic life of the ancient Hindu.

Domestic Ceremonies. — Garbhadhana (ceremony

to cause conception); Pumsavana (ceremony to cause the birth of a male child); Simantonnayana (arranging the hair of the pregnant wife); Jatakarman (ceremony on the birth of a child); naming the child; the first feeding; the tonsure of the head; the initiation; the four vows for the study of the Veda; the bath of completion of studentship; marriage; and the five sacrifices to gods, manes, men, spirits, and to Brahma.

Grihya rites, also called Pakayajnas.—Astaka, or rites performed in winter; Parvana, or new and full moon rites; Sraddha, or sacrifices to departed ancestors; Sravani, a rite performed in the Sravana month; Agrahayani, performed in the Agrahayana month; Chaitri, performed in the month of Chaitra; and Asvayugi, performed in the month of Asvina.

Srauta rites.—These are again divided into two classes, Haviryajna, performed with offerings of rice, milk, butter, meat, and the like, and the Somayajna, performed with libations of the Soma-juice.

The Haviryajna rites are Agnyadhana, Agnihotra, Darsapurnamasa, Agrayana, Chaturmasya, Nirudhapasubandha, and Sautramani.

The Somayajna rites are Agnishtoma, Atyagnishtoma, Ukthya, Shodasin, Vajapeya, Atiratra, and Aptoryama.

Such were the forty sacraments prescribed for householders; but far above the performance of these sacrifices was esteemed the possession of virtue and goodness, which alone led to heaven, so that Gautama says:—

"He who is sanctified by these forty sacraments, but whose soul is destitute of the eight good qualities, will not be united with Brahma, nor does he reach His heaven.

"But he, forsooth, who is sanctified by only a few of these forty sacraments, and whose soul is endowed with the excellent qualities, will be united with Brahma and will dwell in His heaven."

We will now say a few words with regard to those of the forty sacraments which illustrate Hindu life. They include, as stated above, domestic ceremonies, Grihya rites, and Srauta rites. The Srauta rites, which have been briefly described in our account of the Brahmanic Age, throw little light on the manners and life of the people. The domestic ceremonies and Grihya rites, on the other hand, give us glimpses of inestimable value of the manners of the ancient Hindus. The most important of the domestic ceremonies are marriage, ceremonies performed during pregnancy, birth of a child, the first feeding of a child, tonsure, initiation, and return from school on the completion of education.

Marriage.—The bridegroom sent messengers to the house of the girl's father, and if the proposal pleased both parties, the promise of marriage was ratified, both parties touching a full vessel into which flowers, fried grain, barley, and gold had been put, and reciting a formula. The bridegroom then performed a sacrifice. On the appointed day, the bride's relations bathed her with water fragrant with the choicest fruits and scents, clad her in a newly dyed garment, and caused her to sit down by a fire while the family priest performed a sacrifice. The bridegroom, who had also bathed and gone through auspicious ceremonies, was escorted by young unwidowed women to the house of his bride.

The actual marriage ceremony varied in detail in different localities, but agreed in the essential points. The bridegroom took the hand of the bride, and led her three times round a fire, reciting certain verses, such as, "Come, let us marry. Let us beget offspring. Loving, bright, with genial mind, may we live a hundred autumns." Each time he made her tread a millstone, saying, "Like a stone be firm." The bride's brother or guardian filled her hands with *ājya*, or fried grain, which she sacrificed to the fire. The bridegroom then caused the bride to step forward seven steps, reciting suitable words. The going round the fire, treading the stone, sacrificing the fried grain, and stepping forward seven steps, constituted the principal forms of the marriage ceremony. "And she should dwell that night," says Asvalayana, "in the house of an old Brahman woman whose husband is alive and whose children are alive. When she sees the Polar Star, the star of Arundhati, and the Seven Rishis (Ursa Major), let her break silence and say, 'May my husband live, and I get offspring.'" In like manner Sankhayana says, "Let them sit silent, when the sun has set, until the Polar Star appears. He shows her the star with the words, 'Firm be thou, thriving with me.' Let her say,

'I see the polar star; may I obtain offspring.' Through a period of three nights let them refrain from conjugal intercourse."

Pregnancy.—Various were the rites performed during the pregnancy of a wife. In the first place, there was the Garbhadhana rite, which was supposed to secure conception. The Pumsavana rite was supposed to determine the male sex of the child, and the Garbharakshana secured the unborn child from danger, while the Simantonnayana, performed, according to Asvalayana, in the fourth month, and according to Sankhayana, in the seventh month of pregnancy, or even, according to Gobhila, in the fourth, sixth, or eighth month, was a more interesting ceremony, and consisted in the husband's affectionately parting his wife's hair, with certain rites.

Birth of a child.—The rites performed on this occasion were called Jatakarman, or birth ceremony, Medhajananam, or the production of intelligence, and Ayushya, or rite for prolonging life. On this occasion the father gave the child a secret name—of an even number of syllables if the child was a male, and an uneven number if it was a female—and only the father and mother knew that name. On the tenth day, when the mother was convalescent, an appellative for common use was given to the child. "The name of a Brahman should end in Sarman (*e.g.* Vishnu Sarman), that of a Kshatriya in Varman (*e.g.* Lakshmi Varman), and that of a Vaisya in Gupta (*e.g.* Chandra Gupta)."

First feeding of the child with solid food.—This is

the well-known Annaprasana ceremony. The child seems to have been allowed a greater variety of food in the olden days than at the present time. Thus, Asvalayana and Sankhayana declare that he should partake of " goat's flesh, if he be desirous of nourishment; flesh of partridge, if desirous of holy lustre; boiled rice with ghee, if desirous of splendour," to which Paraskara adds such foods as " flesh of that bird called Bharadvaji, if he wishes fluency of speech, and fish, if swiftness be desired."

Tonsure.—This was performed when the child was one year old, according to Sankhayana and Paraskara, or when the child was in his third year, according to Asvalayana and Gobhila. The child's head was shaved with a razor with the recitation of certain Vedic verses (but without them in the case of a girl), and some hair was left and arranged according to the custom of the family.

Initiation.—This was an important ceremony, and was performed when a boy was entrusted by his father or guardian to the teacher for education. The age of initiation, as we have seen before, varied in the case of Brahmans, Kshatriyas, and Vaisyas, and the sacred thread was worn on this occasion by all the three castes.

Return from school.—The student, after he had finished his education, returned to his home, and if he had no ancestral house to go to, had to build a house. This, too, was accompanied by a ceremony, and by the utterance of the hymns of the Rig-Veda to Vastospati, the lord of dwelling-houses, as well as to other divinities. Then followed marriage and the setting up of fires, and the student became a householder, and had other and graver duties to perform.

The most important of the Grihya rites was the Sraddha, or monthly offering to the departed fathers, and the feeding of Brahmans. "Brahmans endowed with learning, moral character, and correct conduct," were invited, and sat down "as representatives of the fathers" to whom the oblations were offered. The sacrificer then offered the Arghya water to the fathers with the words, "Father, this is thy Arghya; Grandfather, this is thy Arghya; Great-grandfather, this is thy Arghya." Gifts of perfumes, garlands, incense, lights, and clothes were then made to the Brahmans. With the permission of the Brahmans, food of the Sthalipaka prepared for the Pindapitriyajna was smeared with ghee and sacrificed in the fire, or in the hands of the Brahmans, together with other food. And when the sacrificer saw that the Brahmans were satiated, he recited the Vedic verse, "They have eaten, they have enjoyed themselves."

Parvana.—This was the rite observed on the new and full moon days, and consisted in fasting, as well as in offering cooked oblations to the deities of those days, with appropriate mantras.

Sravani.—This was a rite observed on the full moon day of the month of Sravana in the rainy season, and the idea was to propitiate serpents, which multiply in India in the rains.

Asvayugi.—This was a rite performed on the full

PROPITIATION OF THE SERPENTS.

moon day of Asvayuga or Asvina month, and is described by Sankhayana as follows:—

"On the full moon day of Asvayuga a milk-rice oblation to Indra.

"Having sacrificed Ajya with the words, 'Hail to the two Asvins! Hail to the two Asvayugas! Hail to the full moon of Asvayuga! Hail to the autumn! Hail to Prajapati! Hail to the tawny one!'

"He shall sacrifice a mixture of curds and butter with this (Vedic) hymn, 'The cows come hither,' verse by verse.

"That night they let the calves join their mothers.

"Then feeding of the Brahmans."

It is impossible not to suspect from this account that the rite is essentially agricultural, and this interpretation is confirmed when Paraskara tells us that the rite was to be followed by a sacrifice to Sita, the goddess of the field furrow.

Agrahayani.—This rite was performed on the full moon day of the Agrahayana month. This particular night was considered to be the consort of the year, or the image of the year, and adoration was offered to the year, to Samvatsara, Parivatsara, Idavatsara, Idvatsara, and to Vatsara, terms designating the different years of the quinquennial period of Yuga.

Ashtaka.—These rites received their name from the fact that they were performed on the eighth day of the three or four successive dark fortnights after the full moon of Agrahayana. Oblations were made with vegetables, flesh, and cakes respectively. Gobhila quoted different opinions as to the object of these oblations, and declared that they might be for the gratification of Agni, or of the Fathers, or of Prajapati, or of the season gods, or of all the gods. It is more probable, however, that they were suggested by the winter season, which is an enjoyable season in India, when the Aman rice is harvested and wheat and barley thrive, and when cakes and flesh and vegetables are not only acceptable to the "season gods," but are also highly gratifying to men.

Chaitri, the last rite in the year, was performed on the full moon day of Chaitra, when Indra and Agni and Rudra and the Nakshatras, or constellations, were propitiated.

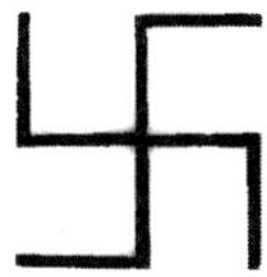

SWASTIKA.

CHAPTER XXIII

SANKHYA AND YOGA

THE true glory of the Philosophic Period consists in the philosophy of Kapila and the religion of Buddha. Both worked to some extent on the same lines; both began with the great object of affording humanity a relief from the suffering which is the lot of all living beings; both rejected the remedies which the Vedic rites offered; both declared knowledge and meditation to be the means of salvation; both adopted the doctrine of transmigration from the Upanishads; both aimed at Nirvana; and both professed an agnostic creed.

But here the parallel ends. Kapila, who probably lived a century before Buddha, started the system of philosophy, but meant it only as philosophy addressed to high thinkers and speculative scholars, and not to the masses. Buddha, on the other hand, who was probably born in the very town sanctified by the memory of the great philosopher, and was well versed in the philosophy of Kapila, possessed a deep and all-embracing sympathy, a feeling for the poor, a tear for the bereaved and the suffering. This was the secret of Buddha's great success.

The object of Kapila's philosophy was to relieve mankind from the three kinds of pain, bodily and mental, natural and extrinsic, divine or supernatural. Vedic rites are inefficacious, because they are tainted with the slaughter of living beings; the complete and final emancipation of the soul is secured by knowledge alone.

Nature and Soul are eternal and self-existent. From Nature (*prakriti*) is produced intellect, consciousness, the five subtle elements, the five grosser elements, the five senses of perception, the five organs of action, and the mind. Soul (*purusha*) produces nothing, but is only linked with Nature, until its final emancipation. Kapila does not accept the orthodox opinion of the Upanishads that all souls are portions of the Universal Soul. He asserts that each soul is separate, and has a separate existence after its emancipation from the bonds of Nature.

It will be seen that, according to Kapila, everything except *purusha*, or Soul, is derived from *prakriti*, or primordial matter, and is therefore material, so that he differs from modern materialistic philosophers only in asserting that there is a soul, independent of matter and eternal, though for a time linked with matter.

The five senses simply receive impressions; the five organs of action, such as the voice, hands, and feet, act according to their functions; but the mind (*manas*) is not what is implied by the English word, being only a sense organ which arranges the impressions and presents them to consciousness. Consciousness individualizes those impressions as "mine," and the intellect distinguishes and discriminates, and forms them into ideas.

ASCETIC AT NASIK.

Kapila recognized only three kinds of evidence, perception, inference, and testimony, and he admitted nothing which could not thus be known, so that, as neither perception, nor inference, nor testimony presented to him the idea of an external Author of all things, the Supreme Deity was not admitted by him as knowable. On the other hand, he recognized causation, and argued the production of all formal existences from *prakriti*, or Nature, on five different grounds. Firstly, specific objects are finite in their nature and must have cause. Secondly, different things have common properties and must be different species of the same primary genus. Thirdly, all things are in a constant state of progression, and show an active energy of evolution which must have been derived from a primary source. Fourthly, the existing world is an effect, and there must be a primary cause. And fifthly, there is an undividedness, a real unity in the whole universe, which argues a common origin.

Purusha, or Soul, however, has a separate existence, first, because matter is apparently collected and arranged with a design, which proves, according to Kapila, not a Designer, but the existence of soul, for which the things must have been arranged. Secondly, matter furnishes materials for pleasure and pain; hence sentient nature, which feels pleasure and pain, must be different from it. Thirdly, there must be a superintending force. Fourthly, there must be a nature that enjoys. And the fifth argument is that the yearning for a higher life points to the possibility of gaining it. These were Kapila's arguments for the existence of soul independent of matter, yet he did not believe in one soul, but held that the souls of different beings are distinct one from the other, thus diverging from the teaching of the Upanishads and the Vedantic school, which is based upon them.

We have already said that Kapila borrowed the doctrine of transmigration of souls from the Upanishads, and having borrowed this idea, he had to adapt it to his own system of philosophy. The soul, according to him, is so passive that the individuality of man is scarcely stamped on it, while the intellect, the consciousness, and the mind all belong to the material part of a man. Hence Kapila was constrained by his own rigid reasoning to assume that a subtle body, consisting of the intellect, the consciousness, the mind, and the subtle principles, migrated with the soul. This subtle body, or *linga sarīra*, forms the personality of an individual, and ascends to a higher region or descends to a lower with the soul, according to the virtues or vices committed in this life, nor does the soul gain final emancipation till it is freed from its subtle body by the knowledge which it acquires through its union with nature.

Even after the soul has obtained complete knowledge, it resides for a time in the body, "as a potter's wheel continues to revolve from the force of the previous impulse." This is the Nirvana of Buddha, a state of quietude, when perfect knowledge has been gained, when all passions have been restrained, all desires have been checked, and the enlightened soul awaits its final emancipation. That separation of soul and matter comes at last. Nature ceases to act, as her purpose has been accomplished, and the soul obtains an abstraction from matter, and both continue to exist eternally isolated from each other and independent of each other.

The great fault of Kapila's philosophy as a creed for the people was its agnosticism, and the Yoga system of philosophy sought to obviate this defect. The Yoga philosophy is ascribed to Patanjali, who probably lived in the second century before Christ. All that we know of the life and history of Patanjali is that his mother was called Gonika, as he himself tells us, and that he resided for a certain time in Kashmir, although he was a native of Gonarda, a place in the eastern part of India. His system is contained in his Yoga Sutra. In the first chapter of this work *yoga* is derived from *yuj*, " to join " or " to meditate," and this meditation is possible only by the suppression of the functions of the mind by constant exercise and

A HINDU DEVOTEE.

by dispassion, thus leading to Yoga, conscious or unconconscious.

The attainment of this coveted state of mind is hastened by devotion to Isvara, or God, who is regarded as a soul untouched by affliction, works, deserts, and desires.

Disease, doubt, and worldly-mindedness are obstacles to the attainment of Yoga, but may be overcome by concentration of the mind, by benevolence, by indifference to happiness or misery, and even by the regulation of the breath.

The first exercises in the performance of Yoga are asceticism, the muttering of a mantra, and devotion to God, which overcome all afflictions like ignorance, egoism, desire, and aversion, or ardent desire to live. These are the motives of work (*karma*), and works must bear their fruits in subsequent births, while the object of Yoga is to devise means to abstain from works, and so to preclude future births.

We have, then, the Sankhya definition of the soul and the intellect; knowledge finally severs the connection between the two, and thenceforward the soul is free, and an end is put to its reincarnation and its suffering. Knowledge passes through seven stages before it is perfect, and eight means (which remind one of the eightfold path of the Buddhists) are prescribed, by which this perfect knowledge can be obtained. The first way is abstinence from evil actions, slaughter, falsehood, theft, incontinence, and avarice; and the second consists of an obligation to perform certain acts, purification, contentment, penance, study, and devotion to God. These two means are prescribed for all, householders and ascetics alike, while the rules for Yogis are supplemented by additional duties. The third stage is the assumption of special postures for meditation; the fourth is regulation of the breath; the fifth is the abstraction of the organs from their natural functions; and the sixth, seventh, and eighth are steadfastness, contemplation, and meditation, which are the essential constituents of Yoga itself. When these three are united, occult powers are acquired, and through them one may know the past and the future, make himself invisible to men, observe the details of what is passing

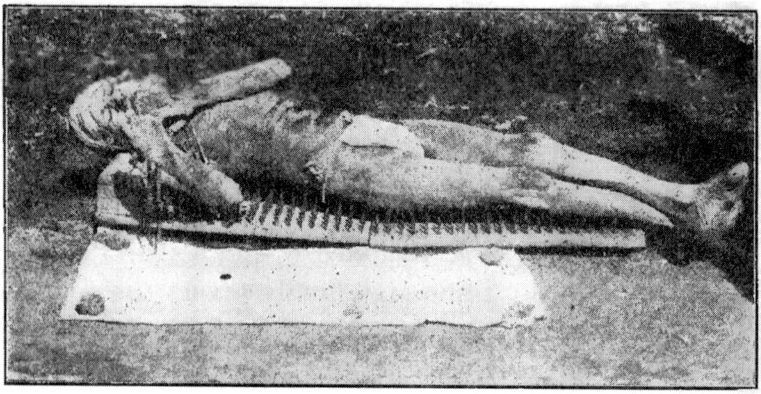

UNDERGOING YOGI PENANCE.
Copyright by Underwood & Underwood.

in distant regions or in the stars and planets, converse with spirits, travel in the air or through water, and acquire various superhuman powers.

It will thus be seen that as a system of philosophy Yoga is valueless; all its fundamental maxims about the soul and intellect and sensations, about the transmigration of souls and their eternity and final emancipation by knowledge, are those of the Sankhya philosophy. In fact Patanjali tried to blend the idea of a Supreme Deity with the philosophy of Kapila; but unfortunately he or his followers mixed up with it much of the superstition and the mystic practices of the age, while in still later times the philosophy of the Yoga system has been completely forgotten, and the system has degenerated into cruel and indecent Tantrika rites, or into the impostures and superstitions of the so-called Yogis of the present day.

CHAPTER XXIV

NYAYA AND VAISESIKA

THE philosopher Gautama was the Aristotle of India, and his system of Nyaya is the Hindu logic, which is still studied in India along the traditional lines, even though the number of teachers and pupils is growing less year by year. The date of Gautama is not known, but he lived in the Philosophic Period, probably a century after Kapila. The Nyaya Sutra, which is ascribed to him, is divided into five books, each subdivided into two " days," or diurnal lessons, and these are again divided into articles, each of which consists of a number of Sutras.

The Nyaya system starts with the subjects to be discussed, which are fourteen in number: proof, problem, doubt, motive, instance or example, determined truth, argument or syllogism, confutation, ascertainment, controversy, jangling, objection, fallacy, perversion, futility, and controversy.

Proof is of four kinds: Perception, inference, analogy, and verbal testimony. Cause (*karana*) is that which necessarily precedes an effect, which could not be without the cause; and effect (*kārya*) is that which necessarily ensues and otherwise could not be. For the relation of cause and effect, the connections might be twofold—simple conjunction (*samyoga*), and constant relation (*samavāya*). Hence cause may be of three kinds: immediate and direct, as the yarn is of cloth; mediate or indirect, as the weaving is of cloth; and instrumental, as the loom is of cloth.

The problems are soul, body, the senses, the objects of sense, intellect, mind (or the internal organ), production, fault, transmigration, retribution, pain, and emancipation.

The soul, which is the seat of knowledge, is different in each person, and is separate from the body and the senses. Each individual soul is infinite and eternal, and transmigrates according to the works performed in life. So far we see an agreement with Kapila's philosophy. But the Nyaya adds that the Supreme Soul is one, the seat of eternal knowledge, and the maker or former of all things. The body is earthly, the five external senses are also material, and the mind is the organ of the senses.

Intellect is twofold, including memory and concept. A concept is true if derived from clear proof, and is wrong if not derived from proof. Similarly, memory may be right or wrong. The objects of sense are odour, taste, colour, touch, and sound.

Acts are the causes of virtue or vice, of merit or demerit; and the only motive to them is the hedonistic desire to attain pleasure or to avoid pain.

Transmigration is the passing of the soul to successive bodies. Pain is the primary evil, and there are twenty-one varieties of evil which are causes of pain. The soul attains its emancipation by knowledge and not by action.

The specialty of Nyaya is its development of inference by the construction of a true syllogism, which, in its Hindu form consists of five parts, which are called the proposition, the reason, the instance, the application of the reason, and the conclusion, as may be illustrated by the following example:—

The hill is fiery.

For it smokes.

Whatever smokes is fiery.

The hill is smoking.

Therefore it is fiery.

Logic has always been a favourite study with learned Hindus, and neither the Ancient Greeks, nor the Mediæval Arabs, nor the European schoolmen of the Middle Ages displayed more acuteness and subtlety in reasoning, or more rigid and scientific strictness in their discussions, than is witnessed in the numerous works of the Hindus on logic.

Kanada's atomic philosophy is supplementary to Gautama's logic, as the Yoga is supplementary to the Sankhya, and therefore need not detain us long. The cardinal principle of Kanada is that all material substances are aggregates of atoms, whence the name *kanāda*, " atom-eater," by which he is known. The atoms are eternal, the aggregates only are perishable by disintegration.

The first compound is of two atoms; the next consists of three double atoms, and so on. The mote visible in the sunbeam is thus a compound of six atoms. In this way two earthly atoms acting under an unseen law constitute a double atom of earth; three binary atoms constitute a tertiary atom; four tertiary atoms make a quaternary atom; and so on to gross, grosser, and grossest masses of earth. In this manner the great earth is produced, the great water is thus produced from aqueous atoms, great light from luminous atoms, and great air from aerial atoms.

INDIAN SCENERY.

Kanada recognizes seven categories of objects: substances, quality, action, community, particularity, coherence, and non-existence.

Under the first of these categories, the nine substances of Kanada are earth, water, light, air (all eternal in atoms, but transient and perishable in aggregates), ether (which transmits sound, and which has no atoms, but is infinite, one, and eternal), time, space (neither of which is material, and therefore is not compounded of atoms), soul, and *manas* (or the internal organ). Light and heat are considered as only different forms of the same essential substance. Ether (*ākāsa*) conveys sound; and *manas*, or the internal organ, is supposed to be extremely small, like an atom.

The second category, quality, embraces seventeen varieties or qualities of the nine substances enumerated above. The qualities are colour, savour, odour, tangibility, number, extension, individuality, conjunction, disjunction, priority, posteriority, intellections, pleasure, pain, desire, aversion, and volition.

The third category, action, is divided into five kinds, upward and downward movement, contraction, dilation, and general motion.

The fourth category, community (genus), denotes qualities common to many objects, and also implies species. These common qualities and species have a real and objective existence, according to Kanada, but not according to the Buddhists, who affirm that only individuals have existence, and that abstractions are unreal conceptions.

The fifth category, particularity, denotes simple objects, devoid of community. They are soul, mind, time, place, the ethereal element, and atoms.

The sixth category, coherence, is connection between things which must be connected so long as they exist, as yarn and cloth.

The seventh category, non-existence, is either universal or mutual.

It will be seen from this brief account that the Vaisesika system of Kanada, in so far as it is an original system, is physics rather than philosophy. It was the first attempt made in India to inquire into the laws of matter and force, of combination and disintegration.

In every system of Hindu Philosophy (except Vedantism) matter is supposed to be eternal, and distinct from soul. The Vedântists alone regard matter as the manifestation of the One Supreme Soul who comprises all and is all. Of this system we shall speak in the next chapter.

INDIAN CARVING.

CHAPTER XXV

PURVA MIMAMSA AND VEDANTA

WE now come to the last two systems of the philosophy of the Hindus, the Purva Mimamsa of Jaimini and the Uttara Mimamsa of Badarayana Vyasa. To the historian of India they are of the utmost importance and value, for the Mimamsa schools represent the conservative phase of the Hindu mind at a time when philosophers and laymen were alike drifting towards agnostic and heterodox opinions. Sankhya philosophy led hosts of thinking men away from the teachings of the Upanishads on the Universal Soul; and the Buddhist religion was embraced by many of the lower classes as a relief from caste inequalities and elaborate Vedic rites. Against this general movement of the day the Mimamsa schools made a stand. The Purva Mimamsa insisted on those Vedic rites and practices which later philosophers had come to regard as useless or even as unholy; and the Uttara Mimamsa proclaimed the doctrine of the Universal Soul which the Upanishads had taught before, and which continues to be the cardinal doctrine of Hinduism to this day.

The controversy, or rather the division in opinion, went on for centuries, but orthodoxy prevailed in India in the end. The great Kumarila Bhatta, who lived in the seventh century after Christ, wrote his celebrated Vartika, or commentary on the Purva Mimamsa Sutras, and was the most redoubted champion of Hinduism, as well as the most uncompromising opponent of Buddhism. He not only vindicated the ancient rites of the Vedas, and inveighed against the heterodox opinions of the Buddhists, but he denied them any consideration, even when they happened to agree with the Veda.

The Uttara Mimamsa also had its champion, a man greater than Kumarila, the celebrated Sankaracharya, who wrote in the first half of the ninth century.

The Sutras of the Purva Mimamsa are ascribed to Jaimini, and are divided into twelve lectures and subdivided into sixty chapters. The first lecture treats of the authority of enjoined duty; the varieties of duty, supplemental duties, and the purpose of the performance of duties are treated in the second, third, and fourth lectures. The order of their performance is considered in the fifth, and the qualification for their performance is treated in the sixth. The subject of indirect precept is treated in chapters seven and eight. Inferable changes are discussed in the ninth, and exceptions in the tenth chapter. Efficacy is considered in the eleventh chapter, and the work closes with a discussion of co-ordinate effect in the twelfth chapter.

The Purva Mimamsa philosophy was, however, merely a philosophy of Vedic rites, and a supplementary system of philosophy was therefore required, this want being supplied by the Uttara Mimamsa or Vedanta. It is the Vedanta which tells us of the Supreme Being, the Universal Soul, the Pervading Breath, as the Purva Mimamsa speaks of rites and sacrifices. The Vedanta is the direct outcome of the Upanishads, as the Purva Mimamsa is the outcome of the Brahmanas, and the two schools of Mimamsa taken together represent orthodox Vedic Hinduism, both in its rites and observances, and in its belief. The two schools taken together were an answer to Buddhist heretics who ignored Vedic rites and denied a Supreme Being, as well as to the agnostic Sankhya system of philosophy, and to other systems which proclaimed the eternity of matter, and thus, when combined, they form the basis of true Hinduism. The great text-book of the Vedanta is the Sariraka Mimamsa Sutra, or Brahma Sutra, which is attributed to Badarayana Vyasa, and which cannot have been compiled very long before the Christian Era.

The Vedanta adopts the syllogism of the Nyaya system, with the obvious improvement of reducing its five members to three, as in the syllogism of Aristotle.

Badarayana's Brahma Sutra is divided into four lectures, and each lecture is subdivided into four chapters. It opens precisely as the Purva Mimamsa, announcing its purport in the very same terms, except that it substitutes Brahma, or God, for Dharma, or

Duty. The author then confutes the Sankhya doctrine that Nature is the material cause of the universe, and declares that a sentient rational Being is the material as well as the efficient First Cause of the universe.

The second lecture continues the confutation of Kapila's Sankhya philosophy, as well as of Patanjali's Yoga system and Kanada's atomic theory. All the universe is rigidly assigned to Brahma, who is the Cause and the Effect.

The soul is active, not passive as the Sankhyas maintain, although its activity is merely adventitious, and it is in reality a portion of the Supreme Ruler, while the corporeal organs and the vital actions are all modifications of Brahma.

The third lecture treats of transmigration of souls, of the attainment of knowledge, of final emancipation, and of the attributes of the Supreme Being. The soul transmigrates, invested with a subtle body, from one state to another. Departing from one body, it experiences the recompense of its works, and returns to occupy a new body with the resulting influence of its former deeds.

The Supreme Being is impassable, unaffected by worldly modifications, as the clear crystal, seemingly coloured by the hibiscus flower, is really pellucid. He is pure Sense, Intellect, Thought.

The reader will perceive that the Vedanta philosophy is a direct and legitimate result of the Upanishads, and the idea of unity is carried to its extreme limit in the Vedanta as in the Upanishads.

The second half of this lecture relates to devout exercises and pious meditation, which are necessary for the reception of divine knowledge.

The fourth and last lecture relates to the fruit of pious meditations properly conducted, and the attainment of divine knowledge. So soon as that knowledge is attained, past sins are annulled and future sins are precluded. In like manner the effects of merit and virtue are also annulled. And " having annulled by fruition other works which had begun to have effect, having enjoyed the recompense and suffered the pains of good and bad actions, the possessor of divine knowledge, on the demise of the body, proceeds to a re-union with Brahma." This, as we know, is the final beatitude taught by the Upanishads.

There are two other less perfect forms of emancipation. One of them qualifies the soul for reception at Brahma's abode, but not for immediate re-union and identity with his being. The other is still less perfect, and is called Jivanmukti, which can be acquired in the present life by Yogis, and enables them to perform supernatural acts, such as evoking the shades of forefathers, assuming different bodies, and going immediately to any place at pleasure.

The attributes of God, according to the Vedanta philosophy, have thus been recapitulated by Colebrooke in his " Philosophy of the Hindus ": " God is the omniscient and omnipotent cause of the existence, continuance, and dissolution of the universe. Creation is an act of His will. He is both efficient and material cause of the world, creator and nature, framer and frame, doer and deed. At the consummation of all things, all are resolved into Him. The Supreme Being is one, sole existent, secondless, entire, without parts, sempiternal, infinite, ineffable, invariable, ruler of all, universal soul, truth, wisdom, intelligence, happiness."

Such are the six systems of philosophy which were developed in India in the Philosophic Period; such are the answers which Hindu philosophers have given to the questions which were started in the Upanishads, to questions which rise in the mind of every reflective man, but which it is not given to him to answer completely — What is God, and what is man?

Summed up as a whole, this rationalistic period of philosophy and laws was rich in results of which every Hindu may be proud. Besides producing the first recorded systems of mental philosophy and logic, and codifying a body of civil and criminal law, it developed the infant sciences of geometry and grammar. The administration of government was perfected in the latter part of this period and the whole of Northern India was brought under a single great ruler. And, lastly, it was in this period that the great reformer Gautama Buddha proclaimed that religion of equality and brotherhood of man which is at the present day the living faith of one-third of the human race. To the story of that great revolution we now turn.

CHAPTER XXVI

BUDDHIST SACRED LITERATURE

IN the sixth century before Christ, India witnessed the commencement of a great revolution. Her ancient religion, which the Hindu Aryans had practised and proclaimed for fourteen centuries, had degenerated into forms. The gods of the Rig-Veda, whom the ancient Rishis had invoked and worshipped, had come to be regarded as mere names; the libations of the Soma juice, and offerings of milk, grain, or flesh, which the Rishis of old had offered to their gods, had developed into cumbrous ceremonials, elaborate rites, unmeaning forms. The descendants or successors of those Rishis had now stepped forth as a powerful and hereditary caste, and claimed the right to perform elaborate religious rites and utter sacred prayers for the people. The people were taught to believe that they earned merit by having these rites performed and these prayers uttered by hired priests. The religious instinct which had inspired the composers of the Vedic hymns was dead, and vast ceremonials alone remained.

But a reaction had taken place. About the eleventh century before Christ, five centuries before the time of

The Golden Temple at Benares.
From a Photograph.

which we are now speaking, earnest and thoughtful Hindus had ventured to go beyond the rituals of the Brahmana literature, and had inquired into the mysteries of the soul and its Creator. The composers of the Upanishads had conceived the bold idea that all animate and inanimate nature proceeded from one universal deity, and were portions of one pervading soul. Inquiries were made into the mysteries of death and the future world, conjectures were made about the transmigration of souls, and doctrines were started containing in a crude form the salient principles of later Hindu philosophy.

Few, however, could devote their lives to these speculations and the abstruse philosophy which they involved. The mass of the Aryan householders—Brahmans, Kshatriyas, and Vaisyas—contented themselves with performing the rites, unintelligible to them, which the Brahmanas had laid down and the Sutras had condensed.

For the Sudras, who had come under the domination of the Aryan religion, there was no religious instruction, no religious observance, no social respect. Despised and degraded in the very community in which they were forced to live, they sighed for a change, and as they increased in number, pursued various useful industries, owned lands and villages, and gained in influence and power, they became more and more conscious of the unbearable conditions to which they were condemned.

To an earnest and inquisitive mind, to a sympathetic and benevolent soul, there was something anomalous in all this. Gautama of the Sakya race was versed in the Hindu learning and religion of the age, but he pondered and asked if what he had learnt could be efficacious or true. His soul rebelled against the distinctions between man and man; and his benevolent heart longed for a means to help the humble, the oppressed, and the lowly. The ceremonials and rites which householders practised appeared as vain and fruitless to him as the penances and mortifications which hermits voluntarily underwent in forests. The beauty of a holy and a sinless life of benevolence became to him as the perfection of human destiny, and with the earnest conviction of a prophet and a reformer he proclaimed this as the essence of religion, inviting the poor and lowly to end their sufferings by cultivating virtue, by eschewing passions and evil desire, and by spreading brotherly love and universal peace. The Brahman and the Sudra, the high and the low, were the same in his eyes; each and all could effect their salvation by a holy life, and he invited every man to embrace his creed of love. Mankind responded to the appeal, and Buddhism in the course of a few centuries became the prevailing faith, not of a sect or a country, but of the continent of Asia.

Nevertheless, it would be wrong to suppose that Gautama Buddha consciously set himself up as the founder of a new religion. On the contrary, he believed to the last that he was proclaiming only the pure and ancient religion which had prevailed among the Hin-

WESTERN GATEWAY OF THE BUDDHIST TOPE AT SANCHI.

dus, but which had been corrupted at a later day. Hinduism itself recognized wandering bodies of ascetics who renounced the world, performed no Vedic rites, and passed their days in contemplation. Such bodies were popularly termed Sramans. Gautama founded only one sect of Sramans among many sects which then existed, and his sect was known as that of the Sakyaputriya Sramans, to distinguish them from others. He taught them renunciation of the world, a holy life, and pious meditation, such as all sects of Sramans recommended and practised.

Gautama's holy and pious life, his universal sympathy, his unsurpassed moral precepts, his gentle and beautiful character, stamped themselves on his teachings, which were not altogether new, gathered round him the meek and lowly, the gentlest and best of the Aryans, converted kings on their thrones and peasants in their cots, and united sect and caste in a communion of love. And the sacred recollections of his life and teachings remained long after he had passed away, uniting the community which cherished his teachings, and in course of time giving his doctrines the character of a distinct religion.

Inspired by his love of purity and a holy, gentle life, Gautama eschewed the rites of the Vedas and the penances of ascetics alike, insisting only on self-culture, on benevolence, on pious resignation. This is what has made Buddhism a living and life-giving religion, when so many rival forms of asceticism have withered away and died.

In its historical development, Buddhism became divided into two great sects, so that the forms of Buddhism prevailing in Nepal and Tibet, China and Japan, are called Northern Buddhism, while the older and purer forms prevailing in Ceylon and Burma are termed Southern Buddhism. The Northern Buddhists furnish us with scanty materials directly illustrating the religion in its earliest form in India, for they embraced Buddhism some centuries after the Christian Era, and the works which they then obtained from India do not represent the earliest form of Hindu Buddhism. The Lalita Vistara, a most important work of the Northern Buddhists, is only a gorgeous poem, composed probably in Nepal in the second or third or fourth century after Christ, although it contains passages—the Gathas—which are of much older date. In China, Buddhism was introduced from the first century after Christ, but did not become the state religion until the fourth century, and the works on Buddhism which were then carried by Chinese pilgrims from India from century to century, and translated into the Chinese language, do not illustrate the earliest phase of Buddhism in India. Buddhism spread to Japan in the sixth century, and to Tibet in the seventh century after Christ, although the latter country has drifted far from primitive Hindu Buddhism, and has adopted forms and ceremonies which were unknown to Gautama and his followers.

The date of Buddha's death was for a long time believed to be 543 B.C.; but it is now generally accepted that the great reformer died about 487 (or 477) B.C., having been born about 567 (or 557) B.C. A council of five hundred monks was held in Rajagriha, the capital of Magadha, immediately after his death, and together they chanted the sacred laws, so as to fix them on their memory. A hundred years later, in 377 B.C., a second council was held in Vaisali, mainly for the discussion and settlement of ten questions on which difference of opinion had arisen. A hundred and thirty-five years after this, the great Asoka, King of the Magadhas, held a third council in Patna about 242 B.C., to determine upon the religious works, or Pitakas.[1] Through the preaching of this monarch's son, Mahinda, a Buddhist whose zeal led him to send missionaries to Ceylon and even to foreign countries, Syria, Macedon, and Egypt, to preach the religion, Ceylon embraced Buddhism in the third century B.C. About a hundred and fifty years after this the Pitakas were formally reduced to writing, and thus we have the most authentic account of the earliest form of Buddhism in Magadha in the Pali Pitakas of Ceylon.

These facts will show that the three Pitakas of the Southern Buddhists can claim a date anterior to 242 B.C., for no work which could not claim a respectable antiquity was included as canonical by the Council of Patna, and there is internal evidence in the Vinaya Pitaka for the hypothesis that the main portions of that Pitaka were settled before the Vaisali Council in 377 B.C.

[1] On the question of the latter date, see vol. ii, p 139.

In the Scriptures of the Southern Buddhists we thus have reliable materials for the history of India for the centuries immediately after the time of Gautama Buddha, while they give a more consistent and a less exaggerated account of the life and work and teachings of Buddha himself than anything which the Northern Buddhists can supply.

The three Pitakas are known as the Sutta Pitaka, the Vinaya Pitaka, and the Abhidhamma Pitaka. The works comprised in the Sutta Pitaka profess to record the sayings and doings of Gautama Buddha himself. Gautama is the actor and the speaker in the earliest works of this Pitaka, and teaches his doctrines in his own words, although occasionally one of his disciples is the instructor, and there are short introductions to indicate where and when Gautama or his disciple spoke.

The Vinaya Pitaka contains very minute rules, often on the most trivial subjects, for the conduct of monks and nuns, the Bhikkhus and the Bhikkhunis who had embraced the holy order. Gautama respected the lay disciple, but he held that to embrace the Holy Order was a quicker path to salvation. As the number of Bhikkhus and Bhikkhunis multiplied, it was necessary to fix elaborate rules, often on very minute subjects, for their proper conduct and behaviour in the Vihara, or monastery. As Gautama lived for nearly half a century after he had proclaimed his religion, there can be no doubt that he himself settled many of these rules, but, at the same time, it is equally certain that many of them grew up after his death, although they are all attributed in the Vinaya Pitaka to the direct order of the Blessed One himself.

And lastly, the Abhidhamma Pitaka contains disquisitions on various subjects, such as the conditions of life in different worlds, personal qualities, the elements, and the causes of existence.

Gautama, disregarding the precedent set by all classical writers and thinkers in India, preached his doctrine and morality to the people of India, not in Sanskrit, but in their own vernacular, and the Chullavagga accordingly says: "There were two brothers, Bhikkhus, by name Yamelu and Tekula, Brahmans by birth, excelling in speech, excelling in pronunciation." And they went up to Gautama and said, "At the present time, Lord, Bhikkhus differing in name, differing in lineage, differing in birth, differing in family, have gone forth. These corrupt the word of the Buddhas by their own dialect. Let us, Lord, put the word of the Buddhas into Sanskrit verse."

But Gautama would have none of this; he worked for the humble and the lowly, his message was for the people, and he wished it to be conveyed to them in their own tongue. "You are not, O Bhikkhus, to put the word of the Buddhas into (Sanskrit) verse. I allow you, O Bhikkhus, to learn the word of the Buddhas each in his own tongue."

CHAPTER XXVII

LIFE OF GAUTAMA BUDDHA

IN the sixth century before Christ, the kingdom of Magadha was rising to power and greatness. The realm, corresponding to the modern South Bihar, extended to the south of the Ganges, and on either side of the Son River. North of the Ganges it had a powerful rival in the haughty confederation of the Lichchhavis. Rajagriha, to the south of the Ganges, was the capital of Bimbisara, King of the Magadhas; and Vaisali, to the north of the Ganges, was the capital of the Lichchhavis. To the east lay the kingdom of Anga, or East Bihar, which is mentioned in connection with Magadha, and Champa was the capital of Anga. Far to the northwest lay the ancient kingdom of the Kosalas, and its capital had been removed from Ayodhya farther northwards to the flourishing town of Sravasti, where Prasenajit reigned at the time of which we are speaking. The equally ancient country of the Kasis, lying to the south, seems to have been subject at this time to the King of Sravasti, and a viceroy of Prasenajit ruled at Benares.

A little to the east of the Kosala kingdom, two

kindred clans, the Sakyas and the Koliyans, lived on the opposite banks of the small stream Rohini, and enjoyed a sort of precarious independence, more through the jealousies of the rival kings of Magadha and Kosala than by their own power. Kapilavastu was the capital of the Sakyas, who were then living in peace with the Koliyans, and Suddhodana, chief of the Sakyas, had married two daughters of the chief of the Koliyans.

Neither queen bore a child to Suddhodana for many years, and the hope of leaving an heir to the principality of the Sakyas was well-nigh abandoned. At last, however, the elder queen promised her husband an heir, and, according to ancient custom, left for her father's house, that her child might be born there. On her way, however, she gave birth to a son in the pleasant grove of Lumbini. The mother and the child were carried back to Kapilavastu, where the former died seven days after, leaving the child to be nursed by his stepmother and aunt, the younger queen.

The boy was named Siddhartha, but Gautama was his family name. He belonged to the Sakya tribe, and is therefore often called Sakyasimha, "Lion of the Sakyas;" and when he had proclaimed his new faith, he was called Buddha, or the "Awakened" or "Enlightened."

Little is known of the early life of Gautama, except that he married his cousin Subhadhra, or Yasodhara, daughter of the chief of Koli, when he was about eighteen years of age. Ten years later, however, he resolved to leave his home and his wife to study philosophy and religion. In the midst of his prosperity, position, and wealth, he felt a secret yearning after something higher, which neither wealth nor position could satisfy; and an irresistible desire to seek for a remedy for the sufferings of men arose in his heart even amid the luxuries of his palace home. It is said that the sight of a decrepit old man, of a sick man, of a decaying corpse, and of a dignified hermit led him to form his resolution to quit his home. The story, whether well-founded or not, represents in a concrete shape the thoughts that arose in his mind with regard to the woes of a worldly life, and the holy calm of a retired existence.

At this very time a son was born to him, but it is said that when the news was announced to him in a garden on the riverside, he only exclaimed, "This is a new, strong tie that I shall have to break."

That night he repaired to the threshold of his wife's chamber, and there by the light of the flickering lamp he gazed on a scene of perfect bliss. The young mother lay surrounded by flowers, with one hand on the infant's head. A yearning arose in his heart to take the babe in his arms for the last time before relinquishing all earthly bliss, but this he might not do, lest the mother awake and by her importunities and tears unnerve his heart and shake his resolution. Silently he tore himself away from the blissful sight, and in that one eventful moment, in the silent darkness of the night, he renounced for ever his wealth and posi-

BRASS IMAGE OF GAUTAMA BUDDHA FROM CEYLON.

He is seated on the Mucalinda Serpent in an attitude of profound meditation, with eyes half-closed, and five rays of light emerging from the crown of his head.

tion and power, his proud rank and his princely fame, the love of his young wife and of his sleeping babe, being determined to become a poor student and a homeless wanderer. He rode quietly out of the city, accompanied only by his faithful servant, named Channa, who asked to be allowed to stay with him and become an ascetic, but Gautama sent him back, and repaired alone to Rajagriha, which lay in a valley surrounded by five hills. Some Brahman ascetics lived in the caves of these hills, sufficiently far from the town for study and contemplation, and yet sufficiently near to obtain supplies. Gautama attached himself first to one and then to another, and learnt from them all that Hindu philosophers had to teach.

Not content with this learning, he retired to the jungles of Uruvela, near the site of the present temple of Bodh Gaya, and for six years, attended by five disciples, he gave himself up to the severest penances and self-mortification. His fame spread far and wide, yet he did not obtain the emancipation that he sought, and, despairing of deriving any profit from penance, he abandoned it.

Deserted then by his disciples, Gautama wandered alone towards the banks of the Niranjara, received his morning meal from the hands of Sujata, the daughter of a villager, and sat himself down under the famous Bo-tree, or the tree of wisdom. Here he was tempted by Mara, the evil spirit, and many legends relate the circumstances and details of this successful struggle with temptation. Long he sat in contemplation, and the scenes of his past life came thronging into his mind, until the doubts cleared away like mists in the morning and the daylight of truth flashed before his eyes. He had made no new discovery, he had acquired no new knowledge. Self-culture and universal love—this was his discovery, this is the essence of Buddhism, and his pious nature and benevolent heart told him that a holy life and an all-embracing love were the panacea to all evils.

Gautama's old teacher Alara was dead, and he therefore went to Benares to proclaim the truth to his five former disciples. In the cool of the evening he entered the Deer Park in the holiest city of India, and there found the followers who had deserted him. To them he explained his new tenets:—

"There are two extremes, O Bhikkhus, which the man who has given up the world ought not to follow: the habitual practice, on the one hand, of those things whose attraction depends upon the passions, and specially of sensuality, a low and pagan way, unworthy, unprofitable, and fit only for the worldly-minded; and the habitual practice, on the other hand, of asceticism, which is painful, unworthy, and unprofitable.

"There is a middle path, O Bhikkhus, avoiding these two extremes, discovered by the Tathagata (Buddha), a path which opens the eyes and bestows understanding, which leads to peace of mind, to the higher wisdom, to full enlightenment, to Nirvana!"

And then he explained to them the four truths concerning suffering, the cause of suffering, the destruction of suffering, and the way which leads to such destruction of suffering.

It is needless to say that the five former disciples were soon converted, and became the first members of the Order, and within five months after his arrival at Benares Gautama had sixty followers. He now called them together and sent them out in different directions to preach the truth for the salvation of mankind. "Go ye now, O Bhikkhus, and wander, for the gain of the many, for the welfare of the many, out of compassion for the world, for the good, for the gain, for the welfare of gods and men. Let not two of you go the same way. Preach, O Bhikkhus, the doctrine which is glorious in the beginning, glorious in the middle, glorious in the end, in the spirit, and in the letter; proclaim a consummate, perfect, and pure life of holiness."

Gautama himself went to Uruvela, where he achieved distinguished success by converting three brothers named Kasyapa, who worshipped fire in the Vedic form, and had high reputation as hermits and philosophers. This event created a sensation, and Gautama, with his new disciples and a thousand followers, walked towards Rajagriha, the capital of Magadha. Tidings of the new prophet soon reached the king, and Seniya Bimbisara, surrounded by numbers of Brahmans and Vaisyas, went to visit Gautama, only to declare himself an adherent of Gautama and invite him to take his meal with him the next day.

The saintly wanderer accordingly went, an honoured guest, to the palace of the king, and the entire population of the capital of Magadha thronged to see the great preacher of the religion of love, who had suddenly appeared in the land. The king then assigned a bamboo grove (Veluvana) close by for the residence of Gautama and his followers, and there Gautama rested for some time, shortly afterward gaining two distinguished converts, Sariputra and Moggallana.

The fame of Gautama had now travelled to his native town, and his old father expressed a desire to see him once before he died. Gautama accordingly went to Kapilavastu, but, according to custom, remained in the grove outside the town. His father and relations came to see him there; and the next day Gautama himself went into the town, begging alms from the people who had once adored him as their beloved prince and master.

The king took his son into the palace, where all the members of the family came to greet him except his wife. The deserted Yasodhara, with a wife's grief and a wife's pride, exclaimed, "If I am of any value in his eyes, he will himself come; I can welcome him better here." Gautama understood this and went to her, attended by only two disciples; and when Yasodhara saw him enter, a recluse with shaven head and yellow robes, her heart failed her, she flung herself on the ground, held his feet, and burst into tears. Then, remembering the impassable gulf between them, she rose and stood aside. She listened to his new doctrines, and when Gautama was subsequently induced to establish an order of female mendicants, she was one of the first to become a Buddhist nun. Gautama's son, Rahula, also became a convert later. The king, his grandfather, was much aggrieved at this, because the celibate tendencies of the religion threatened the royal line with extinction, and asked Gautama to establish a rule that no one should be admitted to the Order without his parents' consent. Gautama consented to this and made a rule accordingly.

On his way back to Rajagriha, Gautama stopped for some time at Anupiya, " a town belonging to the Mallas," and while he was stopping there, he made many converts both from the Koliyan and from the Sakya tribe, some of whom deserve special mention. Anuruddha, the Sakya, went to his mother and asked to be allowed to enter the houseless state. His mother did not know how to stop him, and so told him, " If, beloved Anuruddha, Bhaddiya, the Sakya Raja, will renounce the world, thou also mayest go forth into the houseless state."

Anuruddha accordingly went to Bhaddiya, and it was decided that they would embrace the Order in seven days. " So Bhaddiya, the Sakya Raja, and Anuruddha and Ananda and Bhagu and Kimbila and Devadatta, just as they had so often previously gone out to the pleasure-ground with fourfold array, even so did they now go out with fourfold array, and Upali the barber went with them, making seven in all.

" And when they had gone some distance, they sent their retinue back and crossed over to the neighbouring district, and took off their rich garments and wrapped them in their robes and made a bundle of them, and said to Upali the barber, 'Do you now, Upali, turn back. These things will be sufficient for you to live upon.'" But Upali was of a different mind,

BUDDHIST ROCK-TEMPLE AT KARLI.

and so all the seven went to Gautama and became converts. And when Bhaddiya had retired into solitude he exclaimed over and over, "O happiness! O happiness!" and on being asked the cause, he said:—

"Formerly, Lord, when I was a king, I had a guard completely provided both within and without my private apartments, both within and without the town, and within the borders of my country. Yet though,

Lord, I was thus guarded and protected, I was fearful, anxious, distrustful, and alarmed. But now, Lord, even when in the forest at the foot of a tree, in solitude, I am without fear or anxiety, trustful, and not alarmed; I dwell at ease, subdued, secure, with my mind as peaceful as an antelope."

We have narrated this story because some of the converts, spoken of here, rose to distinction. Ananda became the most intimate friend of Gautama, and after his death led a band of five hundred monks in chanting the Dharma in the Council of Rajagriha. Upali, though a barber by birth, became an eminent member of the Holy Order, and was recognized as an authority in matters connected with Vinaya. Anuruddha lived to become the greatest master of Abhidamma, or metaphysics, but Devadatta, a cousin to the Buddha, subsequently became the rival and opponent of Gautama, and is even said to have advised Ajatasatru, the Prince of Magadha, to kill his own father Bimbasara, and then attempted to kill Gautama himself. Such at least is the orthodox Buddhist tradition.[1]

After spending his second *vassa*, or rainy season, in Rajagriha, Gautama repaired to Sravasti, the capital of the Kosalas, where Prasenajit reigned as king. A wood called Jetavana was presented to the Buddhists, and there Gautama often preached.

The third *vassa* was also passed in Rajagriha, and in the fourth year from the date of his proclaiming his creed Gautama crossed the Ganges, went to Vaisali,

[1] For an account of this tradition see vol. ii, pp. 30–32.

and stopped in the Mahavana grove, but in the following year he again repaired to Kapilavastu, and was present at the death of his father, then ninety-seven years of age.

His widowed stepmother Prajapati Gautami, and his hardly less widowed wife Yasodhara, had now no ties to bind them to the world, and insisted on joining the Order established by Gautama. The sage had not yet admitted women to the Order, and was reluctant to do so, but his mother was inexorable and followed him to Vaisali, begging to be admitted.

Ananda pleaded her cause, but Gautama still replied, "Enough, Ananda! Let it not please thee that women should be allowed to do so." But Ananda persisted, and asked:—

"Are women, Lord, capable—when they have gone forth from the household life and entered the homeless state, under the doctrine and discipline proclaimed by the Blessed One—are they capable of realizing the fruit of conversion or of the second path or of Arhatship?"

There could be only one reply to this. Honour to women has ever been a part of religion in India, and salvation and heaven are not barred to them by the Hindu religion. "They are capable, Ananda," replied the sage, whereupon they were admitted to the Order as Bhikkhunis under some rules making them strictly subordinate to the Bhikkhus.

In the sixth year, after spending the rainy season at Kosambi, near Prayaga, Gautama returned to Rajagriha, and Kshema, the Queen of Bimbisara, was admitted to the Order, while in the same year he is said to have performed miracles at Sravasti, and to have gone to heaven to teach the Law to his mother, who had died seven days after his birth.

In the twelfth year of his ministry Buddha undertook the longest journey he had ever made, going to Mantala and returning by Benares, and then preaching the famous Maha Rahula Sutta to his son Rahula, then eighteen years old. Two years after, Rahula, being twenty, was formally admitted into the Order, and the Rahula Sutta was preached.

In the fifteenth year from the date of his proclaiming his creed, he again visited Kapilavastu, and addressed a discourse to his cousin Mahanama, who had followed Bhadraka, the successor of Suddhodana, as the king of the Sakyas.

In the seventeenth year he delivered a discourse on the death of Srimati, a courtesan; in the next year he comforted a weaver who had accidentally killed his daughter; in the following year he released a deer caught in a snare and converted the angry hunter who had wished to shoot him; and in the twentieth year he converted the famous robber Angulimala of the Chaliya forest.

For twenty-five years more Gautama wandered through the Ganges valley, preaching benevolence and holiness to the poor and humble, making converts among the high and the low, the rich and the poor, and proclaiming his law throughout the length and breadth of the land. He was now eighty years of age.

Most of those whom he had known in his early days were dead, and the aged saint preached to sons and grandsons the same holy law which he had proclaimed to their sires and grandsires, but the faithful Ananda still accompanied him like his shadow, and ministered to his wants. The old King of Rajagriha was no more; his warlike and ambitious son Ajatasatru had ascended the throne of Magadha—it is said by murdering his father—and was now maturing schemes of conquest. It was no part of Ajatasatru's policy to offend so popular and widely respected a person as Gautama, and, outwardly at least, Ajatasatru honoured the reformer.

The powerful Vrijjian clans who occupied the plains on the northern shore of the Ganges, opposite to Magadha, first attracted Ajatasatru's attention. They were a Turanian tribe who had entered into India through the northern mountains and had established a republican form of government in the very centre of Hindu civilization, threatening the conquest of all Magadha.

Gautama was then residing in the Vulture's Peak (Gridhrakuta), a cave on the side of the loftiest of the five hills overlooking the beautiful valley of Rajagriha. Ajatasatru, who was not without some kind of superstitious faith in prophecies, sent his prime minister Vassakara to Gautama to inquire how his expedition against the Vrijjians would end. Gautama was no respecter of kings, and replied that so long as the Vrijjians remained united in their adherence to their ancient customs they would not decline, but prosper.

From the Vulture's Peak Gautama wandered to neighbouring places—to Ambalathika, to Nalanda, and to Pataligrama, the site of the future capital of Magadha, Pataliputra. At the time of Gautama it was an insignificant village, but Sunidha and Vassakara, the chief ministers of Ajatasatru, were building a fortress there to repel the Vrijjians. Such, according to some accounts, was the origin of the town which became the capital of Chandragupta and Asoka, and was the metropolis of India for nearly a thousand years, and which, under the name of Patna, is still one of the largest cities in India. Gautama is said to have visited it upon invitation of the ministers and to have prophesied the greatness of the place, saying to Ananda: "Among famous places of residence and haunts of busy men, this will become the chief, the city of Pataliputra, a centre for the interchange of all kinds of wares." Leaving Pataligrama, Buddha went to Kotigrama, and then to Nadika, where he rested in the "brick hall," which was a resting-place for travellers. There he taught Ananda the lesson that each disciple could ascertain for himself whether he had attained salvation. If he felt within himself that he had faith in the Buddha, that he had faith in the Law, that he had faith in the Order, then he was saved, and thus Buddha, the Law (*Dharma*), and the Congregation (*Sangha*) became the triad of the Buddhists.

From Nadika, Gautama went to Vaisali, the capital of the powerful confederacy of the Lichchhavis to the north of the Ganges. Ambapali, a courtesan, heard that the saint was stopping in her mango grove and came and invited him to a meal, and Gautama accepted the invitation.

From Ambapali's grove, Gautama went to Beluva. He felt his end approaching, and said to the faithful Ananda, "I am now grown old and full of years, my journey is drawing to its close, I have reached the sum of my days, I am turning eighty years of age. . . . Therefore, be ye lamps unto yourselves. Be ye a refuge to yourselves. Betake yourselves to no external refuge. Hold fast to the truth as a lamp. Hold fast as a refuge to the truth."

At Kutagara, Gautama once more proclaimed to his followers the substance and essence of his religion, and enjoined upon them to practise it, to meditate upon it, and to spread it abroad, "in order that pure religion may last long and be perpetuated, in order that it may continue to be for the good and the happiness of great multitudes."

Having paid his last visit to Vaisali, Gautama then wandered through the villages of Bhandagrama, Hastigrama, Ambagrama, Jambugrama, and Bhoganagara, and then went to Pava. There Chunda, a goldsmith and blacksmith, invited him to a meal, and gave him sweet rice and cakes and a quantity of dried boar's flesh. Gautama never refused the poor man's offering, but the boar's flesh did not agree with him. "Now when the Blessed One had eaten the food prepared by Chunda, the worker in metal, there fell upon him a dire sickness, the disease of dysentery, and sharp pain came upon him even unto death. But the Blessed One, mindful and self-possessed, bore it without complaint."

On his way from Pava to Kusinagara, Gautama converted a low-caste man Pukkusa. At Kusinagara, eighty miles due east from Kapilavastu, Gautama felt that his death was nigh. With that loving anxiety which had characterized all his life, he tried on the eve of his death to impress on his followers that Chunda was not to blame for the food he had supplied, but that the humble smith's act, kindly meant, would redound to length of life, to good birth, and to good fortune.

It is said that just before his death the trees were in bloom out of season, and sprinkled flowers on him; that heavenly flowers and sandalwood powder descended on him, and that music and heavenly songs were wafted from the sky. But the great apostle of holy life said, "It is not thus, Ananda, that the Tathagata (Buddha) is rightly honoured, reverenced, venerated, held sacred, or revered. But the brother or the sister, the devout man or the devout woman, who continually fulfils all the greater and the lesser duties, who is correct in life, walking according to precepts—it is he who rightly honours, reverences, venerates, holds sacred, and reveres the Tathagata with the worthiest homage."

On the night of Gautama's death, Subhadra, a Brahman philosopher of Kusinagara, came to ask some questions, but Ananda, fearing that this might be wearisome to the dying sage, would not admit him. Gautama, however, had overheard their conversation, and he would not turn back a man who had come for instruction. He ordered the Brahman to be admitted, and with his dying breath explained to him the principles of his religion. Subhadra was the last disciple whom Gautama converted, and shortly after, at the last watch of the night, the great sage departed this life, with the exhortation to his brother men still on his

RUINS OF THE SAKIYA TOPE, PUT UP BY BUDDHA'S RELATIVES OVER THEIR PORTION OF THE ASHES FROM HIS FUNERAL PYRE.

lips, "Decay is inherent in all component things; work out your salvation with diligence."

The body of Gautama was cremated by the Mallas of Kusinagara, who surrounded his bones "in their council-hall with a lattice-work of spears and with a rampart of bows; and there, for seven days, they paid honour and reverence and respect and homage to them with dance and song and music, and with garlands and perfumes."

It is said that the remains of Gautama were divided into eight portions. Ajatasatru of Magadha obtained one portion, and erected a mound over it at Rajagriha.

The Lichchhavis of Vaisali obtained another portion, and erected a mound at that town. Similarly the Sakyas of Kapilavastu, the Bulis of Allakappa, the Koliyas of Ramagrama, the Mallas of Pava, the Mallas of Kusinagara, and a Brahman named Vethadipaka obtained portions of the relics and erected mounds over them. The Moriyans of Pipphalivana made a mound over the embers, and the Brahman Dona made a mound over the vessel in which the body had been burned.

CHAPTER XXVIII

DOCTRINES OF GAUTAMA BUDDHA

IT is not possible, within the limits of a single chapter, to give our readers anything like a complete summary of the doctrines of Buddha's creed, and our attempt will rather be to present the substance of the great lessons and ideas which Gautama preached and inculcated among his countrymen.

Buddhism is, in its essence, a system of self-culture and self-restraint. Doctrines and beliefs are of secondary importance, for the effort to end human suffering by living a holy life, free from passions and desires, was the cardinal idea with which Gautama was impressed on the day on which he was "enlightened" under the Bo-tree in Bodh Gaya, and it was the central idea which he preached to the last day of his life.

When he went from Bodh Gaya to Benares, and first preached his religion to his five former disciples, he explained to them the Fourfold Wisdom and the Eightfold Path, which form the essence of Buddhism.

"This, O Bhikkhus, is the Noble Truth of Suffering. Birth is suffering, decay is suffering, illness is suffering, death is suffering. Presence of objects we hate is suffering, not to obtain what we desire is suffering. Briefly, the fivefold clinging to existence (the five elements) is suffering.

" This, O Bhikkhus, is the Noble Truth of the Cause of Suffering. Thirst, that leads to rebirth accompanied by pleasure and lust, finding its delight here and there, thirst for pleasure, thirst for existence, thirst for prosperity.

" This, O Bhikkhus, is the Noble Truth of the Cessation of Suffering. It ceases with the complete cessation of thirst—a cessation which consists in the absence of every passion, with the abandoning of this thirst, with the doing away with it, with the deliverance from it, with the destruction of desire.

" This, O Bhikkhus, is the Noble Truth of the Path which leads to the cessation of suffering—the holy Eightfold Path of Right Belief, Right Aspiration, Right Speech, Right Conduct, Right Means of Livelihood, Right Exertion, Right Mindfulness, and Right Meditation."

The substance of this teaching is that life is suffering, the thirst for life and its pleasures is the cause of suffering, the extinction of that thirst is the cessation of suffering, and that such extinction can be brought about only by a holy life. It is impossible to convey in a few words all that is implied by the eight maxims into which a holy life is thus analyzed, but to Buddhists, trained in the traditions of their religion, these aphorisms speak volumes. Correct views and beliefs must be learnt and entertained; high aims and aspirations must always remain before the mind's eye; truthfulness and gentleness must characterize every word; uprightness and absolute integrity must mark the conduct. A livelihood must be sought and adhered to which does no harm to living things; there must be a lifelong perseverance in doing good, in acts of kindness, gentleness, and beneficence; the mind and intellect must be active and watchful; calm and tranquil meditation must fill the life with peace. A more beautiful picture of life was never conceived by poet or visionary; and a more perfect system of self-culture was never proclaimed by philosopher or saint.

The idea of self-culture was no doubt developed during the long course of meditation and good works in which Gautama passed his life. On the eve of his death he called together his brethren and recapitulated the entire system of self-culture under seven heads, and these are known as the Seven Jewels of the Buddhist Law.

"Which, then, O brethren, are the truths which, when I had perceived, I made known to you; which, when you have mastered, it behoves you to practise, meditate upon, and spread abroad, in order that pure religion may last long and be perpetuated, in order that it may continue to be for the good and the happiness of the great multitudes, out of pity for the world, to the good and the gain and the weal of gods and men. They are these: the four earnest meditations, the fourfold great struggle against sin, the four roads to saintship, the five moral powers, the five organs of spiritual sense, the seven kinds of wisdom, and the noble Eightfold Path."

The four earnest meditations here alluded to are the meditations on the body, the sensations, the ideas, and the reason. The fourfold struggle against sin is the struggle to prevent sinfulness, the struggle to put away sinful states which have arisen, the struggle to produce goodness, and the struggle to increase goodness. The fourfold roads to saintship are the four means, the will, the exertion, the preparation, and the investigation, by which *iddhi* is acquired. In later Buddhism *iddhi* implies supernatural powers, but what Gautama probably meant was the influence and power which the mind by long training and exercise can acquire over the body. The five moral powers, and the five organs of spiritual sense, are faith, energy, thought, contemplation, and wisdom; and the seven kinds of wisdom are energy, thought, contemplation, investigation, joy, repose, and serenity. The Eightfold Path has already been described.

It is by such prolonged self-culture and by the breaking of the ten fetters of doubt, sensuality, and all other evils that Nirvana may at last be gained. This was formerly believed to imply final extinction or death, but the majority of scholars now hold that Nirvana does not mean death, but only the extinction of that sinful condition of the mind, that thirst for life and its pleasures, which is the cause of reincarnation. What Gautama meant by Nirvana is attainable in life, for it is the sinless calm of mind, the freedom from passion and desire, the perfect peace, goodness, and wisdom, which continuous self-culture can procure for man.

But is there no future bliss and no future heaven for those who have attained Nirvana? This was a question which often puzzled Buddhists, and many a time they pressed their great Master for a categorical answer.

On this point Gautama's replies are uncertain; nor does he ever appear to have inspired in his followers any hopes of heaven, beyond Nirvana, which is the Buddhist's heaven and salvation.

If a man does not attain to this state of Nirvana in life, he is liable to future births. Gautama did not believe in the existence of a soul; but, nevertheless, the theory of transmigration of souls was too deeply implanted in the Hindu mind to be eradicated, and Gautama therefore adhered to the theory of transmigration by assuming that the *karma*, or deeds, of man cannot die, but must necessarily lead to its legitimate result. When a living being dies, a new being is produced according to the karma of the being that is dead, and Buddhist writers are fond of comparing the relation of one life to the next with that of the flame of a lamp to the flame of another lighted by it.

But the theory of transmigration was not the only doctrine which Gautama accepted from ancient Hinduism and adopted in a modified form into his own religion, for the whole of the Hindu pantheon of the day was taken over and made to square with his cardinal idea of the supreme efficacy of a holy life. The thirty-three gods of the Rig-Veda were recognized, but they were not supreme. Brahma, the Supreme Deity of the Upanishads, was recognized, but was not supreme. For they, too, were struggling through repeated births, to attain to that holy life, that Nirvana, which alone was supreme.

With regard to the caste-system, Gautama respected a Brahman as he respected a Buddhist Sraman, but he respected him for his virtue and learning, not for his caste, which he ignored. When two Brahman youths, Vasishtha and Bharadvaja, began to quarrel on the question, "How does one become a Brahman?" and came to Gautama for his opinion, Gautama delivered to them a discourse in which he emphatically ignored caste, and held that a man's distinguishing mark was his work, not his birth.

At another time Gautama explained to his followers, "As the great streams, O disciples, however many they may be, lose their old name and their old descent when they reach the great ocean, and bear only the one name of ocean, so also do Brahmans, Kshatriyas, Vaisyas, and Sudras." A touching story is also told in the Theragatha, which enables us to comprehend how Buddhism came like a salvation to the lowly in India, and how they eagerly embraced it as a refuge from caste. In this tale Sunita, the *thera*, or elder, says, "I came of a humble family, I was poor and needy. The work which I performed was lowly, sweeping the withered flowers. I was despised of men, looked down upon and lightly esteemed. With submissive mien I showed respect to many. Then I beheld Buddha with his band of monks as he passed to the town of Magadha. I cast away my burden and ran to bow myself in reverence

FOOTPRINTS OF BUDDHA.

before him. From pity for me he halted, that highest among men. Then I bowed myself at the master's feet, drew nigh to him and begged him, the highest among all beings, to accept me as a monk. Then said unto me the gracious master, 'Come hither, O monk' — that was the initiation I received." And the passage concludes with the lesson which Gautama had so often preached, "By holy zeal and chaste living, by restraint and self-repression, thereby a man becomes a Brahman: that is the highest Brahmanhood."

Thus the great teacher who regarded nor wealth, nor rank, nor caste, came to the poor and the despised, as well as to the rich and the noble, urging them to effect their own salvation by a pure and unblemished life. Virtue opened the path of honour to high and low alike; no distinction was known or recognized in the Holy Order. Thousands of men and women responded to this appeal, and merged their caste inequalities in common love for their teacher and common emulation of his virtues.

Yet it would be a mistake to suppose that Gautama

commanded all to retire from the world and embrace the Holy Order. To conquer the yearning for life and its pleasures was his cardinal aim, and he assigned no peculiar virtue to a mere outward act of renunciation of the world. Nevertheless, as it was difficult to conquer that thirst so long as one was actually living in the midst of his family and enjoying the pleasures of life, Gautama recommended the life of a Bhikkhu as the most efficacious means for securing the great end, and so thousands retired from the world and became Bhikkhus, thus forming the Buddhist monastic system, which was probably the first organized monastic system in the world.

These are the leading doctrines of Gautama's religion, whose great distinguishing feature is that it is a training towards a virtuous and holy life on this earth, and takes little thought of reward or punishment. It appeals to the most disinterested feelings in man's nature, sets before him virtue as its own reward, and enjoins a lifelong endeavour towards its attainment. It knows of no higher aim among gods or men than the attainment of a tranquil, sinless life; it speaks of no other salvation than virtuous peace, it knows of no other heaven than holiness. Small wonder, then, that within three centuries from the time when Gautama proclaimed his message of equality and of love in Benares, his creed was the state religion of India, triumphing for a space over Brahmanism under the sway of Asoka, "Beloved of the Gods."

CHAPTER XXIX

MORAL PRECEPTS OF GAUTAMA BUDDHA

A RELIGION, whose great aim is the teaching of holy living in this world, must necessarily be rich in moral precepts, and such maxims are the peculiar beauty of Buddhism, for which the religion is held in honour over all the civilized world. It will be our pleasant task in this chapter to glean some of these graceful precepts, which will give our readers some idea of the essence of Gautama's moral teachings.

Gautama prescribed for lay disciples five prohibitory rules or precepts, which are binding on all Buddhists, whether laymen or Bhikkhus, and are recapitulated thus: "Let not one kill any living being. Let not one take what is not given him. Let not one speak falsely. Let not one drink intoxicating drinks. Let not one be unchaste."

Three other rules are laid down which are not considered obligatory, but which are recommended to austere and pious lay disciples, and run as follows:—

"Let not one eat untimely food at night. Let not one wear wreaths or use perfumes. Let one lie on a bed spread on the earth."

The virtuous and ascetic householder is recommended to take a vow of all these eight precepts, and to them two more are added: to abstain from dancing, music, singing, and stage plays, and to abstain from the use of gold and silver. These Ten Precepts are binding on Bhikkhus, as the Five Precepts are binding on all laymen.

To honour one's father and mother, and to follow an honourable trade, though not included in the Commandments, are duties enjoined upon all householders.

We now turn from Gautama's categories of duties to his precepts of benevolence and love, as when he taught:—

"Hatred does not cease by hatred at any time, hatred ceases by love; this is its nature.

"Let us live happily, not hating those who hate us. Among men who hate us, let us live free from hatred.

"Let one overcome anger by love, let him overcome evil by good. Let him overcome the greedy by liberality, the liar by truth."

Parables were told to impress this great lesson on the followers of the gentle and pure-souled Gautama, and we will here narrate one of these parables as briefly as we can. Trying to heal contentions and differences among his followers, Buddha said:—

"In former times, O Bhikkhus, there lived at Benares a king of the Kasis, Brahmadatta by name, wealthy, rich in treasures, rich in revenues, and rich in troops and vehicles, the lord over a great realm, with full treasuries and storehouses. And there was also a king of the Kosalas, Dighiti by name, not wealthy, poor in treasures, poor in revenues, poor in troops and vehicles, the lord over a small realm, with empty treasuries and storehouses."

As often happens, the rich king robbed the weak one of his realm and treasures, and Dighiti with his queen fled to Benares, and dwelt there in a potter's house in the guise of an ascetic. There the exiled queen gave birth to a child who was called Dighavu, and in course of time the boy reached the years of discretion.

In the meantime King Brahmadatta heard that his former rival was living in the town in disguise with his wife, and he ordered them to be brought before him, and had them cruelly executed.

Their son Dighavu was then living outside Benares, but happened to come to the town at the time of his father's execution. The dying king looked at his son, and with more than human forgiveness left his last injunctions on his son. "Not by hatred, dear Dighavu, is hatred appeased. By love, dear Dighavu, hatred is appeased."

And young Dighavu went to the forest, where he lamented and wept to his heart's content. He then returned to the town, after having formed his resolution, and took employment under an elephant trainer in the royal stables.

Early in the dawn he arose and sang in a beautiful voice and played upon the lute. And the voice was so beautiful that the king inquired who it was that had risen so early and had sung in the elephant stables in so beautiful a voice. And the young boy was taken to the king, who liked him well and employed him as his attendant.

It so happened that on one occasion the king went out to hunt, taking young Dighavu with him. Dighavu's secret resentment was burning within him, and he so drove the royal chariot that the hosts went one way, and the king's chariot went another way.

At last the king was wearied and fell asleep, resting his head in Dighavu's lap.

"And young Dighavu thought, O Bhikkhus, 'This King Brahmadatta, of Kasi, has done much harm to us. By him we have been robbed of our troops and vehicles, our realm, our treasuries, and storehouses. And he has killed my father and mother. Now the time has come for me to satisfy my hatred'—and he unsheathed his sword."

But with the recollection of his father, the last words of his dying parent came to the remembrance of the vengeful prince. "Not by hatred, dear Dighavu, is hatred appeased. By love, dear Dighavu, hatred is appeased"—and the prince put back his sword.

The king dreamed a frightful dream, and started up terrified and alarmed. Dighavu told him the whole truth. The king was astonished, and exclaimed, "Grant me my life, my dear Dighavu! Grant me my life, my dear Dighavu!" whereupon the prince forgave his father's murder by carrying out his father's injunction and granting Brahmadatta his life. And Brahmadatta restored to him his father's troops and vehicles, his realm, his treasures, and his storehouses, and he gave him his daughter.

"Now, O Bhikkhus, if such is the forbearance and mildness of kings who wield the sceptre and bear the sword, so much more, O Bhikkhus, must you so let your light shine before the world, that you, having embraced the religious life according to so well-taught a doctrine and a discipline, may be seen to be forbearing and mild."

Not only forbearance and mildness, but the virtue of good acts is repeatedly and impressively enjoined by Gautama on his followers.

"Like a beautiful flower, full of colour, but without scent, are the fine and fruitless words of him who does not act accordingly.

"A man is not an elder because his head is gray. His age may be ripe, but he is called old in vain.

"He in whom there is truth, virtue, love, restraint, moderation, he who is free from impurity and is wise, he is called an elder."

Again in the Amagandha Sutta of the Sutta Nipata, Gautama explains to a Brahman, Kasyapa by name, that the destruction of life, killing, cutting, binding, stealing, lying, fraud, adultery, backbiting, treachery, cruelty, intoxication, deceit, pride, and a bad mind and wicked deeds are what defile a man, who can be purified neither by abstinence from fish or flesh, nor by nakedness, tonsure, matted hair, dirt, rough garments, penances, hymns, oblations, or sacrifices.

The whole of the Dhammapada is a series of 423 moral precepts which in their beauty and moral worth are unsurpassed by any similar collection of precepts made in any age or country; and a good-sized volume might be compiled from the legends and maxims, the parables and precepts, which are interspersed throughout the Buddhist sacred scriptures, of which the following may serve as specimens:—

"All men tremble at punishment, all men fear death. Remember that you are like unto them, and do not kill, nor cause slaughter."

"The fault of others is easily perceived, but that of oneself is difficult to perceive; a man winnows his neighbour's faults like chaff, but his own fault he hides, as a cheat hides the bad die from the gambler."

"This is called progress in the discipline of the Noble One, if one sees his sin in its sinfulness, and duly makes amends for it, and refrains from it in future."

BUDDHIST TOPE AT SANCHI.

CHAPTER XXX

HISTORY OF BUDDHISM

WE are told in the Chullavagga that, on the death of Gautama, the venerable Mahakasyapa proposed, "Let us chant together the Dhamma and the Vinaya." The proposal was accepted, and 499 Arhats were selected for the purpose; and Ananda, the faithful friend and follower of Gautama, completed the number five hundred.

This was the Council of Rajagriha held in the year of Gautama's death, presumably 487 B. C., to settle the sacred text and, by chanting it together, to fix it on the memory.

A century after the death of Gautama, according to tradition, the Bhikkhus of Vaisali promulgated ten theses, which permitted, among other things, the use of unfermented liquor, and the receipt of gold and silver by Bhikkhus, or monks.

Yasa, the son of Kakandaka, a venerable Bhikkhu, protested against these licenses, and convoked a great

Buddhist council at Vaisali. He sent messengers to the Bhikkhus of the western country, and of Avanti, as well as of the southern country; but in the meantime the Bhikkhus of Vaisali heard that he was obtaining support from the Bhikkhus of the western provinces, and they, in their turn, sought for sanction from the east. Indeed the difference was between the eastern Buddhists of Vaisali and the western Buddhists of the provinces along the higher course of the Ganges, and also of Malwa and the Deccan.

The final decision of the Council, rendered by a committee of four from each side, was against all the proposed innovations except one, which was allowed in certain cases; but this verdict the majority of monks refused to accept. Those who thus renounced western conservatism in favour of the eastern innovations of the Vrijjians, formed the school known as the Northern Buddhism of Nepal, Tibet, China, and Japan, while their orthodox opponents are represented by the Southern Buddhism of Ceylon, Burma, and Siam.

Buddhism first became the state religion of India when Asoka, who had ascended the throne of Magadha about 272, became a convert to the new faith. About the seventeenth year of his reign, he held at his capital, Pataliputra, the third council, which lasted for nine months, under the presidency of Tissa, son of Moggali, and was attended by a thousand elders. After the close of the Council, Asoka sent missionaries to Kashmir and Gandhara, to Mahisa (near modern Mysore), to Vanavasa (probably Rajputana), to Aparantaka (West Panjab), to Maharattha, to Yonaloka (Bactria and Greece), to Himavanta (Central Himalayas), to Subannabhumi (probably Burma), and to Lanka (Ceylon). The edicts of Asoka also inform us that his orders were carried out in Chola (Madras country), Pandya (Madura), Satyapura (Satpura range), Kerala (Travancore), Ceylon, and the land of the Greek King Antiochus of Syria, while in another edict he informs us that he sent em-

BUDDHIST CARVING AT ANURADHAPURA.

bassies to the five Greek kingdoms of Syria, Egypt, Macedon, Epirus, and Cyrene.

We have already seen that Asoka sent his own son Mahendra, or Mahinda, to Ceylon, and that he soon converted King Tissa and spread Buddhism throughout the island. The scenes of Mahinda's labours are still visible in Ceylon. Eight miles from the ruined city of Anuradhapura is the hill of Mihintale, where the Ceylonese king built a monastery for the Indian monks, and here is a great stupa, or cupola, under which rest the ashes of Asoka's son.

After the death of King Tissa and of Mahinda, Ceylon was twice overrun and conquered by Dravidian conquerors, who were finally expelled by Watta Gamini about 88 B. C., when the three Pitakas, which had been so long preserved by word of mouth, are said to have been reduced to writing.

About 450 A. D. Buddhism was introduced into Burma, and in 638 it penetrated to Siam. Java seems to have received Buddhist missionaries about the same time, and Buddhism apparently spread thence to Sumatra. All these countries belonged to the Southern Buddhist school.

Northern Buddhism was the prevailing faith in the northwest of India before the commencement of the Christian Era. Pushpamitra, the King of Kashmir, whose history will be found in the next volume, persecuted the Buddhists early in the second century B. C., and Pushpamitra's son, Agnimitra, met the Greeks on the banks of the Ganges. The Greeks under Menander were victorious, and about 150 B. C. extended their conquests as far as the Ganges. But the victory of the Greeks was no loss to Buddhism, and Nagasena, a renowned Buddhist teacher of the time, had religious controversies with the Greek king, which have been preserved to us in a most interesting Pali work.

Between the first and second centuries after Christ the Yueh-chi under Kanishka conquered Kashmir. Kanishka's vast empire extended over Kabul, over Yarkand and Khotan, over Kashmir and Rajputana, and over the whole of the Panjab, to Gujarat and Sind in the south, and to Agra in the east, and even China had hostages at his court. Kanishka was a zealous Buddhist of the Northern school, and held a council of five hundred monks. If this council had settled the text as the Council of Asoka at Pataliputra did, we should now have in our possession the canon of Northern Buddhism as we have the Three Pitakas of the South. But Kanishka's council satisfied itself with writing three commentaries only, and Northern Buddhism drifted more and more from its primitive form, and assumed different aspects in different lands.

As early as the second century B. C., Buddhist books were taken to the Emperor of China, probably from Kashmir. Another emperor, in 62 A. D., procured more Buddhist works and Buddhism spread rapidly from that date until it became the state religion in the fourth century.[1]

From China the religion spread to Korea in 372 A. D., and thence to Japan in 552 A. D. Cochin-China, Formosa, Mongolia, and other countries received Buddhism from China in the fourth and fifth centuries; while from Kabul the religion travelled to Balkh, Bokhara, and elsewhere.

Buddhism must have penetrated into Nepal at an early date, although the kingdom did not become Buddhist until the sixth century, nor did the first Buddhist King of Tibet send for scriptures from India before 632 A. D.

[1] For an account of the introduction of Buddhism into China see vol. ii, pp. 231–234.

CHAPTER XXXI

HISTORY OF JAINISM

THE Jain religion was long considered an offshoot from the religion proclaimed by Gautama Buddha, but it is now known to be an independent faith which began about the same time as the religion of Gautama, the two creeds flowing in parallel streams for long centuries, until Buddhism declined, while Jainism still continues to be a living faith in some parts of India.

The Jains, both of the Svetambara (with white clothing) and the Digambara (without clothing) sect, allege that Mahavira, the founder of the religion, was the son of Siddhartha of Kundagrama, and belonged to the clan of Jnatrika Kshatriyas. This Kotigrama is identified with the Kundagrama of the Jains, and the Natikas mentioned in the Buddhist Scriptures are identified with the Jnatrika Kshatriyas. Further, Mahavira's mother Trisaa is said to have been the sister of Kataka, King of Vaisali, whose daughter was married to the renowned Bimbisara, King of Magadha. The Jain saint and the Buddha preached, therefore, in Magadha during the reign of the same ruler.

Mahavira, at first called Vardhamana or Jnatriputra, entered the Holy Order at the age of twenty-eight, and after twelve years of self-mortification became a saint and prophet. During the last thirty years of his life he organized his order of ascetics. He was thus a rival of Gautama Buddha, and is mentioned in Buddhist writings under the name of Nataputra as the head of a numerous sect in Vaisali. Mahavira's death occurred some time after 500 B. C., probably shortly before the decease of Buddha.

Jain tradition goes on to say that in the second century after Mahavira's death at Papa there was a famine in Magadha. The renowned Chandragupta was then the sovereign of Magadha. Bhadrabahu, with a portion of his Jain followers, left Magadha under pressure of the famine and went to Karnata. During his absence, the Jains of Magadha settled their scriptures, consisting of the eleven Angas and the fourteen Puvvas, the latter sometimes called the twelfth Anga. On the return of peace and plenty, the Jains again sought Magadha; but within these years a difference in custom had arisen between those who had stayed in Magadha, and those who had gone to Karnata. The former had assumed a white dress, and the latter adhered to the old rule of absolute nudity. The former were accordingly called Svetambaras, and the latter Digambaras. The scriptures which had been settled by the former were not accepted by the latter, and the Digambaras therefore have no Angas. The final division between the two sects is said to have taken place in 83 A. D.

In course of time the scriptures of the Svetambaras

fell into confusion, and were in danger of becoming extinct. It was necessary to record them in writing, and this was done at the Council of Valabhi in Gujarat in 454 or 467 A.D. The operations of the council

JAIN TEMPLE OF VIMALA SAH, MOUNT ABU.

resulted in the redaction of the Jain canon in the form in which we find it at the present day.

Besides these facts and traditions, inscriptions have been discovered on the pedestals of Jain statues at Mathura which prove that the Svetambara sect existed in the first century A. D.

Such is the substance of the evidence on which it is contended that the Jain religion is coæval with Buddhism, and not an offshoot from that religion. From the mention of "Nataputra" and of the "Nirgranthas" in the Buddhist scriptures, it is reasonable to suppose that the Jain sect of unclad ascetics also had its origin about the same time. Indeed, we have already stated repeatedly that various sects of ascetics lived in India at the time when Gautama Buddha lived and taught and led his sect of ascetics. It is difficult to believe, however, that the Jain religion, as we have it now, was professed by the Nirgranthas of the sixth century B. C. The story that the canon was settled by a council in Magadha at the time of Chandragupta is probably a myth; and even if the legend be true, the canon settled in the third century B. C. would be very different from that recorded in the fifth century A. D. For there can be little doubt that the early tenets of the first Nirgranthas had long since been modified and completely transformed, and that the more cultured section of that body, who adopted a white garment, borrowed their maxims and precepts, their rules and customs, their legends and traditions, from Buddhism, which was the prevailing religion of India after the third century B. C. Thus the Jains drifted more and more towards Buddhism for long centuries, until they had adopted the substance of the Buddhist religion as their own, and very little of the early tenets of the unclad Nirgranthas was left. It was then, in the fifth century A. D., that their scriptures were committed to writing, and it is no wonder that those sacred texts read like a copy of the Buddhist scriptures made six centuries before.

Like the Buddhists, the Jains have their monastic order, and they refrain from killing animals, and praise retirement from the world. In some respects they go even further than the Buddhists, and maintain that not only animals and plants, but the smallest particles of

JAIN TEMPLE AT AHMADABAD.

the elements, fire, air, earth, and water, are endowed with life. For the rest, the Jains, like the Buddhists, reject the Veda, they accept the tenets of karma and of nirvana, and believe in the transmigration of souls. They also believe in twenty-five Tirthakaras, or Jinas, as the early Buddhists believed in twenty-four Buddhas who had risen before Gautama Buddha. The sacred books, or Agamas, of the Jains consist of seven divisions, among which the eleven Angas form the first and most important division.

Among the other sects of ascetics which flourished side by side with the Buddhists and the Nirgranthas in the sixth century B.C., the best known in their day were the Ajivakas founded by Gosala. Asoka names them in his inscriptions, along with the Brahmans and Nirgranthas. Gosala was therefore a rival of Buddha and Mahavira; but his sect has now ceased to exist.

The great religious movements that had their rise in the latter part of the sixth century B.C. have been traced here with some attention to detail, not only because of the importance of religion throughout all of India's development, but especially because of the prominent part which Buddhism played in the history of the greatest kings of India during the next thousand years after the date with which this volume closes.

INDEX

A

Abhidhamma Pitaka, contains Buddhist metaphysics, 283
Aborigines, wars with, 30
  Description of, in Rig-Veda, 34–35
  First Hinduized, 37
  Formed Sudra caste, 84
Actions, five, in Vaisesika philosophy, 266
Acts, in Nyaya philosophy, 263
Adhvaryus, class of Vedic priests, duties of, 86
Aditi, Vedic goddess, 69
Adityas, sons of Aditi, 69
  Twelve, the suns of the months, 69
Administration, Megasthenes's account of, 210–212
Adoption, Hindu law of, 58
  Of a son, part of Hindu religion, 166
Adornment, according to Megasthenes, 218–219
Adultery, a criminal offence, 220
Agamas, sacred books of the Jains, 228
Agni, the god of fire, 71–72
Agnihotra, daily milk-libation to sacred fire, 162
Agnimitra, son of Pushpamitra, 321
Agnishtoma, Soma sacrifice, 163
Agnosticism of Sankhya philosophy counteracted by Yoga school, 257
Agnyadhana, ceremony, 163–165
Agrahayani, rite performed in month of Agrahayana, 251
Agrarian laws, 223, 224
Agriculture, 8
  Derivation of Sanskrit word for, 13
  Among the ancient Hindus, 13
Ahura Mazda, Iranian equivalent of Varuna, 63
Aitareya Brahmana, coronation ceremony in, 131–132
Ajatasatru, son of Rajagriha, 298
Ajivakas, a sect of ascetics, 328
Alara, teacher of Buddha, 290
Amrita, the immortal drink, 25
Ananda, convert to Buddhism, 293–295
Ancestor-worship among Hindus, 166
Andaroi (Andhras), Hindu nation, 205
Andhra kingdom, in the Deccan, founding of, 184
  Limits of, 203
Andhras, described by Megasthenes, 205
Anga, kingdom of Ancient India, 284
Animal food, 22
Animals, 7, 29
  Sacrifice of, 22, 160
  In ancient India, 217
Anukramanis, Vedic indexes, 193–194
Anuruddha, convert to Buddhism, 293, 295
Apastamba, Kalpa Sutra of, 191–192
  A teacher who flourished in the fifth century B. C., 202
  Modern followers of, 203
Aranyakas, compilation of, 85
  General character of, 94
  Of the Rig-Veda, 94
  Of the Yajur-Veda, 94–95
Arjuna, one of the five Pandava princes, 101
  Skill of, 102
  Wins the hand of Draupadi, 105
  Recovers cattle stolen from Virata, 108
  Discovery of, 108
  Kills Bhishma, 109
  Conflict of, with Karna, 110
  Kills Karna, 110
  Rise of, as a god, 169
Arrian, Greek historian, 213
Arsha marriage, 238
Aryan settlements in the Panjab, 4
  Derivation of, 8
  Civilization, extension of, 36
  Conquerors, internal strife among, 37
  World, boundaries of, in 1000 B. C., 126, 128
  Nation, formed of Brahmans, Kshatriyas, and Vaisyas, 137
  People principally Vaisyas almost to the Mohammedan conquest, 137

Aryans, development of, in Ancient India, 2–3
A united community, 5
Domestic Economy of, 7
Nomadic life led by, 8
Expansion of, 30, 82, 128–130
Ancient compositions of, preserved traditionally by certain families, 78
Home of, passage concerning, 201
Ascetics, Hindu, 235, 236
Rules for, 241–242
Ashtaka, rites performed in the month of Agrahayana, 251–252
Asia, spread of Buddhism throughout, 322
Asoka, Hindu king, 8
Father of Mahinda, 320
Astronomy, science of, 193
In the Rig-Veda, 156–157
In the Brahmanic period, 156, 157
Asvamedha, horse-sacrifice, 163
Celebrated by Yudhishthira, 110
Celebrated by Rama, 124
Asvapati, a monarch, 163
Asvayugi, rite performed in the month of Asvayuga, 251
Rites described by Sankhayana, 251
Asvins, 20
Known as great physicians, 74
Atharva-Veda, compilation of, 85, 86
Late in gaining canonicity, 90–91
Division of, 91
Character of, 91
Brahmanas of, 93
Atomic theory in Hindu philosophy, 264, 265
Avesta, possible allusions to Aryan customs in, 24
Ayodhya, capital of the Kosalas, 119
Social life in, in the Brahmanic period, 149

B

Badarayana Vyasa, founder of the Vedanta philosophy, 270
Outline of Brahma Sutra of, 270–271
Barbarians, revenge of, 36
Battle of the Ten Kings, 37, 38
Baudhayana, one of the earliest of the Sutrakaras, 200
Benares, a city, 126
Bengal, believed to have been invaded by Pandavas, 106
Hinduized, 203
Bhaddiya, convert to Buddhism, 293
Bhagu, convert to Buddhism, 293
Bharadvaja, a hermitage, 120
Bharata, son of Duhshanta, 132
Son of Kaikeyi, 119
Bharatas, known also as Kurus, a tribe, 98
Bhima, one of the five Pandava princes, 101
Fights with Duryodhana, 102
Kills brother of Queen of Virata, 108
Kills Duhsasana, 109
Bhishma, a renowned warrior, son of Santanu, 100
Killed unfairly by Arjuna, 109
Bhujya, shipwreck of, 20
Bimbisara, King of the Magadhas, 284
Conversion of, to Buddhism, 291
Birds, 17
Brahma, evolution of, 75
Theme of the older Upanishads, 95
His part in creation, 167
True nature of, as taught in the Chhandogya Upanishad, 174–175
Marriage of, 238
Brahmadatta and Dighavu, parable of, 313–316
Brahmana literature, 86
Brahman, caste, 136
Duties of a, 86, 87
Worsted in learning by warrior caste, 114
Only, practise austerities in Krita Age, 136
Allowed to marry into other castes, in Brahmanic and Epic periods, 154
Occupations of, 232, 233
Arrogance toward other castes, 233
Translation from Megasthenes concerning, 234–236
Brahmanas, composition of, 85, 143–144
General character of, 92
Of Rig-Veda, 92–93
Of Sama-Veda, 93
Of Yajur-Veda, 93
Of Atharva-Veda, 93
Brahmanic period, hermit life in, 85, 144
Justice officially administered in, 143
Municipal government in, 143
Students in, 144
Teachers in, 144
Ethical ideal in, 145–146
Metals in, 147
Food in, 147–149
Social life in, 149–154
Plan of towns in, 150
Manufactures in, 150
Child marriage unknown in, 154
Widow marriage not prohibited in, 154
Astronomy a distinct science in, 157
Brihaspati, conception of, 74
Lord of hymns, 74
Buddha, birth of, 281
Religion of, 253
Disapproval of caste by, 276
Beginning of teachings of, 276
Character of, 279

Preaches his doctrines in the vernacular, 283
Marries Subhadhra, 285
Son born to, 286
Leaves home to study philosophy and religion, 286, 289
Converts his former disciples, 291
Sends his sixty followers out to preach, 291
Wife of, a convert, 292
Residence in Veluvana, 292
Guest of Bimbisara, 292
Son of, a convert, 293
Stepmother and wife admitted to order of Buddhist nuns by, 296
Temptation of, 289–290
Work of, in the seventeenth, eighteenth, and twentieth years of his ministry, 297
Still preaching at the age of eighty, 297, 298
Resides on Vulture's Peak, 298
Wanderings of, 296–300
Seized with fatal illness at Pava, 300
Death of, at Kusinagara, 280, 301–302
Cremation of, 302
Body of, said to have been divided into eight portions, 302–303
Teachings of, on caste, 309
Buddhism, spread of, 184
Partial resemblance to Sankhya philosophy, 253
Opposed by Mimamsa philosophies, 270
Prevailing faith of Asia, 276
Spread of, to Tibet, in seventh century A. D., 280
Spread of, to Japan, in sixth century A. D., 280
Becomes state religion in China in fourth century A. D., 280, 322
Divided into two sects, 280
Essentially a system of self-culture and self-restraint, 304
Distinguishing features of, 313
Ten prohibitory rules for monks, 312–313
The precepts of benevolence and love, 313
State religion of India, 319
Early missionary activity of, 319–320
In Ceylon, 320
Introduced into Burma about 450 A. D., 321
Spread of, throughout Asia, 322
Introduced into Siam about 638 A. D., 321
Buddhist books in China in the second century, 322
Law, seven jewels of, 306–307
Monastic system, antiquity of, 311
Missionaries visit Java about 638 A. D., 321
Buddhists, sacred books of the, 281
Triad of the, 299
Burial customs in the Black Yajur-Veda, 165
Customs in the White Yajur-Veda, 165
Hymn on, 60
Practised by the ancient Hindus, 165
Unknown in the Epic period, 165
Building, art of, 28
Burma, Buddhism in, about 450 A. D., 321

C

Cakes, preparation of, from grain, 21
Canons, Jain, codification of, 326
Carpentry, 26
Caste, absence of, among the early Hindus, 5, 50
Unknown in Rig-Veda, 51–52, 143
No priestly, in Vedic period, 76
Brahmanic, rise of the, 83–84
Kshatriya, rise of the, 84, 135
Vaisya, rise of the, 84
Sudra, rise of the, 84
Aborigines formed the Sudra, 84
Reaction against, 84
Among priests, 134
System, beginning of, 135
Brahmanic, 136
Vaisya, 136
Sudra, 136
Not distinguished in the Brahmanic age, 138, 141–142
Developed in Brahmanic and Epic times, 143
Brahmans allowed to marry outside their own, in Brahmanic period, 154
Vaisya, undivided in Philosophic period, 154
Translation from Vasishtha concerning, 233
Vaisya, translation from Megasthenes concerning, 236–237
Kshatriya, translation from Megasthenes concerning, 236
Buddha's teaching on, 309
No distinction of, recognized by Buddhism, 310
Laws varied in severity according to, 220–221
Theoretic origin of, according to Vasishtha, 230
Castes, three highest, educated together, 150
Seven, described by Megasthenes, 234
Categories, seven in Vaisesika philosophy, 265–266

Cattle, 18
Stolen from Virata by princes of Hastinapura, 108
Causation, according to Sankhya philosophy, 255–256
Cause and effect, in Nyaya philosophy, 262–263
Ceylon, discovery of, 203
Believed to have been invaded by the Pandavas, 106
A resort of Hindu traders, 185
Known to Megasthenes and Ælian, 207
Converted to Buddhism, 320
Twice conquered by the Dravidians, 321
Chaitri, a rite performed in the month of Chaitra, 252
Chandalas explained as a caste, 231
Chandragupta, empire of, included whole of Northern India, 204
Army of, 204
Chaturmasya, a sacrifice, 162
Chera, Hindu kingdom, 185, 203
Chhandogya, extracts from, 174–175
Child, rites performed at birth of, 246
Name of, 246
First feeding of, with solid food, 246–247
Marriage unknown in Brahmanic and Epic periods, 154
Marriage not prevalent in Philosophic Age, 239
Children, desire for, 166
China, Buddhism state religion in, in fourth century A. D., 280
Buddhist books in, about the second century, 322
Chola, Hindu kingdom, 185, 203
Chullavagga, translation from, 283
Chumbala, a river, 129
Churning of the ocean of milk, 25
Civilization, Hindu, age of, 1
Aryan, higher state of, 7
Extension of, 36
Development of, in Brahmanic period, 99
Advance of, among Hindus, 133
In the time of Baudhayana, 201
Coherence, category of, in Vaisesika philosophy, 266
Commerce in the Rig-Veda, 18
Conquests, Aryan, determined by course of river systems of Northern India, 126
Corn, preparation of, 8
Coronation of Yudhishthira, 106
Ceremony described in the Aitareya Brahmana, 131–132
Ceremony described in the White Yajur-Veda, 132–133
Corpses burned and ashes buried in Epic period, 165
Cosyri, a Hindu tribe, 205
Council, first Buddhist, at Rajagriha, 281
Second Buddhist, at Vaisali, 281
Third Buddhist, at Patna, 281
Of Rajagriha, 318
At Vaisali, 318–319
Third, at Pataliputra, 319
Creation, two hymns on, 78–80
Legends of, 167–168
Extracts from the Upanishads concerning, 176–178
Extracts in the Aitareya Aranyaka concerning, 178
Cremation, hymn on, 60
Among the Hindus, 165
Of Buddha, 302
Crimes, agrarian, severe punishment of, 222
Criminals tried by the ordeal of fire, 155, 156
Cultivation in Ancient India, 216

D

Dadhikra, a deified war-horse, 29
Daiva marriage, 238
Dandaka, a forest, 120
Darsa-purnamasa, a sacrifice performed on the first day after the full and new moon, 162
Dasaratha, king of the Kosalas, 119
Death of, 120
Dasyus, 33
Reference in Rig-Veda to habitation of, 33–34
Debate between a woman and a priest, 153
Deccan, 126
Hinduized, 203
Delhi, central district of Kuru kingdom, 98
Devadatta, convert to Buddhism, 293, 295
Devas, 10
Worshippers of the, 10
Dhammapada, Buddhist work, extracts from, 317
Dharma Sutras, theme and value of, 189
Source of Manu's code, 189–190
Dhrishtadyumna, brother of Draupadi, 105
Dhritarashtra, grandson of Santanu, 101
Father of Duryodhana, 104
Dyu, primitive sky-god, 63
Digambaras, Jain sect, 323–324
Dighavu and Brahmadatta, parable of, 313–316
Dirghatamas, a Brahman, 132
Dissensions, domestic, 57
Doab, entry of the Kurus into the, 83

Entry of the Panchalas into the, 83
Colonization of the, 98
Domestic ceremonies, value of, for knowledge of Hindu life, 244
Draupadi, svayamvara of, 104
Chooses Arjuna as her husband, 105
Marries the five Pandava princes, 105
Publicly insulted by Duryodhana, 107
Slave of Duryodhana, 107
The Queen of Virata's handmaid, 108
Dravidians, 184
Conquer Ceylon twice, 321
Drona, a warrior, 101
Conquers Drupada, 103
Kills Drupada, 109
Killed by Drupada's son, 109
Drupada conquered by Drona, 103
King of the Panchalas, 104
Alliance of, with the five Pandava princes, 105
Killed by Drona, 109
Duhshanta, father of Bharata, 132
Durga, goddess, 76
Duhsasana killed by Bhima, 109
Duryodhana, son of Dhritarashtra, 102
Fights with Bhima, 102
Publicly insults Draupadi, 107
Flight of, from Bhima, and subsequent return to him, 110

E

Eightfold path, Buddhist, 304–305
Emancipation, final, according to Vedanta philosophy, 272
Epic period, municipal government in, 143
Equality, legal, unknown in ancient India, 220
Ethical ideal in Brahmanic period, 145–146
Evidence, kinds of, recognized by Sankhya philosophy, 255
Evil, true nature of, 216
Exile of Rama, 120
Of Pandava princes, 103, 107

F

False evidence, 222
Famine unknown in India, 217
Fire, various offerings to, 5
Sacred, kept burning in every household, 52, 150
Sacrificial, 76
Ordeal of, criminals tried by, 155–156
Names of, 170
Five Pandava princes, 100–101
Flood, Hindu tradition of, 166–167
Food, vegetable, 21
Animal, 22
In Brahmanic period, 147–148
Foreigners explained as castes, 232
Forest hermits in the Brahmanic period, 144
Fourfold wisdom, Buddhist, 304–306
Future life, hymn on, 59–60

G

Gambling match of Yudhishthira, 107
Gandharva marriage, 238
Ganges, river, 97, 126
Valley of, reached by the Hindus, 82
Exploration of shores of, 97
Gautama, see also Buddha
Buddha, 3
Haridrumata, a Vedic teacher, 139–141
Founder of the Nyaya philosophy, 262
Gayatri, the, 70
Genus, in Buddhism, 266
In Vaisesika philosophy, 266
Geometry, 192, 194
Godavari, a river of ancient India, 120
Gods of the Rig-Veda still worshipped in Brahmanic and Epic times, 169
Gosala, founder of sect of Ajivakas, 328
Government, 9
Grammar, science of, in India, 193
Greek knowledge of India, 197–198, 204–207
Grain, names of, in Rig-Veda, 21
Grihya Sutras, regulations concerning domestic rites, 190
Value of, for knowledge of Hindu life, 191, 244
Gujarat, Hinduized, 203

H

Hanuman, commander-in-chief of the non-Aryan army, 121
Restores Sita to Rama, 121
Haoma, Iranian name for Soma, 24
Hastinapura, capital of the Kurus, 100
Ruins of, said to be near Delhi, 100
Social life of, in the Brahmanic period, 149
Harvests, two annually in India, 218
Hercules, identified with Krishna, 207
Hermit life, in the Brahmanic period, 85, 86
Hermits, rules for, 241, 242
Hetairism, 7
Hindu Aryans, a united body in the Vedic Age, 136
Civilization, age of, 1
Civilization, expansion of, 112
Literature, ancient, 2
Pantheon adopted and modified by Buddha, 308–309

Religion, cardinal principle of, 179
Religion, explanation of, by Rig-Veda, 11
Villages, manage their own affairs, 150
Women, Sita model of, 125
World, Panchalas and Kurus centre of, 99
Hindus, Vedic, character of, 4
Vedic, settlement of, on Indus, 4
Agriculture among, 13
Separation of, from the Iranians, 24
Effect of climate of Ganges valley on, 83
Gradual enervation of, 83
Cremation among, 165
Ancestor-worship among, 166
Advance of civilization among, 133
Rules of, to regulate domestic and social duties, 143
Spread of civilization among, 198–200
As described by Megasthenes, 124–215
Food and clothing of, 216
Home, early Aryan, controversy concerning, 6
Horatoi (Saurashtras), Hindu nation, 206
Horse, sacrifice of a, 22, 23, 24, 163
Sacrificial, captured by Rama's sons and his subsequent recognition of them, 125
Horses, 16
Hospitality, 145, 150, 241
Hotris, Vedic priests, duties of, 86, 88
Household worship, 50
Householders, students as, 145
Forty sacraments of, 242–243
Hymn to the rivers, historical significance of, 49
Recounting Indra's slaying of Vritra, 66–67
Relating to the storm-myth of Indra, 69–70
Hymns, sung by professional priests, 5
Certain families proficient in composing, 77
Of the Vedas still repeated as texts in Brahmanic and Epic times, 169

I

Idols, unknown in the Vedic period, 5, 52
India, oldest records of, 1
Political life, decadence of, 3
History, value of, 3–4
Early civilization centred in, 6
Buddhism state religion of, 319
Indian tribes, number one hundred and eighteen, 215
Indo-Iranians in Asia, 9
Indra, 33–35
Hymn to, 32–33
First among Vedic gods, 63
Slays Vritra, 65
Storm-myth of, 67
An Aditya, 69
As leader, 69
Indrajit, son of Ravana, 122
Killed by Lakshmana and revived by a powerful medicine, 122
Indraprastha, city in ancient India, 106
Indus, sacred river of the Panjab, 49, 126
Industries, 7
Inheritance, law of, 58, 227–229
Initiation into religious life, 239–241
Age of, varies in different castes, 247
Inscriptions on Jain statues, 325
Intellect, in Nyaya philosophy, 263
Interest, six forms of, according to Gautama, 226–237
Internecine wars of the Kurus, 83
Wars of the Panchalas, 83
Invocation of the bright gods, 5
Iranians, separation of, from the Hindus, 24
Irrigation in the Panjab, 15
Reference to, in the tenth book of the Rig-Veda, 17
In ancient India, 217
Isari, Hindu tribe, 205
Isa Upanishad, extract from, 176

J

Jabala, mother of Satyakama, 139–140
Jaimini, founder of the Purva Mimamsa philosophy, 269
Outline of sutras of, 269
Jainism, a religion of India, 323
Coæval with Buddhism, 325
Approximation to Buddhism, 326
Jains, division of, into two sects, 324
Refrain from killing animals, 327
Monastic order of, 327
Beliefs of, 333
Sacred books of, 333
Janaka, king of the Videhas, 114
In the Ramayana, 117
Quotation from Brihadaranyaka Upanishad relating to, 152
Janamejaya, son of Parikshit, 132
Japan, Buddhism in, in the sixth century A. D., 280
Java, Buddhist missionaries visit, 321
Jnatrika Kshatriyas, Hindu clan, 323
Judicial procedure still crude in Brahmanic and Epic periods, 155
Jumna, a river, 95, 126
Exploration of shores of, 97
Justice officially administered in the Brahmanic period, 143

K

Kaikeyi, queen of Dasaratha, 119
Kali, goddess, 76
Kalidasa, poetry of, 3
Kalingoi, army of, 205
Kalpa sutra, 191
Kampilya, capital of the Panchalas, 104
  Social life in, in the Brahmanic period, 149
Kanada, founder of the Vaisesika philosophy, 264
Kanchi, capital of the Cholas, 185
Kanishka, early Buddhist monarch, 321
  Extent of territory of, 321
  Council of, 322
Kapila, founder of the Sankhya philosophy, 3, 253
Kapilavastu, capital of the Sakyas, 285
  Buddha's return to, 292, 296, 297
Karna knighted to fight with Arjuna, 103
  Fights with Arjuna, 110
  Killed by Arjuna, 110
Kashmir, 321
Kasis, a nation of ancient India, 82, 112, 143, 284
Kasyapa, conversion to Buddhism of three brothers named, 291
  A Brahman, 316
Katha Upanishad, extract from, concerning Nachiketas, 181–183
Kausalya, queen of Dasaratha, 119
Kavasha, father of Tura, 132
  Legend of, 139
Kena Upanishad, extract from, 175–176
Kimbila, a convert to Buddhism, 293
Kingdoms, Hindu, account of, in the Aitareya Brahmana, 125–126
Kings, customs relating to coronation of, in the Rig-Veda, 41–42
  Performing religious rites, 77
  Invested by priests at the coronation ceremony, 132
  Palaces of, centre of life in the Brahmanic and Epic times, 150
  Rules for, regarding subjects, 208–209
  Occupations of, 212–213
Koliyans, Hindu clan, 285
Kosalas, 119
  A nation of ancient India, 112
  Capital of, changed to Sravasti, 284
Krishna, a leader of the aborigines, 34
  Chief of the Yadavas of Gujarat, 106
  Entirely human in the Upanishads, 170
  Dvaipayana Vyasa, reputed author of the Mahabharata, 120
Krita age, 135, 136
Kshatriya caste, 135
Kshatriyas, 3
  Religious speculations of, 85, 114
  Occupations of, 232, 233
Kshema, queen of Bimbisara, admitted to the order of Buddhist nuns, 296
Kumarila, argument of, 167–168
  Bhatta, Hindu philosopher, 269
Kundagrama identified with Buddhist Kotigrama, 323
Kuru country divided, 105–106
Kurukshetra, battle of, 109
Kurus, known also as Bharatas, a Hindu nation, 84, 100
  Entry into the Doab, 83
  Provenience of, a mooted question, 98
  And Panchalas centre of the Hindu world, 99
Kusa, son of Sita and Rama, 123
Kusinagara, place of Buddha's death, 301
Kutsa, a warrior, 33

L

Lakshmana, son of Sumitra, 119
  Accompanies his half-brother Rama into exile, 120
Lakshmi, 76
Lalita Vistara, poem of the Northern Buddhists, 280
Lanka besieged by a non-Aryan army, 122
Lava, son of Sita and Rama, 123
Law as laid down in the Brihadaranyaka Upanishad, 155
  Of property, 225
  Of inheritance, 227–229
  Varied in severity according to castes, 220, 221
  Agrarian, passage from Apastamba on, 223
  Agrarian, passage from Gautama on, 223–224
  Usury, of ancient India, 226
Learning, branches of, in the Brahmanic and Epic periods, 157–158
Legends, development of Puranic, from poets of the Rig-Veda, 25
Lichchhavis, nation of ancient India, 284
Literature, ancient Hindu, 2
  Brahmana, 88
Lord of the Field, hymn to, 13–14
Lunar asterisms, enumerated, 157

M

Madhava, legend of king, 113
Magadha, Hinduized, 184
  Kingdom of, 284
  Jain council of, 226
Magadhas, explained as a caste, 231
Mahabharata, Sanskrit epic, 83
  Description of Kuru-Panchala war in, 98
  Lessons of the, 111

A work of later ages, 136
Maha Rahula Sutta, preached, 327
Mahavira, son of Siddhartha of Kundagrama, 323
Founder of Jainism, 323, 324
Entered the Holy Order at the age of twenty-eight, 324
Death of, 324
Mahinda, son of Asoka, 320
Maitreyi, discussion of, with Yajnavalkya, 151–152
Malwa, Hindu kingdom, 126
Man, as protector and head of the family, 7
Manu, legend of, in Satapatha Brahmana, 166–167
Manufactures, commencement of, 7
Allusions to, in Rig-Veda, 26–27
In Brahmanic and Epic periods, 150
Of ancient India known to the Greeks, 218
Mara, an evil spirit, 289
Maritime travel not forbidden in ancient India, 50
Marriage, not compulsory in Vedic India, 54
Vedic ceremony of, 55–57
Of students, 145
Among blood relations prohibited, 154
Eight varieties of, 238–239
Among kinsfolk prohibited by Vasishtha and Apastamba, 239
Among kinsfolk permitted by Baudhayana, 239
Of widows, 239
Ritual of, 244–246
Maruts, storm gods, legend of, 72
Mathura (Madura), capital of the Pandyas, 207
Matriarchy, no trace of, in India, 7
Matter, in Hindu philosophy, 267
Meat, eating of, 8, 50
Megasthenes' account of India, 204, 205–207, 210–212, 214, 219, 234, 235
Takes up residence in India, 204
Subdivides the philosophers into Brahmans and Sramans, 236
Metals, in ancient India, 9, 218
In the Rig-Veda, 26
Knowledge of, in Brahmanic times, 147
Metre, science of, 192
Mihintale, seat of an Indian monastery, 320
Mind, according to Sankhya philosophy, 254–255
Mithila, social life in, in Brahmanic period, 149
Mitra, an Aditya, 69
Modo-Galingoi (Madhya-Kalingas), Hindu tribe, 205
Moggali, father of Tissa, 319
Moggallana, convert to Buddhism, 292
Monastery, Indian, at Mihintale, 320
Money, in the Rig-Veda, 19–20
Monotheism, 172–173
In the Rig-Veda, 80–81
Moon, regulation of sacrificial rites by position of, 157
Morning hymn to the sun, 70
Municipal government in the Brahmanic and Epic periods, 141

N

Nachiketas, story of, 181–183
Nagasena, a renowned Buddhist teacher, 321
Nakula, one of the Pandava princes, 102
Narada, 132
Nature, according to Sankhya philosophy, 254
Nearchos, a Greek historian, 216
Nirvana, parallel to, in Sankhya philosophy, 257
Meaning of, 307–308
Gained by breaking the ten fetters, 308
Nomadic life among the Aryans, 8
Non-existence, category of, in Vaisesika philosophy, 266
Northern Buddhism, the form prevailing in Nepal and Tibet, China, and Japan, 280, 319

O

Occult power, gained by Yoga, 260
Ocean, churning of, 25
Order of Buddhist nuns founded, 296
Orissa, Hinduized, 203

P

Paisacha marriage, 239
Palace, description of, in the sutras, 208
Panchala kingdom, the, in 1400 B. C., 99
Panchalas, a nation of ancient India, 82
Provenience of, a mooted question, 98
Entry into the Doab, 83
Settlement of, near the modern Kanouj, 98
And Kurus, centre of the Hindu world, 99
Pandava princes, five, 104–105
Princes, exhibition of skill in the use of arms, 104
Princes, the five, wed Draupadi, 109
Princes, slaves of Duryodhana, 107
Pandavas, refuse to fight with Karna, 103
First exile of, 103
House of the, burnt, 104
Disguised as Brahmans, 104

Alliance of, with Drupada, 105
Military campaigns of, 106
Believed to have invaded Bengal and Ceylon, 110
Second exile of, 107
In thirteenth year of exile take service under the king of Virata, 108
Send an envoy to Hastinapura to claim back their kingdom, 109
Go to Hastinapura, 110
Pandoi (Pandyas), Hindu nation, 206
Pandu, grandson of Santanu, 100
Pandya, a Hindu kingdom, 203
Pandyas, kingdom of, 185
History of, 206–207
Panini, Sanskrit grammarian, 193
Panjab, Aryan settlements in, 4
Irrigation by means of wells in, 15
Seven rivers of the, 49
Colonized by Aryans, 97
Pantheon, Hindu, adopted and modified by Buddha, 308–309
Parasurama, legend of, 117
Parikshit, father of Janamejaya, 132
Parishads, schools, 144
Parthalis, capital of the Kalingoi, 205
Particularity, category of, in Vaisesika philosophy, 266
Parvana, a rite performed on new and full moon days, 248
Parvata, 132
Pasturage in Early India, 17
Pataliputra (Patna), metropolis of India for nearly a thousand years, 299
Capital of the Prachyas, 204
Council at, 319
Patanjali, founder of Yoga philosophy, 257–258
Paulkasas, explained as a caste, 231
Philosophic period, summary of, 273
Philosophy, its debt to the Kshatriya caste, 85
Six schools of Hindu, 194–195
Mimamsa, 268
Purva Mimamsa, 268–270
Uttara Mimamsa, 268–269
Nyaya, 262–264
Sankhya, 254–257, 268, 271
Vaisesika 264–266, 271
Vedanta, 195, 268–273
Yoga, 258–261, 271
Phonetics, science of, 192
Pindapitri-yajna, sacrifice to departed ancestors, 162
Ceremony of, 165–166
Pitakas, sacred books of the Buddhists, 281–282
Date of, 281
Said to have been reduced to writing about 88 B. C., 321
Plants of ancient India, 217
Political life, decadence of, in India, 3
Polygamy, 154
Allowed among kings and rich people in Vedic times, 57
Polyandry unknown in ancient India, 154
Prachyas, the most powerful nation in the fourth century B. C., 204
Boundary of, 205–206
Prajapati, his part in creation, 167–168
Prajapatya marriage, 239
Pratisakhyas, 192
Pregnancy, rites of, 246
Priestly caste, rise of the, 83–84
Priests, professional, 5, 77
Studied nature, 78
Divisions of, 86–87
Sacrificial duties, 86
And kings become separate castes in the Epic Age, 136
And soldiers mingle and intermarry with the people, 150
Prisni, the storm cloud, 72
Problems, in Nyaya philosophy, 263
Proof, in Nyaya philosophy, 262–263
Puranic legends, development of, from the myths of the Rig-Veda, 25
Purusha, 176
Pushan, an Aditya, 69
Hymn to, 17–18
Sun-god of the shepherds, 70
Pushpamitra, king of Kashmir, 321

Q

Qualities, seventeen, in Vaisesika philosophy, 266

R

Rahula, a convert to Buddhism, 293
Son of Buddha, admitted to the order, 297
Rajagriha, Council of, 318
Rajasuya, imperial coronation sacrifice, 163
Rajputana, a desert, 126
Described by Megasthenes, 206
Rama, son of Kausalya, 119
An incarnation of Vishnu, 116
A recrudescence of Indra, 116
Wins Sita at a svayamvara, 119
Husband of Sita, 116
Goes into exile, 120
Preparations of, for the recovery of Sita, 121
Alliance of, with non-Aryan tribes, 121
Kills Vali, 121
Exiles Sita, 123
Kills Ravana, 123

Return to Ayodhya and ascends the throne, 123
Celebrates the Asvamedha sacrifice, 124
Sons of, capture the sacrificial horse, 125
Ideal Hindu man, 125
Ramayana, the second great epic of India, 83, 115
Value of, 116
Decline in warlike spirit in, 117
Characters of heroes of, 118
A means of moral education to the Hindus, 125
A work of later ages, 136
Ravana, the demon-king of Lanka, 120
Steals Sita, 121
Killed by Rama, 123
Religion, Hindu, explanation of, by the Rig-Veda, 11
Of the Rig-Veda, 62–81
Kshatriyas speculate on, 85
Vedic, decline of, 86
Later, essence of the, 86
Religious discussions in Brahmanic and Epic times, 144
Life, initiation into, 229–241
Revealed literature, 85
Right of way, passage from Vasishtha, on, 224–225
Rig-Veda, earliest date of, 1
Composition of, 10
Composers of, 11
Divisions of, 11
Tenth book of, 12
Wells in, 16
Commerce in, 18
Voyages in, 20
Money in, 20
Grains named in, 21
Metals in, 26
Allusions to aborigines in, 31
Weapons in, 39, 41, 42
Coronation customs in, 41–42
Religion of, 62, 81
Preservation of, by youths of priestly houses, 78
Monotheism in, 80–81
Brahmanas of, 92–93
Aranyakas of, 94
Astronomy in, 156–157
Translations from, 13–14, 15, 17–18, 19, 20, 25, 29, 31, 32–35, 38–42, 44–46, 52–53, 55–57, 58, 59–60, 61, 63, 64, 65, 66–68, 70, 73–74, 75–76, 78–81
Rishis, Vedic bards, 76
Not a separate class, 50–51
As warriors, 77
Rivers, hymns to, in the Rig-Veda, 44–46
Robbers, allusion to aboriginal, in the Rig-Veda, 31
Royal caste, rise of, 135
Courts, the seats of learning, 143
Rudra, father of the Maruts, one of the Hindu Triad, 11, 72
Development of, as a deity, 169
Not yet identified with Siva in the Brahmanas, 169
Rules, prohibitory, of Buddhism, 312–313

S

Sacred books of the Jains, 327
Sacred fire in the household, 52, 150
Sacraments inferior to virtue, 244
Sacrifice, increasing importance of, 86
Importance of, in Brahmanic and Epic periods, 159
Human, no reference to, in Rig-Veda, 160–161
Human, in ancillary Vedic literature, 161–162
Performed by professional priests, 5
Sacrifices, accompanied by gifts in Brahmanic and Epic periods, 159
Seven Paka, 191
Sacrificial fire, 5
Rites regulated by the position of the moon, 157
Fire, setting up of the, 163
Sadanira, a river, 113
Sahadeva, one of the five Pandava princes, 102
Sakai, a tribe of the fourth century B.C., 215
Sakyaputriya Sramans, a sect founded by Gautama, 236–279
Sakyas, a clan, 285
Sale-transaction, a verse on, 19
Salvation, doctrine of, from the Brihadaranyaka Upanishad, 181
Sama-Veda, compilation of, 85–86
Duplicate verses found in the Rig-Veda, 89
Selections from Rig-Veda set to music, 89
Brahmanas of, 93
Sankaracharya, a Hindu philosopher, 167, 269
Santanu, king of Hastinapura, 109
Father of Bhishma, 100
Saranyu, the dawn, 73
Sarasvati, sacred river of the Panjab, 49, 97
Goddess of speech, 75–76
Sariputra, a convert to Buddhism, 292
Satapatha Brahmana, various strata in, 93
Satrughna, son of Sumitra, 119
Satyakama, story of, 139–140
Saurashtras, Hinduized, 185

Sautramani, sacrifice in expiation of an overindulgence in Soma, 163
Savitri, a sun-god, 69–71
Schopenhauer, on Upanishads, 183
Self-defence, right of, 222
Settlements, Aryan, in the Panjab, 4
Settlers, Aryan, earliest home of, 50
Seven jewels of the Buddhist law, 306–307
  Rivers of the Panjab, 49
Siam, Buddhism in, about 638 A. D., 321
Siddhartha, see Buddha
Sisupala of Chedi, killed by Krishna, 107
Sita, described as the daughter of Janaka, 116
  Originally a goddess of the furrow, 116
  Won by Rama at a svayamvara, 119
  Accompanies Rama into exile, 120
  Stolen by Ravana, 121
  Proof of purity required of, 123
  Exiled by Rama, 123
  Mythical character of, 125
  Ideal Hindu woman, 125
  Death of, 125
Skepticism, Hindu, 171
Sky, the most prominent object of worship in early India, 62
Social customs, had force of laws in ancient India, 99
Soldiers and priests mingle and intermarry with the people, 150
Soma, plant, 24
  Juice, 24, 76
  As a deity, 24
  Celebrated in an entire book of the Rig-Veda, 24
  Mixed with milk, 25
  Iranian name of, 24
  Hymn to, 25
  Indra's fondness for, 69
  Hymn to, containing an allusion to the future life, 73–74
Soul, according to Sankhya philosophy, 254–256
  In Nyaya philosophy, 263
Nature of, according to Vedanta philosophy, 271
Souls, transmigration of, 308
South Behar, 126
Southern Buddhism, the form prevailing in Ceylon and Burma, 280, 319
Southern India from the writings of Baudhayana, 202
Sraddha rite, a monthly offering to departed ancestors, 248
Sramans, Hindu hermits, 279
  Translation from Megasthenes concerning, 235
Srautra Sutras, extant, 188
Sravani, a rite performed in the month of Sravana, 249
Sravasti, new capital of the Kosalas, 284
Stone, uses of, for architectural purposes, 28
Student life, termination of, 241, 247
Students, 186
  In Brahmanic period, 144
  Marriage of, 145
  Duties as householders, 145, 247
Subhadhra, wife of Buddha, 285, 302
Substances, nine, in Vaisesika philosophy, 265
Subtle body, according to Sankhya philosophy, 256–257
Sudas, Vedic king, 37, 132
  Hymns to, 38–39
Suddhodana, chief of the Sakyas and the father of Buddha, 285
Sudra caste, 136
  Rise of the, 84
  Formed of aborigines, 138
  Religious knowledge forbidden to, 234
  Oppression of, 275
Sugriva, brother of Vali, 121
  Wins Vali's kingdom and widow, 121
  Marches his army to Lanka, 121
Suicides, 222
Sumitra, queen of Dasaratha, 119
Sunidha, chief minister of Ajatasatru, 299
Sunita, story of, 309–310
Supreme being, not recognized by Sankhya philosophy, 255
  Being, in Yoga philosophy, 266
  Being, in Nyaya philosophy, 263
  Being, according to Vedanta philosophy, 271, 272–273
  Deity, Vishnu developed into, 70–71
Surya, a sun-god, 69
Sutras, character of, 185
  Human compositions, 186
  Schools of, 186
  Classes of, 186
Sutta Pitaka, record of sayings and doings of Gautama Buddha, 282
Sutlaj, river of the Panjab, 4, 97
  Reached by the Hindus, 82
Suttee, supposed Vedic basis for, 61
Svayamvara, of Draupadi, 104
Svetaketu, story of, 174
Svetambaras, a sect of Jains, 323–324
  Existence of, in first century A. D., 325
Syllogism, in Hindu philosophy, 264, 270

T

Taprobane, Greek name of Ceylon, 207
Taxes, 209–210
  Some exempt from paying, 209
Teachers, individual, in Brahmanic period 144

Teaching of the Golden Mean, 290
Temples, unknown in the Vedic period, 5
  Not mentioned in the Rig-Veda, 52, 76
Ten fetters, Buddhist, breaking of the, 307
  Kings, battle of the, 37, 38
Theft, punishment of, 221
Tibet, Buddhism in, in the seventh century A. D., 280
Tissa, son of Moggali, 319
Tonsure, ceremony of, 247
Towns, stone-built, 27
  Plan of, in Brahmanic and Epic periods, 150
Transmigration of souls, 308
  Doctrine of, 179
  Extract concerning, in the Brihadaranyaka Upanishad, 179–180
  According to Sankhya philosophy, 256–257
  In Nyaya philosophy, 263–264
  According to Vedanta philosophy, 271
Travel, maritime, not forbidden in ancient India, 50
Treta age, 136
Triad of the Buddhists, 299
Tribes, chiefs of, as kings, 5
  Five, of the Panjab, 50
  Indian, number of, one hundred and eighteen, 215
Trisaa, mother of Mahavira, 323
Tura, son of Kavasha, 132
Twice-born men, caste of, 136–137

U

Udgatris, Vedic priests, duties of, 87
Ugrasena, father of Yudhamsraushti, 132
Uma Haimavati, a female theologian, 170
Universal soul, doctrine of, in the Upanishads, 172–176
Upali, convert to Buddhism, 293–295
Upanishads, 172
  Compilation of, 85
  Number and enumeration of principal, 95
  Contain religious speculations of the warrior caste, 114
  Doctrines of, 172
  Pantheism in, 173
  Passage of Schopenhauer on, 183
  Continued by Vedanta philosophy, 271
  Basic concept of, 275
Uruvela, place of Buddha's residence for six years, 289
Ushas, goddess of dawn, 75
  Hymn to, in the Rig-Veda, 75–76
Uttara Kurus, 98

V

Vaidehas, Hindu nation, explained as a caste, 231
Vaisali, capital of Lichchhavis, 284
  Buddhist council at, 318–319
Vaisya caste, 136
  Rise of the, 84
  Undivided in Philosophic period, 232
  Occupations of the, 232–233
Vali, king among the non-Aryans, 121
  Brother of Sugriva, 121
  Killed by Rama, 121
Valabhi, council of, records the scriptures of the Svetambaras in writing about 457–67 A. D., 325
Valmiki, the reputed author of the Ramayana, 120
  Instructor of Rama's sons, 124
Varanavata, place of exile of the Pandava princes, 103
Varuna, Hindu deity, 20
  The sky-god, 63
  Three hymns to, 63–65
  An Aditya, 69
Vasishtha, Hindu legislator, 132, 222
  Dharmasastra of, translation from, 230–231
Vassakara, chief minister of Ajatasatru, 299
Vayu, god of air, 72
  Purana, describes the beginnings of the caste system, 135
Vedangas, 192–193
Vedanta philosophy, 270–273
Vedas, compilation of, 85–86
  Indexes of, 193–194
Vedic hymns, study of, 1–2
  Period, 4
  Religion, decline of, 86, 274
  Age, Hindu Aryans a united body in, 136
  Religion, reaction against, 274–275
Vegetable food, 21
Vibhishana, brother of Ravana, 122
Videhas, rise of kingdom of, 82, 112–114
  Most prominent kingdom of Northern India, 114
  Court of the, 143
Vijaya, conquers Ceylon, 207
Vinaya Pitaka, record of minute rules for Buddhist monks and nuns, 282
Virata, king of, taught by the Pandava princes, 108
Vishnu, Hindu deity, 11
  An Aditya, 69
  Developed into a supreme deity, 70–71
  Legends of, 170
Visvamitra, hymn of, 3
  First a warrior, then a priest, 37

Hymn of, to the rivers, 49
Visvavara, woman of the Vedic period, 54
Vivasvat, the rising sun, 73
Voyages, no prohibition against, in the Rig-Veda, 20
Vratyas, 171
Vrijjians, a Turanian tribe, 298
Vritra slain by Indra, 65

W

War, 8
With the aborigines, 30
Kuru-Panchala, 83, 100
Not stopped by advance of civilization, 100
Equipment, account of, by Arrian, 213–214
Laws of, among Hindus, 214–215
Warrior caste, rise of the, 84
Warriors, Vedic, 42–43
Water, manner of obtaining, for cultivation, 16
Wealth, in Brahmanic period, 146–150
Weapons, 8
Allusions to, in the Rig-Veda, 39, 41, 42
Weaving, 25
Widow-marriage, 61
Not prohibited in Brahmanic and Epic periods, 154
Wives and husbands in Vedic sacrifices, 52
Women take part in Vedic sacrifices, 50, 52
Freedom of, in Vedic India, 53–55
Influence of, in ancient India, 100
Absolute seclusion of, unknown in ancient India, 150, 151
Privileges accorded to, 151
Hold honoured place in ancient India, 151, 153–154
Worship, household, 50
Writing known in India in the Philosophic period, 216

Y

Yadavas, a Hindu nation, 206–207
Yajnavalkya, discussion of, with Maitreyi, 151–152
Yajur-Veda, compilation of, 85, 86, 89
Brahmanas of, 93
Aranyakas of, 94, 95
Account of coronation ceremony in, 132–133
Verse from, descriptive of kingly duty, 133
Burial customs in, 165
Yama, god of the heaven of the righteous, 58
God of the dead, 73
In the Puranas, 73
Stanzas concerning older conception of, 73
Yaska, plan of, to reduce Vedic gods to three, 71
Yasodhara, wife of Buddha, 292
Yavanas (Greeks) explained as a caste, 230
Yoga, meaning of the word, 258
Obstacles to, 258–259
Rules to attain to, 259–260
Yudhamsraushti, son of Ugrasena, 132
Yudhisthira, one of the five Pandava princes, 101
Appointed crown prince, 103
Coronation ceremony of, 106
Gambling match of, 106
Becomes king, 110
Celebrates the Asvamedha ceremony, 110
Said to have subdued every monarch in Aryan India, 110
Yueh-chi, conquer Kashmir, 321

Published by

Facsimile Publisher
Ashok Vihar, Delhi-110052 (India)
Website: www.facsimilepublisher.com

Distributed by

Gyan Books Pvt. Ltd.
5, Ansari Road, Daryaganj, New Delhi-110002 (India)
E-mail: books@gyanbooks.com, Website: www.gyanbooks.com

8 888000 714521